NEVER GIVE A LADY

A RESTIVE HORSE

A 19th Century Handbook of Etiquette

Selections reprinted without change from the pages of Professor Thomas E. Hill's justly famous volumes on 19th century rules of etiquette: Hill's Manual of Social & Business Forms; and Hill's Album of Biography and Art.

HILL'S MANUAL

NEVER GIVE A LADY

A RESTIVE HORSE

A 19th Century Handbook of Etiquette

DIABLO PRESS
Berkeley:1967

© 1967 by Diablo Press
Berkeley and San Francisco
Box 7084, Berkeley, California 94717
Cover design by Andrew Hoyem and Robert Grabhorn

1st Printing, October, 1967
2nd Printing, February, 1968

Printed in the United States of America.

PREFACE.

IN 1873 the stock market collapsed, the steamer *Atlantic* sank with 547 passengers, an earthquake rocked Dayton, Ohio, and P. T. Barnum was robbed of a diamond stickpin. But the year had a bright side: "Prof." Thos. E. Hill of Aurora, Illinois, brought out the first edition of his *Manual of Social and Business Forms.*

The *Manual* was exactly what Victorian Americans craved. It told them how to write, think, and act in every situation that Hill's fertile mind could conceive. By the turn of the century, he had sold nearly 400,000 copies—equaling sales of Robert Louis Stevenson's *Treasure Island,* and a phenomenal number by any standard.

The popularity of the *Manual* encouraged Hill to produce companion volumes. One of these, the *Album of Biography and Art,* he published himself in 1881 after having become wealthy enough to buy out his early publisher, Moses Warren. He continued to revise and reissue the *Manual* until the ultimate edition appeared in 1911 bearing the impressive subtitle, "The New and Improved 20th Century Edition Revised and Enlarged."

There is a breathtaking variety in these books. They are, like the age in which they were written, simultaneously stern and kindly, hilarious and pathetic, and shrewd and muddled. Hill spoke to an America of adolescent complexity, and he taught it how to copy its own new aristocracy—the industrial barons and professional people who shouldered aside the genteel patricians of ante bellum society. The light of Hill's advice illuminated every facet of Victorianism—dressing, eating, sleeping, bathing, riding, visiting, emoting.

Hill's books of manners followed a tradition at least as old as Aristotle, a tradition that persists today, despite the collapse of formality, in hundreds of volumes on proper behavior. In his own time, Hill had to compete with such social arbiters as Mrs. Clara Sophia Bloomfield-Moore, who wrote *Sensible Etiquette of the Best Society, Custom, Manners, Morals, and Home Culture,* and Alexander Murdoch Gow, author of *Good Morals and Good Manners for Schools and Families.* During this period, an average of five new titles in adult etiquette appeared each year.

Hill simply overwhelmed his competition with his network of salesmen. Bookstores were scarce in the hinterland, where Hill's drummers descended with boxes of books and wills of iron. (For a salesman's conquest of President Grant, see page 144.) Every customer could find *something* in Hill's treasure store. Consider what you may discover in these pages—which we think include the wisest and richest in his two major books:

☞ How to write someone you love—whether or not you know her.

☞ How to be beautiful though symmetrical.

☞ How to breed pleasant and agreeable manners in your horse, dog, or child, saving them all from bad reputation.

☞ How to borrow a pistol on Friday.

☞ How to give a speech when speechless.

The man from whom all this advice flowed was born in rural Vermont in 1832. In his early twenties, he set out for Waukegan, Illinois, to seek his fortune as a door-to-door salesman. He also taught penmanship, and when his students thrust the title of "professor" upon him, he did not flinch. Victorian Americans believed in working hard, and Hill never practiced one profession at a time.

While still a teacher he set himself up as a correspondent for Chicago's daily newspapers. In the 1860s he answered a call to rehabilitate the floundering Aurora Silver Plate Factory. We don't know how he worked that wonder, but he made enough money to establish a daily newspaper, the Aurora *Herald*. He also bought an ornate mansion in Aurora. From its veranda he could see the town's horses and dogs drink from a fountain at his curb; indeed, he soon developed the habit of walking Aurora's streets with bags of food for needy animals.

Anything that impressed Hill was likely to find a place in his books, and his interests were so diverse that the arrangement of his material didn't make much difference to him. For example, a section on humane treatment of animals appears in the *Album* between biographies of Baron von Humboldt and Louis Agassiz. Hill's Etiquette of Traveling (see page 29) probably evolved during the many hours he spent on trains between Chicago and Aurora transporting packages and messages for merchants of the two cities—another of his business enterprises. Then, too, in 1876 he was elected mayor of Aurora. The exquisitely detailed guidance on how to organize a Fourth of July parade must have grown out of his public leadership. As mayor he is chiefly remembered for his successful campaign to rid Aurora of the 600 cattle that roamed its streets, breaking fences and disturbing authors at their work. For the heritage of that event, see page 44.

Hill moved to nearby Glen Ellyn in 1885 to speculate in land. There, he converted a swamp into a full-fledged lake whose winter ice he cut and stored for summer sale. He made a small killing on the adjacent land, and to no one's surprise he shortly issued *Hill's Guide for Land Seekers*. He also wrote a handful of books on history and government, but none of them, alas, was as warmly received as the *Manual* and *Album*.

Hill died July 13, 1915, in the waning days of what is now called the Age of Progress. He did not live to see the business of etiquette fall on hard times after the Great War. It is just as well, we suspect, for he must have believed in what he wrote. No matter how fussy Hill may look from this distance, he can't be faulted for lack of sincerity. Anyone who would take the trouble to combine, in one volume, such advice as "Resolution Thanking a Conductor and Commending a Railway" and "Feet, How to Care for Them" must have been a genuinely considerate person.

We enthusiastically offer Thomas Edie Hill—wholesaler of etiquette, publisher, management consultant, teacher, real estate promoter, politician, and iceman—to the 20th century reader who would like a well-mannered glimpse of Victorian ideals in America. We hope you will enjoy a few chuckles at the manners of Hill's era—just as we hope that a future generation will be able to laugh at ours.

DAVID MACKENZIE
W. B. BLANKENBURG

Los Altos, California
August, 1967

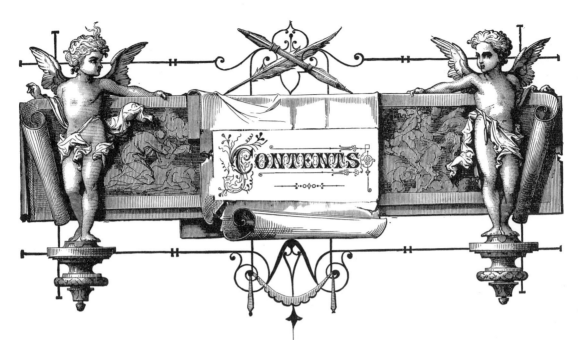

Contents

THE LAWS of ETIQUETTE. WHAT TO SAY AND HOW TO DO.

PLEASANT WORDS AND AGREEABLE MANNERS.

O be loved is the instinctive desire of every human heart. To be respected, to be honored, to be successful, is the universal ambition. The ever constant desire of all is to be happy. This never varying instinct lies at the foundation of every action; it is the constantly propelling force in our every effort.

To be happy, we strive for the acquisition of wealth, for position and place, for social and political distinction. And when all is obtained, the real enjoyment in its possession comes from the thousand little courtesies that are exchanged between individuals — pleasant words and kindly acts, which the poor may enjoy as well as the rich.

In reality it need not take much to make one happy. Our real wants are very few. To be fed and clothed, and provided with comfortable shelter, are the prime necessities. Added to these are kindness and love from those with whom we associate. Given all these, with a contented spirit, and, however lowly our position, we may be very happy.

There is one perpetual law, however, running through all our intercourse with others, which is that we may rightly possess nothing without rendering therefor just compensation. This law is recognized in the commercial world, and it should be strictly observed in the etiquette of social life.

In short, in the many varied amenities of life, the fundamental rule of action should be the golden rule: "To do unto others as we would that others should do unto us."

We are at ease, we are made peaceful, satisfied and happy, by words and acts of kindly feeling extended to us; and in like manner we may strew the pathway of others with roses and sunshine, by courteous action, and kind, gentle and loving conduct; to do which may cost us no effort, but on the contrary may afford us real pleasure.

In a business, social and artistic view, it is of very great advantage to most people to be possessed of ease and grace of manner. By the possession of confidence and self-command, a single individual will oftentimes cause a large company, that otherwise would be socially very inharmonious, to be satisfied, composed and perfectly at ease; and in a thousand ways such a person will scatter happiness and blessings among those with whom he or she may come in contact.

Natural and Acquired Politeness.

To some, a pleasing manner comes very naturally. If born to the possession of an easy flow of language, agreeableness of address, poetical and imaginative power, and large knowledge of human nature, the whole accompanied by judicious training, good education and wide opportunities, such persons will most surely, without studied effort, be self-possessed and at ease in any company, upon any occasion.

On the contrary, if the natural advantages have been few, and the opportunities for acquiring polished deportment limited, then we may very appropriately make a study of the subject of how to please; and hence the necessity for special instruction on the subject of Etiquette.

It is of the utmost importance, however, that there be no labored effort to behave by rule, and that the forms of etiquette be not carried too far. The law of common sense should rest at the basis of our intercourse with society, and a kindly desire to make happy everybody with whom we

come in contact, should actuate our conduct. Still, with all this, there are thousands of people of the kindest intentions, with much breadth of intellect, who continually violate the common usages of society, and who are liable to do the wrong thing at important times, and thus embarrass their warmest friends. Hence, the need of a treatise on general conduct is evidently as much a necessity as is the text-book on grammar, penmanship or mathematics.

If the soldier is more efficient by drill, the teacher more competent by practice, the parliamentarian more influential by understanding the code of parliamentary law, then equally is the general member of society more successful by an understanding of the laws of etiquette, which teach how to appear, and what to do and say in the varied positions in which we may be placed.

In the study of etiquette, much may be learned by observation, but much more is learned by practice. We may listen to the finest oratory for a dozen years, and yet never be able to speak in public ourselves; whereas, by practice in the art of declamation, with passable talent, we may become quite proficient in half that time. We may thoroughly study the theory and art of language for twenty years, and yet be very poor talkers. We may practice the art of conversation by familiar and continuous intercourse with the cultured and refined, and become fluent and easy in communicating thought in a few years.

Such is the difference between theory and practice. Both are necessary—the former in pointing the way; the latter by making use of theory in practical application. Thus we may acquire ease and grace of manner: First, by understanding the regulations which govern social etiquette; and secondly, by a free intermingling in society, putting into continual practice the theories which we understand. To avail ourselves, however, to the fullest extent of society advantages, we must have acquaintance; and hence, we introduce the rules of etiquette by a chapter on the forms of presentation—the art of getting acquainted.

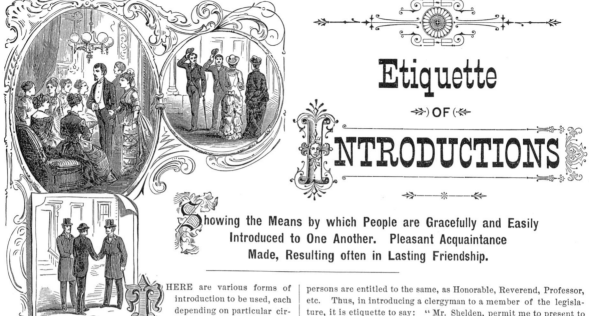

Etiquette
OF
INTRODUCTIONS

Showing the Means by which People are Gracefully and Easily Introduced to One Another. Pleasant Acquaintance Made, Resulting often in Lasting Friendship.

HERE are various forms of introduction to be used, each depending on particular circumstances. Thus, when introducing a gentleman to a lady, the party introducing them will say, bowing to each as the name of each is pronounced, "Miss Williamson, allow me to introduce to you my friend Mr. Grant; Mr. Grant, Miss Williamson."

Some prefer the word "present" instead of the word "introduce." The choice of words is not material. The form is all that is essential.

Of two gentlemen being introduced, one of whom is more eminent in position, look first at the elder or superior, with a slight bow, saying, "Mr. Dunham, I make you acquainted with Mr. Stevens; Mr. Stevens, Mr. Dunham."

The last clause, repeating the names, "Mr Stevens, Mr. Dunham," may be justly regarded as a useless formality, and is not necessary unless for the purpose of making the names more distinct by their repetition.

Persons being introduced have an opportunity for conversation, and are immediately set at ease by the person introducing giving the place of residence and the business of each, with the introduction, thus: "Mr. Snow, allow me to make you acquainted with Mr. Burton. Mr. Burton is extensively engaged in mining in Colorado. Mr. Snow is one of our lawyers in this city." He may still continue, if he wishes to aid those whom he is introducing, by saying, "Mr. Burton comes East for the purpose of disposing of mining stock to some of our capitalists, and it is possible, Mr. Snow, that with your large acquaintance you can give him some information that will aid him." Such an introduction will immediately lead to a general conversation between the parties, and the person having introduced them can then retire if he so desires.

It is always gratifying to any one to be highly esteemed, hence you will confer pleasure by always conveying as favorable an impression as possible when giving the introduction.

Always apply the titles when making introductions, where the

persons are entitled to the same, as Honorable, Reverend, Professor, etc. Thus, in introducing a clergyman to a member of the legislature, it is etiquette to say: "Mr. Shelden, permit me to present to you the Reverend Mr. Wing." Addressing Mr. Shelden, he says: "Mr. Wing is the pastor of the First Presbyterian church at Troy, New York." Addressing Mr. Wing, he continues: "Mr. Shelden is at present our representative in the State Legislature, and author of the 'Shelden Letters' which you have so admired."

If there are many introductions to be made, the simple words, "Mr. Smith, Mr. Jones," will serve the purpose. Mr. Smith and Mr. Jones will then take up the weather or some other topic, and proceed with their conversation. A very proper reply for either party to make when introduced is, "I am glad to meet you," or, "I am happy to make your acquaintance."

If several persons are introduced to one, mention the name of the single individual but once, as follows: "Mr. Belden, allow me to introduce Mr. Maynard, Mr. Thompson, Miss Hayward, Mrs. Rice, Mr. Harmon, Mr. Brown," bowing to each as the name is mentioned.

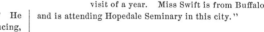

Introduction on the Street.

When introducing a couple that may be somewhat diffident, the parties will be materially aided in becoming sociable and feeling at ease, by a very full introduction, thus: "Miss Kennicott, allow me to present to you my friend Miss Swift. Miss Kennicott is from the far-famed city of New Haven, Connecticut; and, upon the close of her visit here, is going to California for a visit of a year. Miss Swift is from Buffalo, New York, and is attending Hopedale Seminary in this city."

General Suggestions About Introductions.

Ladies being introduced should never bow hastily, but with slow and measured dignity.

The inferior is to be introduced to the superior; the younger to the older; the gentleman to the lady.

It is the lady's privilege to recognize the gentleman after an introduction, and his duty to return the bow.

Introductions on the streets or in public places should be made so quietly as not to attract public attention.

Perfect ease and self-possession are the essentials to the making and receiving of graceful and happy introductions.

Etiquette requires that a gentleman always raise his hat when introduced to either a lady or gentleman on the street.

Introduce to each other only those who may find acquaintance agreeable. If any doubt exists on the subject, inquire beforehand.

When introducing parties pronounce the names distinctly. If you fail to understand the name when introduced, feel at liberty to inquire.

One of the duties of the host and hostess of a private party is to make the guests acquainted with each other. Guests may, however, make introductions.

Introductions are often dispensed with at a private ball, it being taken for granted that only those are invited who ought to be acquainted. Thus acquaintance may begin without formal introduction. If upon any occasion you are introduced at a friend's house to even your bitterest enemy, courtesy requires that you salute him, or her, and give no sign of ill-feeling while you are the guest of your friend.

If casually introduced to a stranger, when making a call at the house of a friend, etiquette does not require a subsequent recognition. It is optional with the parties whether the acquaintance be continued or not after such accidental meeting and introduction.

Always pronounce the surname when giving the introduction. To be introduced to "my cousin Carrie" leaves the stranger at a loss how to address the lady. In introducing a relative, it is well to say, "My brother, Mr. Wells;" "My mother, Mrs. Briggs," etc.

To shake hands when introduced is optional; between gentlemen it is common, and oftentimes between an elderly and a young person. It is not common between an unmarried lady and a gentleman, a slight bow between them when introduced being all that etiquette requires.

The married lady will use her discretion when introduced to gentlemen. Two persons meeting on the street, accompanied by friends, may stop and speak to each other without the necessity of introducing their friends, though, when parting, it is courtesy for each to give a friendly salutation as though acquaintance had been formed.

Parties who may meet by chance at your house, when making calls, need not necessarily be introduced to each other. If, however, they continue their calls together, it may be agreeable to make them acquainted in order to more pleasantly carry forward conversation.

If you are a gentleman, do not let the lack of an introduction prevent you from rendering services to any unattended lady who may need them. Politely offer your protection, escort or assistance, and, when the service has been accomplished, graciously bow and retire.

A visitor at your house should be introduced to the various callers, and the acquaintance should continue while the friend remains your guest. All callers should aim to make the visit of the friend as pleasant as possible, treating the guest as they would wish their friends to be treated under similar circumstances.

If thrown into the company of strangers, without the formality of an introduction, as is often the case when traveling and at other times, acquaintance may be formed between gentlemen and ladies, with proper reserve, but duty requires that the slightest approach toward undue familiarity should be checked by dignified silence.

Persons who have been properly introduced have claims upon the acquaintance of each other which should call for at least a slight recognition thereafter, unless there be very decided reasons for cutting the acquaintance entirely. To completely ignore another to whom you have been rightly introduced, by meeting the person with a vacant stare, is a mark of ill-breeding.

Introductions at Court and Presidential Receptions.

In paying your respects to the President of the United States, you will be introduced by the master of ceremonies on public occasions. At other times, to send in your card will secure you audience, although the better way is to be introduced by a mutual acquaintance, or a member of Congress. Introductions at Court in foreign countries are accompanied by a good deal of formality. At the English Court, the stranger, having the credential of the American Ambassador, will be introduced, if a lady, by a lady; if a gentleman, by a gentleman. Elsewhere abroad the proper method in each case can be best learned from our national representative at each capital. Court etiquette requires that the lady appear in full dress, and the gentleman in black suit, with white vest, gloves and necktie.

Forms of Salutation.

Common forms of salutation, in America, are the bow, the kiss, words of address, and shaking hands.

Street Salutation.

Acquaintances are usually entitled to the courtesy of a bow. It is poor policy to refuse recognition because of a trifling difference between parties.

The young lady should show similar deference to an elderly lady, or to one in superior position, that a gentleman does to a lady.

A gentleman who may be smoking when he meets a lady should, in bowing, remove the cigar from his mouth and from her presence.

When bowing to ladies, it is etiquette for the gentleman to raise his hat from his head. If passing on the street, the hat should be raised and salute given with the hand farthest from the person addressed.

A bow or graceful inclination should be made by ladies when recognizing their acquaintances of the opposite sex. It is the privilege of the lady to bow first.

A gentleman on horseback should grasp whip and reins in his left hand, and raise his hat with his right, when saluting a lady. The lady salutes by bowing slightly.

To a casual acquaintance you may bow without speaking; but to those with whom you are well acquainted greater cordiality is due. A bow should always be returned; even to an enemy it is courtesy to return the recognition.

When a gentleman, accompanied by a friend, meets a lady upon the street, it is courtesy in the salutation for the gentleman's friend to bow slightly to the lady also, as a compliment to his companion, even though unacquainted with the lady.

On meeting a party, some of whom you are intimately acquainted with, and the others but little, the salutation should be made as nearly equal as possible. A slight recognition of some and great demonstration of pleasure toward others is a violation of etiquette.

A gentleman should return a bow made him on the street, even if the one making the same is not recognized. The person may possibly be a forgotten acquaintance; but, even if a mistake has been made, there will be less embarrassment if the bow is returned.

A gentleman should not bow from a window to a lady on the street, though he may bow slightly from the street upon being recognized by a lady in a window. Such recognition should, however, generally be avoided, as gossip is likely to attach undue importance to it when seen by others.

A warm cordiality of manner, and a general recognition of acquaintances, without undue familiarity, is a means of diffusing much happiness, as well as genial and friendly feeling. In thinly-settled localities the habit of bowing to every one you meet is an excellent one, evincing, as it does, kindliness of feeling toward all.

When meeting a lady who is a stranger, in a hallway, upon a staircase, or in close proximity elsewhere, courtesy demands a bow from the gentleman. In passing up a stairway, the lady will pause at the foot and allow the gentleman to go first; and at the head of the stairway he should bow, pause, and allow her to precede him in the descent

How to Address Others—Nicknames.

Use the title, when speaking to others, whenever possible. Thus, addressing John Brown, a Justice of the Peace, say "Squire;" Dr. Bell you will address as "Doctor;" Mayor Williams, as "Mayor;" Senator Snow, as "Senator;" Governor Smith, as "Governor;" Professor Stevens, as "Professor," etc.

Before all public bodies, take pains to address those in authority very respectfully, saying to the presiding officer, "Mr. President," or if he be a Mayor, Judge, or Justice, address him as "Your Honor," etc.

When stopping at the house of a friend, ascertain the Christian names of all the children, and of those servants that you frequently have to address; and then always speak respectfully to each, using the full Christian name, or any pet name to which they may be accustomed.

To approach another in a boisterous manner, saying, "Hello, Old Fellow!" "Hello, Bob!" or using kindred expressions, indicates ill-breeding. If approached, however, in this vulgar manner, it is better to give a civil reply, and address the person respectfully, in which case he is quite likely to be ashamed of his own conduct.

Husbands and wives indicate pleasant conjugal relation exist-ing where they address each other in the family circle by their Christian names, though the terms of respect, "Mr." and "Mrs.," may be applied to each among strangers. When speaking of each other among near and intimate relatives, they will also use the Christian name; but among general acquaintances and strangers, the surname.

Never call any one by a nickname, or a disrespectful name. Treat all persons, no matter how lowly, in addressing them, as you would wish to be addressed yourself. You involuntarily have more respect for people, outside of your family or relatives, who call you "Mr. Smith," or "Mr. Jones," than for those who call you "Jack," or "Jim." Hence, when you speak to others, remember that you gain their favor by polite words of address.

When speaking to a boy under fifteen years of age, outside of the circle of relatives, among comparative strangers, call him by his Christian name, as "Charles," "William," etc. Above that age, if the boy has attained good physical and intellectual development, apply the "Mr." as "Mr. Brown," "Mr. King," etc. To do so will please him, will raise his self-respect, and will be tendering a courtesy, which you highly valued when you were of the same age.

It is an insult to address a boy or girl, who is a stranger to you, as "Bub" or "Sis." Children are sometimes very sensitive on these points, resenting such method of being addressed, while they very highly appreciate being spoken to respectfully. Thus, if the child's name is unknown, to say "My Boy," or "My Little Lad," "My Girl," or "My Little Lady," will be to gain favor and set the child a good example in politeness. Children forever gratefully remember those who treat them respectfully. Among relatives, nicknames should not be allowed. Pet names among the children are admissible, until they outgrow them, when the full Christian name should be used.

Upon the meeting of intimate friends among ladies, at the private house, the kiss as a mode of salutation is yet common; but even there it is not as customary as formerly. The custom ought to be abolished for physiological and other reasons.

Upon the meeting or departure of a young person, as between parents and children, or guardians and wards, the kiss is not inappropriate in public. Between all other parties it is a questionable propriety in public places, it being etiquette to avoid conduct that will attract the attention of strangers.

Etiquette of Shaking Hands—Ways of Clasping Hands.

ACCOMPANYING the salutation of hand-shaking, it is common, according to the customs of English-speaking people, to inquire concerning the health, news, etc.

Offer the whole hand. It is an insult, and indicates snobbery, to present two fingers (Fig. 1) when shaking hands. It is also insulting to return a warm, cordial greeting with a lifeless hand (Fig. 2),

Fig. 1. The snob that sticks out two fingers when shaking hands.

and evident indifference of manner, when hand-shaking. Present a cordial grasp (Fig. 3) and clasp the hand firmly, shaking it warmly for a period of two or three seconds, and then relinquishing the grasp entirely. It is rude to grasp the hand very tightly or to shake it over-vigorously. To hold it a very long time is often very embarrassing, and is a breach of etiquette. It is always the lady's privilege to extend the hand first. In her own house a lady should give her hand to every guest.

If both parties wear gloves, it is not necessary that each remove them in shaking hands; if one, however, has ungloved hands, it is courtesy for the other to remove the glove, unless in so doing it would cause an awkward pause; in which case apologize for not removing it, by saying, "Excuse my glove." The words and forms will always very much depend upon circumstances, of which individuals can themselves best judge. Kid and other thin gloves are not expected to be removed in hand-shaking; hence, apology is only necessary for the non-removal of the thick, heavy glove.

As a rule in all salutations, it is well not to exhibit too much haste. The cool, deliberate person is the most likely to avoid mistakes. The nervous, quick-motioned impulsive individual will

Fig 3. The generous, frank, whole-souled individivial, that meets you with a warm, hearty grasp.

need to make deliberation a matter of study; else, when acting on the spur of the moment, with possibly slight embarrassment, ludicrous errors are liable to be made. In shaking hands, as an evidence of cordiality, regard and respect, offer the right hand, unless the same be engaged; in which case, apologize, by saying "Excuse my left hand." It is the right hand that carries the sword in time of war, and its extension is emblematic of friendliness in time of peace.

Fig. 2. The cold-blooded, languid person, that exhibits only indifference as you shake the hand.

Etiquette of Calling.

THE morning call should be very brief. This formal call is mainly one of ceremony, and from ten to twenty minutes is a sufficient length of time to prolong it. It should never exceed half an hour.

In making a formal call, a lady does not remove her bonnet or wraps.

Unless there be a certain evening set apart for receiving, the formal call should be made in the morning.

It is customary, according to the code of etiquette, to call all the hours of daylight morning, and after nightfall evening.

Calls may be made in the morning or in the evening. The call in the morning should not be made before 12 M., nor later than 5 P. M.

A gentleman, making a formal call in the morning, must retain his hat in his hand. He may leave umbrella and cane in the hall, but not his hat and gloves. The fact of retaining hat indicates a formal call.

When a gentleman accompanies a lady at a morning call (which is seldom), he assists her up the steps, rings the bell, and follows her into the reception-room. It is for the lady to determine when they should leave.

All uncouth and ungraceful positions are especially unbecoming among ladies and gentlemen in the parlor. Thus (Fig. 6), standing with the arms akimbo, sitting astride a chair, wearing the hat, and smoking in the presence of ladies, leaning back in the chair, standing with legs crossed and feet on the chairs — all those acts evince lack of polished manners.

If possible, avoid calling at the lunch or dinner hour. Among society people the most fashionable hours for calling are from 12 M. to 3 P. M. At homes where dinner or lunch is taken at noon, calls may be made from 2 to 5 P. M.

Should other callers be announced, it is well, as soon as the bustle attending the new arrival is over, to arise quietly, take leave of the hostess, bow to the visitors, and retire, without apparently doing so because of the new arrivals. This saves the hostess the trouble of entertaining two sets of callers.

To say bright and witty things during the call of ceremony, and go so soon that the hostess will desire the caller to come again, is much the more pleasant. No topic of a political or religious character should be admitted to the conversation, nor any subject of absorbing interest likely to lead to discussion.

A lady engaged upon fancy sewing of any kind, or needlework, need not necessarily lay aside the same during the call of intimate acquaintances. Conversation can flow just as freely while the visit continues.

During the visits of ceremony, however, strict attention should be given to entertaining the callers.

Gentlemen may make morning calls on the following occasions: To convey congratulations or sympathy and condolence, to meet a friend who has just returned from abroad, to inquire after the health of a lady who may have accepted his escort on the previous day. (He should not delay the latter more than a day.) He may call upon those to whom letters of introduction are given, to express thanks for any favor which may have been rendered him, or to return a call. A great variety of circumstances will also determine when at other times he should make calls.

Evening Calls.

Evening calls should never be made later than 9 P. M., and never prolonged later than 10 P. M.

In making a formal call in the evening, the gentleman must hold hat and gloves, unless invited to lay them aside and spend the evening.

In making an informal call in the evening, a gentleman may leave hat, cane, overshoes, etc., in the hall, provided he is invited to do so, and the lady may remove her wraps.

The evening call should not generally be prolonged over an hour. With very intimate friends, however, it may be made a little longer; but the caller should be very careful that the visit be not made tiresome.

General Suggestions.

Calls from people living in the country are expected to be longer and less ceremonious than from those in the city.

When it has been impossible to attend a dinner or a social gathering, a call should be made soon afterwards, to express regret at the inability to be present.

A gentleman, though a stranger, may with propriety escort an unattended lady to the carriage, and afterwards return and make his farewell bow to the hostess.

Should a guest arrive to remain for some time with the friend, those who are intimate with the family should call as soon as possible, and these calls should be returned at the earliest opportunity.

Unless invited to do so, it is a violation of etiquette to draw near the fire for the purpose of warming one's self. Should you, while waiting the appearance of the hostess, have done so, you will arise upon her arrival, and then take the seat she may assign you.

When a lady has set apart a certain evening for receiving calls, it is not usual to call at other times, except the excuse be business reasons.

FIG. 6. UNGRACEFUL POSITIONS.

No. 1. Stands with arms akimbo.
" 2. Sits with elbows on the knees.
" 3. Sits astride the chair, and wears his hat in the parlor.
" 4. Stains the wall paper by pressing against it with his hand; eats an apple alone, and stands with his legs crossed.
No. 5. Rests his foot upon the chair-cushion.
" 6. Tips back his chair, soils the wall by resting his head against it, and smokes in the presence of ladies.

THE USE OF CARDS WHEN CALLING.

The gentleman's card should bear nothing but the name and address of the caller, in small script or card text. In addition, the lady's card may bear the "Mrs." or the "Miss," thus:

CHARLES BELDEN
Cambridge, Mass.

MRS. H. B. KING,
17 Belmont Place.
At Home Thursday Evenings.

The eldest daughter and unmarried sisters often adopt the following:

MISS CLARA D. WELLS,
No. 44 Birch Street.

THE MISSES HAMMOND,
No. 1 Day Street.

The physician may have his professional title, as

DR. ROBERT HOLLAND, or ROBERT HOLLAND, M. D.
No. 70 Henderson St. *No. 70 Henderson St.*

The officers of the army and navy may have their titles thus:

LIEUT. HENRY H. WEBSTER, U. S. A.

LIEUT. HARVEY B. SNOW, U. S. N.

A card left, during your illness, should be answered by a call as soon as your health will permit.

The honorary titles of Prof., Hon., Esq., etc., are not allowable upon the calling card in the United States.

When about leaving town, the card which is left will bear on the lower left-hand corner the letters "P. P. C."—"Presents parting compliments," from the French *"Pour Prendre Conge"*—to take leave. The card may also be sent by mail or private carrier, the latter mode of conveyance showing most respect. *

A card sent to a person who is ill or in affliction, from the loss of a relative, should be accompanied by verbal inquiries regarding the person's health.

Cards may be left immediately where a death is known, but a call of sympathy and condolence is not usually made within a week after the bereavement.

The lady in mourning who may not desire to make calls, will send mourning cards instead of making calls for such period of time as she may not desire to mingle in general society.

Should the servant reply to a gentleman that the lady of the house, to whom the call is made, is not at home, but the daughter is, he should send in his card, as it is not usual for young ladies to receive calls from gentlemen unless they are quite intimate friends.

It is well to have cards in readiness at every call. If a servant meets you at the door, to send up a card will save mispronouncing your name, and if the lady is not at home it will show that you have called. Should there be two or more ladies in the household, to turn down one corner of the card will signify that the call was designed for all the family.

The handsomest style of card is that which is engraved; next is that which is prettily written. Succeeding, comes the printed card, which, with some of the modern script or text types, makes a most beautiful card if neatly printed. Extra ornament is out of place.

When desirous of seeing anyone at a hotel or parlor, send up your card by the waiter, while you wait in the reception-room or office.

The hostess should, if not desiring to see anyone, send word that she is "engaged" when the servant first goes to the door, and not after the card has been sent up. Should she desire certain persons only to be admitted, let the servant understand the names definitely.

* P. P. C. cards are no longer left when leaving home to be absent a few months.

WHAT SHOULD BE AVOIDED WHEN CALLING.

Do not stare around the room.

Do not take a dog or small child.

Do not linger at the dinner-hour.

Do not lay aside the bonnet at a formal call.

Do not fidget with your cane, hat or parasol.

Do not make a call of ceremony on a wet day.

Do not turn your back to one seated near you.

Do not touch the piano, unless invited to do so.

Do not handle ornaments or furniture in the room.

Do not make a display of consulting your watch.

Do not go to the room of an invalid, unless invited.

Do not remove the gloves when making a formal call.

Do not continue the call longer when conversation begins to lag.

Do not remain when you find the lady upon the point of going out.

Do not make the first call if you are a new-comer in the neighborhood.

Do not open or shut doors or windows or alter the arrangement of the room.

Do not enter a room without first knocking and receiving an invitation to come in.

Do not resume your seat after having risen to go, unless for important reasons.

Do not walk around the room, examining pictures, while waiting for the hostess.

Do not introduce politics, religion or weighty topics for conversation when making calls.

FIG. 7. GENTILITY IN THE PARLOR.

The figures in the above illustration represent graceful postures to be assumed by both ladies and gentlemen in the parlor. As will be seen, whether holding hat or fan, either sitting or standing, the positions are all easy and graceful.

To assume an easy, genteel attitude, the individual must be self-possessed. To be so, attention must be given to easy flow of language, happy expression of thought, study of cultured society and the general laws of etiquette.

Do not prolong the call if the room is crowded. It is better to call a day or two afterwards.

Do not call upon a person in reduced circumstances with a display of wealth, dress and equipage.

Do not tattle. Do not speak ill of your neighbors. Do not carry gossip from one family to another.

Do not, if a gentleman, seat yourself upon the sofa beside the hostess, or in near proximity, unless invited to do so.

Do not, if a lady, call upon a gentleman, except officially or professionally, unless he may be a confirmed invalid.

Do not take a strange gentleman with you, unless positively certain that his introduction will be received with favor.

Do not, if a gentleman, leave the hat in the hall when making merely a formal call. If the call is extended into a visit, it may then be set aside. Whether sitting or standing (Fig. 7), the hat may be gracefully held in the hand.

Duty of the Hostess.

She should greet each guest with quiet, easy grace.

She should avoid leaving the room while guests are present.

She should furnish refreshments to those callers who come a long distance to see her.

She should be aided, upon important occasions, by a gentleman, in the reception of guests.

She should avoid speaking disrespectfully of those who have previously called upon her; she should equally divide her attentions among the several callers, that none may feel slighted.

The Inquisitive, Disagreeable Caller.

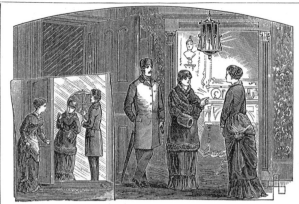

Ready to Go, Yet Waiting.

AMONG the disagreeable callers are the husband and wife who come with a child and a small dog; the husband making himself familiar with the hostess, the dog barking at the cat, the child taking the free run of the house, while the wife, in the meantime, passes around the room, handling and examining the ornaments.

Other unpleasant callers are the man with the muddy boots, and the individual just in out of the rain, from whose overcoat and umbrella the water drips on the carpet.

SOME evening callers make themselves odious by continuing their visit too long, and even when they have risen to depart they lack decision of purpose to go, but will frequently stand several minutes before taking final leave, and then when wraps are on and they are nearly gone, they will stand in the doorway to tell one more story while the hostess protects herself as best she can from the incoming gusts of wind and storm, sometimes thus taking a cold that ends in death. When the guest is ready to go—*go*.

New Year's Calling.

OF LATE years it has become fashionable for ladies in many cities and villages to announce in the newspapers the fact of their intention to receive calls upon New Year's day, which practice is very excellent, as it enables gentlemen to know positively who will be prepared to receive them on that occasion; besides, changes of residence are so frequent in large cities as to make the publication of names and places of calling a great convenience.

The practice of issuing personal notes of invitation, which is sometimes done, to a list of gentlemen acquaintances, stating that certain ladies will receive on New Year's day, is not to be commended. It looks very much like begging the gentlemen to come and see them; moreover, should the practice generally prevail, it would, in a brief time, abolish New Year's calls altogether, as gentlemen would not feel at liberty to make calls unless personally invited; and thus the custom would soon go into disuse.

Upon calling, the gentlemen are invited to remove overcoat and hat, which invitation is accepted unless it is the design to make the call very brief. If refreshments are provided, the ladies will desire to have the gentlemen partake of them, which cannot conveniently be done in overcoat, with hat in hand. Gloves are sometimes retained upon the hand during the call, but this is optional. Cards are sent up, and the gentlemen are ushered into the reception-room. The call should not exceed ten or fifteen minutes, unless the callers are few and it should be mutually agreeable to prolong the stay.

Gentlemen Making New Year's Calls.

Best taste will suggest that a lady having the conveniences shall receive her guests at her own home, but it is admissible and common for several ladies to meet at the residence of one and receive calls together. Whether ladies make announcement or not, however, it will be usually safe for gentlemen to call on their lady friends on New Year's, as the visit will generally be received with pleasure.

It is customary for the ladies who announce that they will receive to make their parlors attractive on that day, and present themselves in full dress. They should have a bright, cheerful fire, if the weather

be cold, and a table, conveniently located in the room, with refreshments, consisting of fruits, cakes, bread and other food, such as may be deemed desirable, with tea and coffee. No intoxicating drinks should be allowed. Refreshments are in no case absolutely essential. They can be dispensed with if not convenient.

Ladies expecting calls on New Year's should be in readiness to receive from 10 A. M. to 9 P. M. It is pleasant for two or more ladies to receive calls together on that occasion, as several ladies can the more easily entertain a party of several gentlemen who may be present at one time. While gentlemen may go alone, they also frequently go in pairs, threes, fours or more. They call upon all the ladies of the party, and where they are not acquainted introductions take place, care being taken that persons do not intrude themselves where they would not be welcome. Each gentleman should be provided with a large number of cards, with his own name upon each, one of which he will present to every lady of the company where he calls.

The ladies keep these cards for future reference, it being often pleasant to revive the incidents of the day by subsequent examination of the cards received upon that occasion.

An usher should be present wherever many calls are expected, to receive guests and care for hats and coats. The calls are necessarily very brief, and are made delightfully pleasant by continual change of face and conversation. But, however genial and free may be the interchange of compliments upon this occasion, no young man who is a stranger to the family should feel at liberty to call again without a subsequent invitation.

The two or three days succeeding New Year's are the ladies' days for calling, upon which occasion they pass the compliments of the season, comment upon the incidents connected with the festivities of the holiday, the number of calls made, and the new faces that made their appearance among the visitors. It is customary upon this occasion of ladies' meeting to offer refreshments and to enjoy the intimacy of a friendly visit.

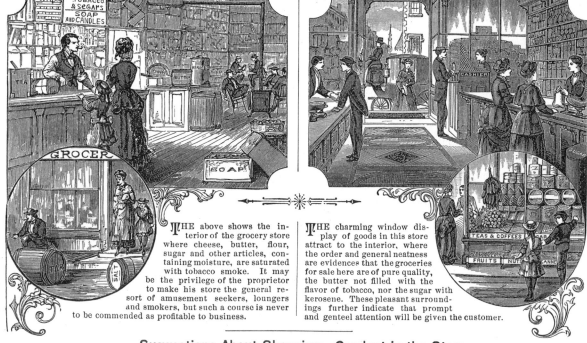

THE above shows the interior of the grocery store where cheese, butter, flour, sugar and other articles, containing moisture, are saturated with tobacco smoke. It may be the privilege of the proprietor to make his store the general resort of amusement seekers, loungers and smokers, but such a course is never to be commended as profitable to business.

THE charming window display of goods in this store attract to the interior, where the order and general neatness are evidences that the groceries for sale here are of pure quality, the butter not filled with the flavor of tobacco, nor the sugar with kerosene. These pleasant surroundings further indicate that prompt and genteel attention will be given the customer.

Suggestions About Shopping. Conduct in the Store.

PURCHASERS should, as far as possible, patronize the merchants of their own town. It is poor policy to send money abroad for articles which can be bought as cheaply at home.

Do not take hold of a piece of goods which another is examining. Wait until it is replaced upon the counter before you take it up.

Injuring goods when handling, pushing aside other persons, lounging upon the counter, whispering, loud talk and laughter, when in a store, are all evidences of ill-breeding.

Never attempt to "beat down" prices when shopping. If the price does not suit, go elsewhere. The just and upright merchant will have but one price for his goods, and he will strictly adhere to it.

It is an insult to a clerk or merchant to suggest to a customer about to purchase that he may buy cheaper or better elsewhere. It is also rude to give your opinion, unasked, about the goods that another is purchasing.

Never expect a clerk to leave another customer to wait on you; and, when attending upon you, do not cause him to wait while you visit with another. When the purchases are made let them be sent to your home, and thus avoid loading yourself with bundles.

Treat clerks, when shopping, respectfully, and give them no more trouble than is necessary. Ask for what is wanted, explicitly, and

if you wish to make examination with a view to future purchase, say so. Be perfectly frank. There is no necessity for practicing deceit.

The rule should be to pay for goods when you buy them. If, however, you are trusted by the merchant, you should be very particular to pay your indebtedness when you agree to. By doing as you promise, you acquire habits of promptitude, and at the same time establish credit and make reputation among those with whom you deal.

It is rude in the extreme to find fault and to make sneering remarks about goods. To draw unfavorable comparisons between the goods and those found at other stores does no good, and shows want of deference and respect to those who are waiting on you. Politely state that the goods are not what you want, and, while you may buy, you prefer to look further.

If a mistake has been made whereby you have been given more goods than you paid for, or have received more change than was your due, go immediately and have the error rectified. You cannot afford to sink your moral character by taking advantage of such mistakes. If you had made an error to your disadvantage, as a merchant, you would wish the customer to return and make it right. You should do as you would be done by. Permanent success depends upon your being strictly honest.

Say "No" Politely.

A COMMON saying is, "A man's manners make his fortune." This is a well-known fact, and we see it illustrated every day. The parents who considerately train a child amid kindness and love, rear a support for their declining years. The teacher that rules well and is yet kind, is beloved by his pupils. The hotel proprietor, by affability and an accommodating spirit, may fill his hotel with guests. The railway conductor who has a pleasant word for the lonely traveler, is always remembered with favor. The postoffice clerk who very carefully looks through a pile of letters and says, "not any" very gently, pleasantly adding a word of hope by saying, "it may come on the afternoon train," we always gratefully

recollect. When the time comes that we can return the kindness, we take great pleasure in doing so.

The man who shows himself to be a gentleman, even though he may not buy what we have to sell when we solicit him, we always know will get his reward. His affability, when he declined, demonstrated that he could say "no" with a pleasant word. The very fact of his impressing us so favorably, even when he did not purchase, clearly indicated that he was thoroughly schooled in the ways of politeness, and that he lived up to the golden rule of doing to others as he desired others to do to him.

Etiquette of Conversation.

HOW, WHEN AND WHERE TO SPEAK.

TO ACQUIRE the art of conversation in a superior degree, there must be intimacy with those who possess refinement and general information. There must also be observed certain general rules in order to accomplish the best results, prominent among which are the following:

In the first place, in order to converse well, there must be knowledge; there must be a command of language, assisted by imagination; there must be understanding of the rules of construction to frame sentences aright; there must be confidence and self-possession, and there must be courage to overcome failure.

To be an excellent conversationalist is a very desirable accomplishment. We talk more than we do anything else. By conversation we may make friends, we may retain them, or we may lose them. We may impart information; we may acquire it. We may make the company with whom we associate contented with itself, or we can sow inharmony and discord. Our success in life largely rests upon our ability to converse well; therefore, the necessity of our carefully studying what should and what should not be said when talking.

How to Please in Conversation.

Use clear, distinct words to express your ideas, although the tone of your voice should be subdued.

Be cool, collected and self-possessed, using respectful, chaste and appropriate language.

Always defend the absent person who is being spoken of, as far as truth and justice will permit.

Allow people that you are with to do their full share of the talking if they evince a willingness to converse.

Beware of talking much about yourself. Your merits will be discovered in due time without the necessity of sounding your own praises.

Show the courtesy, when another person joins the group where you

Coarse and Boisterous.

THE refinement and culture of an individual can be largely determined by the tone of voice and the manner of speaking. In ordinary conversation the wild gesticulation, the coarse and boisterous laugh, and the uncouth position are all indicative of ill-breeding. In such a domestic group as is here represented the ties of nature may be quite as strong as in more refined circles, and yet the tendency is to introduce a variety of topics into the general conversation that were better not discussed. The rude jest, the coarse criticism of absent ones, the unclean song and the foolish retort, are the natural outgrowth of such a gathering. Education and knowledge of the rules that govern polite society would have prevented such a scene as this by providing instruction and lessons of culture and refinement. While there is at the present day every facility for improving the minds of the young, it is no less true that politeness and respect for superiors are not properly taught.

are relating an incident, of recapitulating what has been said, for the advantage of the new-comer.

Recollect that the object of conversation is to entertain and amuse; the social gathering, therefore, should not be made the arena of dispute. Even slight mistakes and inaccuracies it is well to overlook, rather than to allow inharmony to present itself.

Aim to adapt your conversation to the comprehension of those with whom you are conversing. Be careful that you do not undervalue them. It is possible that they are as intelligent as yourself, and their conversation can, perhaps, take as wide a range as your own.

Remember that the person to whom you are speaking is not to blame for the opinion he entertains. Opinions are not made *by* us, but they are made *for* us by circumstances. With the same organization, training and circumstances around us, we would have the same opinions ourselves.

Remember that people are fond of talking of their own affairs. The mother likes to talk of her children, the mechanic of his workmanship, the laborer of what he can accomplish. Give every one an opportunity, and you will gain much valuable information besides being thought courteous and well-bred.

Be patient. The foreigner cannot, perhaps, recall the word he desires; the speaker may be slow of speech; you may have heard the story a dozen times; but even then you must evince interest and listen patiently through. By so doing you gain the esteem of the person with whom you are conversing.

What to Avoid in Social Conversation.

Do not manifest impatience.

Do not engage in argument.

Do not interrupt another when speaking.

Do not find fault, although you may gently criticise.

Do not talk of your private, personal and family matters.

Do not appear to notice inaccuries of speech in others.

Do not allow yourself to lose temper or to speak excitedly.

Do not allude to unfortunate peculiarities of any one present.

Do not always commence a conversation by allusion to the weather.

Do not, when narrating an incident, continually say "you see," "you know," etc.

Do not introduce professional or other topics in which the company generally cannot take an interest.

Do not talk very loud. A firm, clear, distinct, yet mild, gentle and musical voice has great power.

Do not be absent-minded, requiring the speaker to repeat what has been said that you may understand.

Do not speak disrespectfully of personal appearance when any one present may have the same defects.

Do not try to force yourself into the confidence of others. If they give their confidence, never betray it.

Do not use profanity, vulgar terms, slang phrases, words of double meaning, or language that will bring the blush to any person.

Do not intersperse your language with foreign words and high-sounding terms. It shows affectation, and will draw ridicule upon you.

Do not carry on a conversation with another in company about matters of which the general company knows nothing. It is almost as impolite as to whisper.

Do not allow yourself to speak ill of the absent if it can be avoided; the day may come when some friend will be needed to defend you in your absence.

Do not speak with contempt and ridicule of a locality where you may be visiting. Find something to truthfully praise and commend; thus make yourself agreeable.

Do not make a pretense of gentility, nor parade the fact that you are a descendant of any notable family. You must pass for just what you are, and must stand on your own merit.

Do not contradict. In making a correction say, "I beg your pardon, but I had an impression that it was so and so." Be careful in correcting, as you may be wrong yourself.

Do not be unduly familiar; you will merit contempt if you are.

Neither should you be dogmatic in your assertions, arrogating to yourself much consequence in your opinions.

Do not be too lavish in your praise of various members of your own family when speaking to strangers; the person to whom you are speaking may know some faults that you do not.

Do not allow yourself to use personal abuse when speaking to another, as in so doing you may make that person a life long enemy. A few kind, courteous words might have made him a life-long friend.

Do not discuss politics or religion in general company. You probably would not convert your opponent, and he will not convert you. To discuss those topics is to arouse feeling without any good result.

Do not make a parade of being acquainted with distinguished or wealthy people, of having been to college, or of having visited foreign lands. All this is no evidence of any real genuine worth on your part.

Do not use the surname alone when speaking of your husband or wife to others. To say to another, that "I told Jones," referring to your husband, sounds badly. Whereas, to say, "I told Mr. Jones," shows respect and good-breeding.

Do not feel it incumbent upon yourself to carry your point in conversation. Should the person with whom you are conversing feel the same, your talk will lead into violent argument.

Do not yield to bashfulness. Do not isolate yourself, sitting back in a corner, waiting for some one to come and talk with you. Step out; have something to say. Though you may not say it very well, keep on. You will gain courage and will improve. It is as much your duty to entertain others as theirs to amuse you.

Do not attempt to pry into the private affairs of others by asking what their profits are, what things cost, whether Melissa ever had a beau, and why Amarette never got married. All such questions are extremely impertinent, and are likely to meet with rebuke.

Cultured and Refined.

IN the social gathering here brought to view we have a strong contrast to that on the opposite page. The positions are graceful and easy, with quietude and gentleness of manner, and the self-possession which true politeness always produces. An air of refinement in dress and gesture indicates a degree of mental culture secured by early training and the careful observance of the rules of social etiquette. In such a circle we should naturally expect the utterance of only the finest sentiments, the earnestness of sincerity, the purest of wit. Nothing is strained, far-fetched or improper, and the conversation is of that character that all may take a part in it and impart or receive lessons of truth and beauty, the remembrance of which will last as long as life itself. It is not necessary, in order to reap these advantages, to amass immense wealth. Even in the humblest households politeness, good nature and an easy demeanor may be cultivated with the happiest effects.

Do not whisper in company; do not engage in private conversation; do not speak a foreign language which the general company present may not comprehend, unless it is understood that the foreigner is unable to speak your own language.

Do not take it upon yourself to admonish comparative strangers on religious topics; the persons to whom you speak may have decided convictions of their own in opposition to yours, and your over-zeal may seem to them an impertinence.

Do not aspire to be a great story-teller; an inveterate teller of long stories becomes very tiresome. To tell one or two witty, short, new stories, appropriate to the occasion, is about all that one person should inflict on the company.

Do not indulge in satire; no doubt you are witty, and you could say a most cutting thing that would bring the laugh of the company upon your opponent, but you must not allow it, unless to rebuke an impertinent fellow who can be suppressed in no other way.

Do not forget that "words are the chariot wheels of thought," and that Dr. Samuel Johnson, Addison and Goldsmith won honor by the grace and eloquence of their language.

Do not spend your time in talking scandal; you sink your own moral nature by so doing, and you are, perhaps, doing great injustice to those about whom you talk. You probably do not understand all the circumstances. Were they understood, you would, doubtless, be much more lenient.

Do not flatter; in doing so you embarrass those upon whom you bestow praise, as they may not wish to offend you by repelling it, and yet they realize that if they accept it they merit your contempt. You may, however, commend their work whenever it can truthfully be done; but do not bestow praise where it is not deserved.

Etiquette of the Table.

THE TABLE--HOW TO SET AND ARRANGE IT.

THE dinner-hour will completely test the refinement, the culture and good breeding which the individual may possess. To appear advantageously at the table, the person must not only understand the laws of etiquette, but he must have had the advantage of polite society. It is the province of this chapter to show what the laws of the table are. It will be the duty of the reader, in the varied relations of life, to make such use of them as circumstances shall permit.

Rules to be Observed.

Sit upright, neither too close nor too far away from the table.

Open and spread upon your lap or breast a napkin, if one is provided—otherwise a handkerchief.

Do not be in haste; compose yourself; put your mind into a pleasant condition, and resolve to eat slowly.

Keep the hands from the table until your time comes to be served. It is rude to take knife and fork in hand and commence drumming on the table while you are waiting.

Possibly grace will be said by some one present, and the most respectful attention and quietude should be observed until the exercise is passed.

It is the most appropriate time, while you wait to be served, for you to put into practice your knowledge of small talk and pleasant words with those whom you are sitting near. By interchange of thought, much valuable information may be acquired at the table.

Do not be impatient to be served. With social chit-chat and eating, the meal-time should always be prolonged from thirty minutes to an hour.

Taking ample time in eating will give you better health, greater wealth, longer life and more happiness. These are what we may obtain by eating slowly in a pleasant frame of mind,thoroughly masticating the food.

If soup comes first, and you do not desire it, you will simply say, "No, I thank you," but make no comment; or you may take it and eat as little as you choose. The other course will be along soon. In receiving it you do not break the order of serving; it looks odd to see you waiting while all the rest are partaking of the first course. Eccentricity should be avoided as much as possible at the table.

The soup should be eaten with a medium-sized spoon,so slowly and carefully that you will drop none upon your person or the table-cloth. Making an effort to get the last drop, and all unusual noise when eating, should be avoided.

Fig. 9   The general arrangement of the table set for a party of twelve persons. The plates are often left off, and furnished by the waiter afterwards.

Fig. 10. Relative position of plate, napkin, goblet, salt-cup, knife and fork, when the table is set.

If asked at the next course what you desire, you will quietly state, and upon its reception you will, without display, proceed to put your food in order for eating. If furnished with potatoes in small dishes, you will put the skins back into the dish again; and thus where there are side-dishes all refuse should be placed in them—otherwise potato-skins will be placed upon the table-cloth, and bones upon the side of the plate. If possible, avoid putting waste matter upon the cloth. Especial pains should always be taken to keep the table-cover as clean as may be.

Eating with the Fork.

Fashions continually change. It does not follow, because he does not keep up with them, that a man lacks brains; still to keep somewhere near the prevailing style, in habit, costume and general deportment, is to avoid attracting unpleasant attention.

Fashions change in modes of eating. Unquestionably primitive man conveyed food to his mouth with his fingers. In process of time he cut it with a sharpened instrument, and held it, while he did so, with something pointed. In due time, with the advancement of civilization, there came the two-tined fork for holding and the broad-bladed knife for cutting the food and conveying it to the mouth. As years have passed on, bringing their changes, the three and four-tined forks have come into use, and the habit of conveying food with them to the mouth; the advantage being that there is less danger to the mouth from using the fork, and food is less liable to drop from it when being conveyed from the plate. Thus the knife, which is now only used for cutting meat, mashing potatoes, and for a few other purposes at the table, is no longer placed to the mouth by those who give attention to the etiquette of the table.

Set the table as beautifully as possible. Use only the snowiest of linen, the brightest of cutlery, and the cleanest of china. The setting of the table (Fig. 9) will have fruit-plates, castors and other dishes for general use, conveniently placed near the center. The specific arrangement (Fig. 10) of plate, knife, fork, napkin, goblet and salt-cup, is shown in the accompanying illustration.

It is customary for the gentleman who is the head of the household, in the ordinary family circle, to sit at the side of the table, in the center, having plates at his right hand, with food near by. When all the family are seated, and all in readiness, he will serve the guests who may be present; he will next serve the eldest lady of the household, then the ladies and gentlemen as they come in order. The hostess will sit opposite her husband, and preside over the tea, sauces, etc.

ERRORS TO BE AVOIDED.

DO NOT speak disrespectfully to the waiters, nor apologize to them for making them trouble; it is their business to bring forward the food called for. It is courtesy, however, when asked if you desire a certain article, to reply, "If you please;" "Not any, I thank you," etc.; when calling for an article, to say, "Will you please bring me," etc.; and when the article has been furnished, to say, "Thank you."

Never eat very fast.

Never fill the mouth very full.

Never open your mouth when chewing.

Never make noise with the mouth or throat.

Never attempt to talk with the mouth full.

Never leave the table with food in the mouth.

Never soil the table-cloth if it is possible to avoid it.

Never carry away fruits and confectionery from the table.

Never encourage a dog or cat to play with you at the table.

Never use anything but fork or spoon in feeding yourself.

Never explain at the table why certain foods do not agree with you.

Never introduce disgusting or unpleasant topics for conversation.

Never pick your teeth or put your hand in your mouth while eating.

Never cut bread; always break it, spreading with butter each piece as you eat it.

Never come to the table in your shirt-sleeves, with dirty hands or disheveled hair.

Never express a choice for any particular parts of a dish, unless requested to do so.

Never hesitate to take the last piece of bread or the last cake; there are probably more.

Never call loudly for the waiter, nor attract attention to yourself by boisterous conduct.

Never hold bones in your fingers while you eat from them. Cut the meat with a knife.

Never use your own knife when cutting butter. Always use a knife assigned to that purpose.

Never pare an apple, peach or pear for another at the table without holding it with a fork.

Never wipe your fingers on the table-cloth, nor clean them in your mouth. Use the napkin.

Never allow butter, soup or other food to remain on your whiskers. Use the napkin frequently.

Never wear gloves at the table, unless the hands from some special reason are unfit to be seen.

Never, when serving others, overload the plate nor force upon them delicacies which they decline.

Never pour sauce over meat and vegetables when helping others. Place it at one side, on the plate.

Never make a display of finding fault with your food. Very quietly have it changed if you want it different.

Never pass your plate with knife and fork on the same. Remove them, and allow them to rest upon a piece of bread.

Never make a display when removing hair, insects or other disagreeable things from your food. Place them quietly under the edge of your plate.

Never make an effort to clean your plate or the bones you have been eating from too clean; it looks as if you left off hungry.

Never tip back in your chair nor lounge upon the table; neither assume any position that is awkward or ill-bred.

Never, at one's own table or at a dinner-party elsewhere, leave before the rest have finished without asking to be excused. At a hotel or boarding house this rule need not be observed.

Never feel obliged to cut off the kernels with a knife when eating green corn; eaten from the cob, the corn is much the sweetest.

FIG. 11. BAD MANNERS AT THE TABLE.

No. 1. Tips back his chair.
" 2. Eats with his mouth too full.
" 3. Feeds a dog at the table.
" 4. Holds his knife improperly.
" 5. Engages in violent argument at the meal-time.
" 6. Lounges upon the table.
" 7. Brings a cross child to the table.
No. 8. Drinks from the saucer, and laps with his tongue the last drop from the plate.
" 9. Comes to the table in his shirt-sleeves, and puts his feet beside his chair.
" 10. Picks his teeth with his fingers.
" 11. Scratches her head and is frequently unnecessarily getting up from the table.

Never eat so much of any one article as to attract attention, as some people do who eat large quantities of butter, sweet cake, cheese or other articles.

Never expectorate at the table; also avoid sneezing or coughing. It is better to arise quietly from the table if you have occasion to do either. A sneeze is prevented by placing the finger firmly on the upper lip.

Never spit out bones, cherry pits, grape skins, etc., upon your plate. Quietly press them from your mouth upon the fork, and lay them upon the side of your plate.

Never allow the conversation at the table to drift into anything but chit-chat; the consideration of deep and abstruse principles will impair digestion.

Never permit yourself to engage in a heated argument at the table. Neither should you use gestures, nor illustrations made with a knife or fork on the table-cloth. The accompanying engraving (Fig. 11) very forcibly illustrates several faults to which many people are addicted.

Never pass forward to another the dish that has been handed to you, unless requested to do so; it may have been purposely designed for you, and passing it to another may give him or her what is not wanted.

Never put your feet so far under the table as to touch those of the person on the opposite side; neither should you curl them under nor at the side of your chair.

Never praise extravagantly every dish set before you; neither should you appear indifferent. Any article may have praise.

POLITENESS AT THE TABLE.

PROPERLY conducted, the dinner-party should be a pleasant affair; and if rightly managed, from the beginning to the end, it may prove a very enjoyable occasion to all in attendance, the dinner being from 5 to 8 P. M., the guests continuing at the table from one to two hours.

For a very pleasant social affair the rule is not to have the company when seated exceed twelve in number. With a party of that size the conversation can be general, and all are likely to feel more at ease than if the number be larger, provided a selection of guests is made that are congenial to each other. None of them should be conspicuously superior to the others, and all should be from the same circle of society.

Having determined upon the number of guests to be invited, the next thing in order will be the issuing of notes of invitation, by special messenger, which should be sent out ten or twelve days before the dinner is given. Their form will be—

Mr. and Mrs. L—— request the pleasure of the company of Mr. and Mrs. T—— at dinner on Wednesday, the 10th of March, at six o'clock P. M.
R. S. V. P.

The answer accepting the invitation may read—

Mr. and Mrs. T—— accept with much pleasure Mr. and Mrs. L——'s invitation for dinner on the 10th of March.

If declined, the form may be as follows:

Mr. and Mrs. T—— regret that a previous engagement (or for other reasons which may be given) will prevent their accepting Mr. and Mrs. L——'s kind invitation for dinner on the 10th of March.

Should the invitation be declined, the declination, which should state the reason for non-acceptance of the invitation, should be sent immediately by a messenger, that the hostess may have an opportunity for inviting other guests in the place of those who decline.

Should the invitation be accepted, nothing but serious difficulty should prevent the appointment being fulfilled. Should anything happen to prevent attendance, notification should be given the hostess immediately.

It is of the utmost importance that all of the company be punctual, arriving from ten to fifteen minutes before the appointed time. To be ten minutes late, keeping the dinner waiting, is a serious offense which no one should be guilty of.

The host, hostess and other members of the family should be early in the drawing-room to receive guests as they arrive, each of whom should be welcomed with a warm greeting.

The hostess having determined who shall accompany each other to the table, each gentleman should be informed what lady he is expected to escort. The hour having arrived, the host offers his right arm to the most honored or possibly the eldest lady guest, and the gentleman most distinguished will escort the lady of the house.

Proceeding to the dining-room when all is in readiness, the host will take his seat at the foot of the table, and the hostess at the head, the lady escorted by the host taking her seat at his right, and the escort of the hostess sitting also at *her* right. The next most honored seat is at the *left* of the hostess. The illustration (Fig. 12) upon this page shows a company thus seated.

It is fashionable to have cards laid upon the table, bearing the name, sometimes printed very beautifully upon silk, indicating where each guest shall sit, which saves confusion in being seated. The ladies having taken their places, the gentlemen will be seated, and all is in readiness for the dinner to be served, unless grace be said by a clergyman present or by the host.

Let us hope if there is any carving, it will be done before the meat is brought to the table, and the time of the company saved from this sometimes slow and tedious work. Should soup be passed, it is well for each one to take it, and also the various courses as they are served, making no special comment on the food.

The gentleman will, when a dish is brought, having seen the lady he escorted provided for, help himself and pass it on; he will pay no attention to the other lady near him, but will leave that to her escort. In all cases he will be careful and attentive to the wants of the lady in his charge, ascertaining her wishes and issuing her orders to the waiters.

No polite guest will ever fastidiously smell or examine any article of food before tasting it. Such conduct would be an insult to those who have invited him; neither will the host or hostess apologize for the cooking or find fault with each other, the cook or the waiters; all having done the best they could, there is nothing left to do but to make the best of everything that is provided.

Especial pains should be taken by the host and hostess, as well as all the company, to introduce topics of conversation that shall be agreeable and pleasing, that the dinner hour may be in the highest degree entertaining. When all the guests have finished their eating, the hostess, with a slight nod to one of the leading members of the party, will rise, as will all the company, and repair to the drawing-room, where, in social converse, the time should be spent for the next two or three hours. Etiquette demands that each member of the company remain at least an hour after the dinner is finished, it being impolite to hurry away immediately after rising from the table. Should he do so, however, he will ask to be excused.

FIG. 12. GENTILITY IN THE DINING-ROOM.

The evidences of good breeding with a party of ladies and gentlemen seated about a table, who are accustomed to the usages of polite society, are many. Among these will be the fact that the table is very beautifully and artistically spread. This need not require much wealth, but good taste is necessary to set it handsomely.

Again, the company evince gentility by each assuming a genteel position while eating. It is not necessary that an elaborate toilet be worn at the table, but careful attention should always be given to neatness of personal appearance, however plain may be the dress which is worn.

Another evidence of good manners is the self-possession with which the company deport themselves throughout the meal.

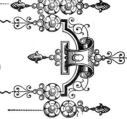

Etiquette of Visiting.

WHEN, WHERE AND HOW TO VISIT.

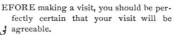

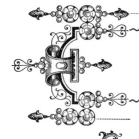

EFORE making a visit, you should be perfectly certain that your visit will be agreeable.

It is common for some people to be very cordial, and even profuse in their offers of hospitality. They unquestionably mean what they say at the time, but when they tender you an invitation to come and tarry *weeks*, it may seriously incommode them if you should pay them a visit of even a few *days*.

As a rule, a visit should never be made upon a general invitation. Should you visit a city where a friend resides, it will be best to go first to the hotel, unless you have a special invitation from the friend. From the hotel you will make a polite call, and if then you are invited, you can accept of the hospitality.

In all cases when you contemplate a visit, even with relatives, it is courtesy to write and announce your coming, giving, as nearly as possible, the day and exact time of your arrival.

An invitation to visit a friend should be answered as soon as may be; stating definitely when you will come, and how long you intend to stay.

When near your destination, it is well to send a prepaid telegram, stating upon what train you will arrive. As a reward for this forethought, you will probably find your friends waiting for you at the depot, and the welcome will be very pleasant.

What is Expected of the Guest when Visiting.

You are expected to pleasantly accept such hospitality as your friends can afford.

If no previous understanding has been had, the visit should be limited to three days, or a week at most.

You should make your visit interfere as little as possible with the routine work of the household in which you are a guest.

You should aim to conform your action, as much as may be, to the rules of the house, as to times of eating, retiring to rest, etc.

You should state upon your arrival how long you intend to stay, that your friends may arrange their plans to entertain accordingly.

Letters and papers being received in the presence of the host, hostess and others, the guest should ask to be excused while reading them.

Furnish your own materials in doing work for yourself when you are visiting, as much as possible, and never depend upon your entertainers.

A kind courtesy, while you remain, will be to execute some work representing your own skill, to be given the hostess as a memento of the occasion.

You should in shopping or transacting business, when you desire to go alone, select the hours of the day when your friends are engaged in their own duties.

The guest should beware of making unfavorable comment about the friends of the host and hostess, or of offering unfavorable criticism upon what they are known to favor or admire.

Should you happen to injure any article or other property while visiting, you should have the same immediately repaired, and, if possible, the article put in better condition than it was before.

You should not treat your friend's house as if it was a hotel, making your calls, visiting, transacting business about the town, and coming and going at all hours to suit your own convenience.

Never invite a friend who may call upon you to remain to dinner or supper. This is a right which belongs to the hostess, and it is for her to determine whether she wishes your guest to remain or not.

The guest should aim to render efficient assistance in case of sickness or sudden trouble at the house where the visit may be made. Oftentimes the best service will be rendered by considerately taking your leave.

Invitations accepted by the lady-guest should include the hostess, and those received by the hostess should include the guest. Thus, as much as possible, at all places of entertainment hostess and guest should go together.

While husbands and wives are always expected to accompany each other, where either may be invited, it is a trespass upon the generosity of the friend to take children and servants unless they are included in the invitation.

Never invite a friend who calls upon you into any other room than the parlor, unless it is suggested by the hostess that you do so. While you may have the right to enter various rooms, you have no authority for extending the privilege to others.

Immediately upon the return to your home, after paying a visit, you should write to your hostess, thanking her for hospitality and the enjoyment you received. You should also ask to be remembered to all of the family, mentioning each one by name.

Expenses which the friends may incur in removal and care of baggage, in repairs of wardrobe, or any other personal service requiring cash outlay, the guest should be careful to have paid. Washing and ironing should be sent elsewhere from the place where the guest is visiting.

The lady-guest should beware of receiving too many visits from gentlemen, and if invited to accompany them to places of amusement or on rides, she should consult with the hostess and learn what appointments she may have, and whether the going with others will be satisfactory to her.

Should a secret of the family come into your possession while on a visit, you should remember that the hospitality and privileges extended should bind you to absolute secrecy. It is contemptibly mean to become the possessor of a secret thus, and afterwards betray the confidence reposed in you.

Be careful that you treat with kindness and care servants, horses, carriages and other things at your friend's house which are placed at your disposal. To pluck choice flowers, to handle books roughly, to drive horses too fast, to speak harshly to servants—all this indicates selfishness and bad manners.

The visitor should beware of criticism or fault-finding with the family of the hostess. It is also in extremely bad taste for the guest to speak disparagingly of things about the home or the town where the visit is being made, being at the same time enthusiastic in praise of people and places elsewhere.

When a child is taken along, the mother should be very watchful that it does no injury about the house, and makes no trouble. It is excessively annoying to a neat housekeeper to have a child wandering about the rooms, handling furniture with greasy fingers, scattering crumbs over the carpets, and otherwise making disturbance.

The gentleman visitor should be certain that smoking is not offensive to the various members of the family, before he indulges too freely in the pipe and cigar about the house. For the guest, without permission, to seat himself in the parlor (Fig. 16), and scent the room with the fumes of tobacco, is a serious impoliteness.

When you can at times render assistance to those you are visiting, in any light work, you will often make your visit more agreeable. A lady will not hesitate to make her own bed if there be few or no servants, and will do anything else to assist the hostess. If your friend, however, declines allowing you to assist her, you should not insist upon the matter further.

Guests should enter with spirit and cheerfulness into the various plans that are made for their enjoyment. Possibly some rides will be had, and some visits made, that will be tiresome, but the courteous guest should find something to admire everywhere, and thus make the entertainers feel that their efforts to please are appreciated.

Of various persons in the family where the guest may be visiting, gifts may most appropriately be given to the hostess, and the baby or the youngest child. If the youngest has reached its teens, **then it may be best to give it** to the mother. The visitor will, however, use discretion in the matter. Flowers and fancy needle-work will always be appropriate for the lady. Confectionery and jewelry will be appreciated by the children. Small articles of wearing apparel or money will be suitable for servants who have been particularly attentive to the guest.

Special pains should be taken by guests to adapt themselves to the religious habits of those with whom they are visiting. If daily prayers are had, or grace is said at meals, the most reverent attention should be given; though when invited to participate in any of these exercises, if unaccustomed to the same, you can quietly ask to be excused. As a rule, it is courtesy to attend church with the host and hostess. Should you have decided preferences, and go elsewhere, do so quietly and without comment, and under no circumstances should there be allowed religious discussion afterwards. You visit the home of your friends to entertain and be entertained. Be careful that you so treat their opinions that they will wish you to come again.

Hints to the Host and Hostess.

Take the baggage-checks, and give personal attention to having the trunks conveyed to your residence, relieving the guest of all care in the matter.

Having received intelligence of the expected arrival of a guest, if possible have a carriage at the depot to meet the friend. Various members of the family being with the carriage will make the welcome more pleasant.

Have a warm, pleasant room especially prepared for the guest, the dressing-table being supplied with water, soap, towel, comb, hair-brush, brush-broom, hat-brush, pomade, cologne, matches, needles and pins. The wardrobe should be conveniently arranged for the reception of wearing apparel. The bed should be supplied with plenty of clothing, a side-table should contain writing materials, and the center-table should be furnished with a variety of entertaining reading matter.

Arrange to give as much time as possible to the comfort of the guest, visiting places of amusement and interest in the vicinity. This should all be done without apparent effort on your part. Let your friends feel that the visit is a source of real enjoyment to you; that through their presence and company you have the pleasure of amusements and recreation that would, perhaps, not have been enjoyed had they not come. Treat them with such kindness as you would like to have bestowed upon yourself under similar circumstances.

Fig. 17. The Visitor who Converts the Parlor into a Smoking-Room.

At the close of their stay, if you would be happy to have the visitors remain longer, you will frankly tell them so. If they insist upon going, you will aid them in every way possible in their departure. See that their baggage is promptly conveyed to the train. Examine the rooms to find whether they have forgotten any article that they would wish to take. Prepare a lunch for them to partake of on their journey. Go with them to the depot. Treat them with such kindness and cordiality to the close that the recollection of their visit will ever be a bright spot in their memory. Remain with them until the train arrives. They would be very lonely waiting without you. You will ever remember with pleasure the fact that you made the last hours of their visit pleasant. And thus, with the last hand-shaking, and the last waving of adieu, as the train speeds away, keep up the warmth of hospitality with your guests to the very end. It is, perhaps, the last time you will ever see them.

CONDUCT AT PLACES OF PUBLIC AMUSEMENT.

While a quiet conversation is allowable in the intervals after the opening of the performance, close attention should be given to the stage. Should it be a concert, the utmost stillness should be observed, as the slightest whisper will disturb the singers. This considerate attention should be given to the very end. It is in exceedingly bad taste, near the close of the last act, for the audience to commence moving about, putting on wraps and outer clothing, preparatory to leaving. Those who do so, lose the choicest part of the entertainment; they distract others who wish to be attentive, and they advertise the fact that they have no private carriage of their own, but on the contrary go by some public conveyance, and with characteristic selfishness they intend to rush out first and secure the best seats.

If the entertainment be a fancy fair, where goods which have been manufactured by a company of ladies are sold for church or charitable purposes, good sense will immediately suggest that as large a price should be realized as possible, and hence it is not etiquette for the purchaser to attempt to buy under price. It is also courtesy for the saleswoman, when a larger sum is presented than is charged, to deduct the price and promptly return the change, unless the surplus be donated to the charity.

Bad Manners.

Do not forget, while you make yourself comfortable, that others have rights which should be always considered.

Do not talk loudly, laugh boisterously, or make violent gestures.

Do not talk or whisper so loudly during the entertainment as to disturb those sitting near you.

Do not make a display of secrecy, mystery, or undue lover-like affection with your companion.

Do not prevent your companion from giving attention to the exercises, even though they may be without interest to yourself.

Do not, in a picture-gallery, stand conversing too long in front of pictures. Take seats, and allow others to make examination.

Do not, if a lady, allow a gentleman to join you, and thus withdraw your attention from your escort. And do not, if a gentleman, allow your attention to be taken up, to any great extent, with a lady other than the one you have in charge.

Do not, if a gentleman, be continually going from the hall between the acts of the play. To be passing up and down the aisle, eating peppers and cardamom seeds, advertises the fact that you are addicted to the too frequent use of liquors.

Do not join a party about to visit a place of amusement unless invited to do so. Should the party consist of one gentleman and two ladies, a gentleman, if well acquainted, may ask the privilege of attending one of the ladies. Should a ticket be furnished him, he should return the favor by an equal politeness bestowed upon the party, if possible, during the evening.

CONDITIONS THAT PROMOTE HAPPINESS.

THE happiness of married life comes from pleasant, harmonious relations existing between husband and wife. If rightly mated in the conjugal state, life will be one continual joy. If unhappily wedded, the soul will be forever yearning, and never satisfied; happiness may be hoped for, may be dreamed of, may be the object ever labored for, but it will never be realized.

In view, therefore, of the great influence that marriage has upon the welfare and happiness of all those who enter the conjugal relation, it becomes the duty of everyone to study the laws which make happy, enduring companionships between husbands and wives. It is a duty which not only the unmarried owe themselves, but it is an obligation due to society, as the well-being of a community largely rests upon the permanent, enduring family relation.

Very properly does the highest civilization not only recognize one woman for one man, and one man for one woman, but it ordains that marriage shall be publicly solemnized; and in view of its sacred nature and its vast influence on the welfare of society, that its rights shall be jealously guarded, and that a separation of those who pledge themselves to each other for life shall be as seldom made as possible.

The young should, therefore, be thoroughly imbued with the idea that the marriage state may not be entered upon without due and careful consideration of its responsibilities, as explained in the introductory remarks found in the department devoted to "Love Letters."

The province of this chapter is to consider the etiquette of courtship and marriage, not its moral bearings; and yet we may in this connection very appropriately make a few suggestions.

Whom to Marry.

There are exceptions to all rules. Undoubtedly parties have married on brief acquaintance, and have lived happily afterwards. It is sometimes the case that the wife is much older than the husband, is much wiser, and much his superior in social position, and yet happiness in the union may follow. But, as a rule, there are a few fundamental requisites, which, carefully observed, are much more likely to bring happiness than does marriage where the conditions are naturally unfavorable.

Of these requisites, are the following:

Marry a person whom you have known long enough to be sure of his or her worth—if not personally, at least by reputation.

Marry a person who is your equal in social position. If there be a difference either way, let the husband be superior to the wife. It is difficult for a wife to love and honor a person whom she is compelled to look down upon.

Marry a person of similar religious convictions, tastes, likes and dislikes to your own. It is not congenial to have one companion deeply religious, while the other only ridicules the forms of religion. It is not pleasant for one to have mind and heart absorbed in a certain kind of work which the other abhors; and it is equally disagreeable to the gentle, mild and sweet disposition to be united with a cold, heartless, grasping, avaricious, quarrelsome person. Very truthfully does Luna S. Peck, in the "Vermont Watchman," describe one phase of inharmony, in the following poem:

MISMATED.

A HAWK once courted a white little dove,
With the softest of wings and a voice full of love;
And the hawk — O yes, as other hawks go —
Was a well-enough hawk, for aught that I know.
    But she was a dove,
    And her bright young life
    Had been nurtured in love,
    Away from all strife.

Well, she married the hawk. The groom was delighted;
A feast was prepared, and the friends all invited.
(Does anyone think that my story's not true?
He is certainly wrong — the facts are not new.)
    Then he flew to his nest,
    With the dove at his side,
    And soon all the rest
    Took a squint at the bride.

A hawk for his father, a hawk for his mother,
A hawk for his sister, and one for his brother,
And uncles and aunts there were by the dozens,
And oh, such a number of hawks for his cousins!
    They were greedy and rough —
    A turbulent crew,
    Always ready enough
    To be quarrelsome, too.

To the dove all was strange; but never a word
In resentment she gave to the wrangling she heard.
If a thought of the peaceful, far-away nest
Ever haunted her dreams, or throbbed in her breast,
    No bird ever knew;
    Each hour of her life,
    Kind, gentle and true
    Was the hawk's dove-wife.

But the delicate nature too sorely was tried;
With no visible sickness, the dove drooped and died;
Then loud was the grief, and the wish all expressed
To call the learned birds, and hold an inquest.
    So all the birds came,
    But each shook his head:
    No disease could he name
    Why the dove should be dead;

'Till a wise old owl, with a knowing look,
Stated this: "The case is as clear as a book;
No disease do I find, or accident's shock;
The cause of her death was *too much hawk!*
Hawk for her father, and hawk for her mother,
Hawk for her sister, and hawk for her brother,
Was more than the delicate bird could bear;
She hath winged her way to a realm more fair!
    She was nurtured a dove,
    Too hard the hawk's life —
    Void of kindness and love,
    Full of hardness and strife."

And when he had told them, the other birds knew
That this was the cause, and the verdict was true!

Natural Selection.

In the first place, observation proves that selections made in nature by the beasts of the field and fowls of the air, of couples which pair, the male is always the strongest, generally the largest, the most brave, and always the leader. The female follows, trusting to her companion, leaving him to fight the heavy battles, apparently confident in his bravery, strength and wisdom.

If nature teaches anything, it is what observation and experience in civilized life has also proved correct, that of husband and wife, rightly mated, the husband should represent the positive—the physical forces, the intellectual and the strongly-loving; while the wife will represent the negative—the sympathetic, the spiritual, and the affectional. The husband should be so strong as to be a natural protector to his family. He should be brave, that he may defend his companion. He should be wise, and he should be so thoroughly true and devoted to his wife that he will delight in being her guardian and support.

The wife, confident in the husband's strength and wisdom, will thus implicitly yield to his protecting care. And thus both will be happy—he in exercising the prerogatives which belong naturally to the guardian and protector; and she in her confidence, love and respect for her companion, whom she can implicitly trust.

Peculiarities Suitable for Each Other.

Those who are neither very tall nor very short, whose eyes are neither very black nor very blue, whose hair is neither very black nor very red,—the mixed types—may marry those who are quite similar in form, complexion and temperament to themselves.

Bright red hair and a florid complexion indicate an excitable temperament. Such should marry the jet-black hair and the brunette type.

The gray, blue, black or hazel eyes should not marry those of the same color. Where the color is very pronounced, the union should be with those of a decidedly different color.

The very corpulent should unite with the thin and spare, and the short, thick-set should choose a different constitution.

The thin, bony, wiry, prominent-featured, Roman-nosed, cold-blooded individual, should marry the round-featured, warm-hearted and emotional. Thus the cool should unite with warmth and susceptibility.

The extremely irritable and nervous should unite with the lymphatic, the slow and the quiet. Thus the stolid will be prompted by the nervous companion, while the excitable will be quieted by the gentleness of the less nervous.

The quick-motioned, rapid-speaking person should marry the calm and deliberate. The warmly impulsive should unite with the stoical.

The very fine-haired, soft and delicate-skinned should not marry those like themselves; and the curly should unite with the straight and smooth hair.

The thin, long-face should marry the round-favored; and the flat nose should marry the full Roman. The woman who inherits the features and peculiarities of her father should marry a man who partakes of the characteristics of his mother; but in all these cases where the type is not pronounced, but is, on the contrary, an average or medium, those forms, features and temperaments may marry either.

Etiquette of Courtship.

But however suitable may be the physical characteristics, there are many other matters to be considered before a man and woman may take upon themselves the obligation to love and serve each other through life, and these can only be learned by acquaintance and courtship, concerning which the following suggestions may be appropriate:

Any gentleman who may continuously give special, undivided attention to a certain lady, is presumed to do so because he prefers her to others. It is reasonable to suppose that others will observe his action. It is also to be expected that the lady will herself appreciate the fact, and her feelings are likely to become engaged. Should she allow an intimacy thus to ripen upon the part of the gentleman, and to continue, it is to be expected that he will be encouraged to hope for her hand; and

hence it is the duty of both lady and gentleman, if neither intends marriage, to discourage an undue intimacy which may ripen into love, as it is in the highest degree dishonorable to trifle with the affections of another. If, however, neither has objections to the other, the courtship may continue.

The Decisive Question.

At length the time arrives for the gentleman to make a proposal. If he is a good judge of human nature, he will have discovered long ere this whether his favors have been acceptably received or not, and yet he may not know positively how the lady will receive an offer of marriage. It becomes him, therefore, to propose.

What shall he say? There are many ways whereby he may introduce the subject. Among these are the following:

He may write to the lady, making an offer, and request her to reply. He may, if he dare not trust to words, even in her presence write the question on a slip of paper, and request her laughingly to give a plain "no" or "yes." He may ask her if in case a gentleman very much like himself was to make a proposal of marriage to her, what she would say. She will probably laughingly reply that it will be time enough to tell what she would say when the proposal is made. And so the ice would be broken. He may jokingly remark that he intends one of these days to ask a certain lady not a thousand miles away if she will marry him, and asks her what answer she supposes the lady will give him; she will quite likely reply that it will depend upon what lady he asks. And thus he may approach the subject, by agreeable and easy stages, in a hundred ways, depending upon circumstances.

Engaged.

An engagement of marriage has been made. The period of courtship prior to marriage has been passed by the contracting parties, doubtless pleasantly, and we trust profitably.

Let us hope that they have carefully studied each other's tastes, that they know each other's mental endowments, and that by visits, rides and walks, at picnics, social gatherings and public entertainments, they have found themselves suited to each other.

Upon an engagement being announced, it is courtesy for various members of the gentleman's family, generally the nearest relatives, to call upon the family of the lady, who in turn should return the call as soon as possible. Possibly the families have never been intimate; it is not necessary that they should be so, but civility will demand the exchange of visits. If the betrothed live in different towns, an exchange of kind and cordial letters between the families is etiquette, the parents or near relatives of the gentleman writing to the lady or her parents.

A present of a ring to the lady, appropriately signalizes the engagement of marriage. This is usually worn on the fore-finger of the left hand. If the parties are wealthy, this may be set with diamonds; but if in humble circumstances, the gift should be more plain. Other presents by the gentleman to the lady, of jewelry, on birthdays, Christmas or New Year's, will be very appropriate; while she, in turn, may reciprocate by gifts of articles of fancy-work made with her own hands.

Aside from the engagement-ring, a gentleman should not, at this period of acquaintance, make expensive presents to his intended bride. Articles of small value, indicative of respect and esteem, are all that should pass between them. Should the marriage take place, and coming years of labor crown their efforts with success, then valuable gifts will be much more appropriate than in the earlier years of their acquaintance.

Arrangements for a Permanent Home.

It remains to be seen whether the intended husband will prove a financial success or not. He may be over benevolent; he may be too ready to become security for others; he may prove a spendthrift; he may lose his property in a variety of ways. It is therefore wise for the lady and her friends to see that, previous to the marriage, if she have money in her own right, a sufficient sum be settled upon her to provide for all contingencies in the future. This is a matter that the gentleman should himself insist upon, even using his own money for the purpose, as many a man has found, when his own fortune was wrecked, the provision made for his wife to be his only means of support in declining years.

Conduct During the Engagement.

An engagement having been made, it is desirable that it be carried to a successful termination by marriage. To do this, considerable depends upon both parties.

The gentleman should be upon pleasant terms with the lady's family, making himself agreeable to her parents, her sisters and her brothers. Especially to the younger members of her family should the gentleman render his presence agreeable, by occasional rides and little favors, presents of sweetmeats, etc.

He should also take pains to comply with the general regulations of the family during his visits, being punctual at meals, and early in retiring; kind and courteous to servants, and agreeable to all.

He should still be gallant to the ladies, but never so officiously attentive to anyone as to arouse uneasiness upon the part of his affianced. Neither should he expect her to eschew the society of gentlemen entirely from the time of her engagement.

The lady he has chosen for his future companion is supposed to have good sense, and while she may be courteous to all, receiving visits and calls, she will allow no flirtations, nor do anything calculated to excite jealousy on the part of her fiancé.

The conduct of both after the engagement should be such as to inspire in each implicit trust and confidence.

Visits should not be unduly protracted. If the gentleman makes them in the evening, they should be made early, and should not be over two hours in length. The custom of remaining until a late hour has passed away in genteel society. Such conduct at the present time, among the acquaintance of the lady, is certain to endanger her reputation.

For the gentleman and lady who are engaged to isolate themselves from others when in company, or do anything that shall attract the attention of the company to themselves, is in bad taste. Such conduct will always call forth unfavorable comments. The young ladies will sneer at it from jealousy, the young men will pronounce it foolish, and the old will consider it out of place.

And yet, by virtue of engagement, the gentleman should be considered the rightful escort, and upon all occasions the lady will give him preference; and he will especially see, however thoughtful he may be of others, that her wants are carefully attended to.

Should a misunderstanding or quarrel happen, it should be removed by the lady making the first advances towards a reconciliation. She thus shows a magnanimity which can but win admiration from her lover. Let both in their conduct towards the other be confiding, noble and generous.

The Wedding.

The wedding-day having arrived, the presents for the bride, if there be any, which may be sent at any time during the previous week, will be handsomely displayed before the ceremony. The presents, which have the names of the donors attached, are for the bride — never the bridegroom, although many of them may be sent by friends of the latter.

The form and ceremony of the wedding will be as various as are the peculiarities of those who marry, and comprise every description of display, from the very quiet affair, with but a few friends present, to the elaborate occasion when the church is filled to repletion, or in the palatial residence of the father of the bride, "the great house filled with guests of every degree."

We will suppose that the parties desire a somewhat ostentatious wedding, and the marriage takes place in church. In arranging the preliminaries, the bride may act her pleasure in regard to bridesmaids. She may have none; she may have one, two, three, four, six or eight; and, while in England it is customary to have but one groomsman, it is not uncommon in the United States to have one groomsman for every bridesmaid.

The bridegroom should make the first groomsman the manager of affairs, and should furnish him with money to pay necessary expenses.

Ushers are selected from the friends of the bride and groom, who, designated by a white rosette worn on the left lapel of the coat, will wait upon the invited guests at the door of the church, and assign them to their places, which will be a certain number of the front seats.

The bridegroom should send a carriage at his expense for the officiating clergyman and his family. He is not expected to pay for the carriage of the parents of the bride, nor for those occupied by the bridesmaids and groomsmen.

The latter will furnish the carriages for the ladies, unless otherwise provided. The invited guests will go in carriages at their own expense.

The clergyman is expected to be within the rails, and the congregation promptly in their seats, at the appointed hour. The bridegroom will proceed to the church, accompanied by his near relatives, and should precede the bride, that he may hand her from the carriage, if not waited upon by her father or other near relative.

The bride goes to the church in a carriage, accompanied by her parents, or those who stand to her in the relation of parents (as may other relatives, or legal guardian), or she may be accompanied by the bridesmaids.

When the bridal party is ready in the vestibule of the church, the ushers will pass up the center aisle, the first groomsman, accompanied by the first bridesmaid, coming next, the others following in their order. The groom walks next with the bride's mother upon his arm, followed by the father with the bride. At the altar, as the father and mother step back, the bride takes her place upon the left of the groom.

Another mode of entering the church is for the first bridesmaid and groomsman to lead, followed by the bride and groom. When in front of the altar, the groomsman turns to the right, the bridesmaid to the left, leaving a space in front of the minister for the bride and groom; the near relatives and parents of the bride and groom follow closely, and form a circle about the altar during the ceremony.

The former mode is, however, established etiquette. At the altar the bride stands at the left of the groom, and in some churches both bride and groom remove the right-hand glove. In others it is not deemed necessary. When a ring is used, it is the duty of the first bridesmaid to remove the bride's left-hand glove. An awkward pause is, however, avoided by opening one seam of the glove upon the ring finger, and at the proper time the glove may be turned back, and the ring thus easily placed where it belongs, which is the third finger of the left hand.

The responses of the bride and groom should not be too hastily nor too loudly given.

Following the ceremony, the parents of the bride speak to her first, succeeded by the parents of the groom before other friends.

Essentially the same ceremonies will be had, the same positions will be assumed, and the same modes of entering will be observed, in the parlors at the residence, as at the church.

The bride and groom, after the ceremony, will go in the same carriage from the church to the home or to the depot.

Should a breakfast or supper follow the ceremony, the bride will not change her dress until she assumes her traveling apparel. At the party succeeding the ceremony, the bridesmaids and groomsmen should be invited, and all may, if they prefer, wear the dresses worn at the wedding.

The Wedding Trousseau.

It is customary, at the wedding, for the young bride to wear only pure white, with a wreath of orange flowers to adorn the full veil of lace. The widow or elderly lady will wear pearl color or tinted silk, without wreath or veil. The bridesmaid of the youthful bride may wear colors, but a very beautiful effect is produced by pure white, with colored trimmings. In some cases, one-half of the bridesmaids will wear one color, and the other half another color. No black dresses should be worn by the guests. Any in mourning may, for the time, wear purple, lavender, iron-gray and other quiet colors.

The bridegroom and groomsmen will wear white gloves, vest and neckties.

The bride's traveling dress should be very quiet and modest, and not such as in any way to attract attention.

Only the bridegroom is congratulated at the wedding; it is he who is supposed to have won the prize. Acquaintances of both should speak to the bride first; but if acquainted with but one, they will address that one first, when introductions will take place.

At the wedding breakfast or supper the bride sits by the side of her husband, in the center of the table, at the side; her father and mother occupy the foot and head of the table, and do the honors of the occasion, as at the dinner-party.

The festivities of the occasion being over, and the hour of departure having arrived, the guests disperse, it being etiquette for them to make a formal call on the mother of the bride in the succeeding two weeks.

Etiquette Between Husbands and Wives.

Let the rebuke be preceded by a kiss.

Do not require a request to be repeated.

Never should both be angry at the same time.

Never neglect the other, for all the world beside.

Let each strive to always accommodate the other.

Let the angry word be answered only with a kiss.

Bestow your warmest sympathies in each other's trials.

Make your criticism in the most loving manner possible.

Make no display of the sacrifices you make for each other.

Never make a remark calculated to bring ridicule upon the other.

Never deceive; confidence, once lost, can never be wholly regained.

Always use the most gentle and loving words when addressing each other.

Let each study what pleasure can be bestowed upon the other during the day.

Always leave home with a tender good-bye and loving words. They may be the last.

Consult and advise together in all that comes within the experience and sphere of each individually.

Never reproach the other for an error which was done with a good motive and with the best judgment at the time.

The Wife's Duty.

Never should a wife display her best conduct, her accomplishments, her smiles, and her best nature, exclusively away from home.

Be careful in your purchases. Let your husband know what you buy, and that you have wisely expended your money.

Let no wife devote a large portion of her time to society-work which shall keep her away from home daytimes and evenings, without the full concurrence of her husband.

Beware of entrusting the confidence of your household to outside parties. The moment you discuss the faults of your husband with another, that moment an element of discord has been admitted which will one day rend your family circle.

If in moderate circumstances, do not be over ambitious to make an expensive display in your rooms. With your own work you can embellish at a cheap price, and yet very handsomely, if you have taste. Let the adornings of your private rooms be largely the work of your own hands.

Beware of bickering about little things. Your husband returns from his labors with his mind absorbed in business. In his dealings with his employes, he is in the habit of giving commands and of being obeyed. In his absent-mindedness, he does not realize, possibly, the change from his business to his home, and the same dictatorial spirit may possess him in the domestic circle. Should such be the case, avoid all disputes. What matters it where a picture hangs, or a flower-vase may sit. Make the home so charming and so wisely-ordered that your husband will gladly be relieved of its care, and will willingly yield up its entire management to yourself.

Be always very careful of your conduct and language. A husband is largely restrained by the chastity, purity and refinement of his wife.

A lowering of dignity, a looseness of expression and vulgarity of words, may greatly lower the standard of the husband's purity of speech and morals.

Whatever may have been the cares of the day, greet your husband with a smile when he returns. Make your personal appearance just as beautiful as possible. Your dress may be made of calico, but it should be neat. Let him enter rooms so attractive and sunny that all the recollections of his home, when away from the same, shall attract him back.

Be careful that you do not estimate your husband solely by his ability to make display. The nature of his employment, in comparison with others, may not be favorable for fine show, but that should matter not. The superior qualities of mind and heart alone will bring permanent happiness.

To have a cheerful, pleasant home awaiting the husband, is not all. He may bring a guest whom he desires to favorably impress, and upon you will devolve the duty of entertaining the visitor so agreeably that the husband shall take pride in you. A man does not alone require that his wife be a good housekeeper. She must be more; in conversational talent and general accomplishment she must be a companion.

The Husband's Duty.

A very grave responsibility has the man assumed in his marriage. Doting parents have confided to his care the welfare of a loved daughter, and a trusting woman has risked all her future happiness in his keeping. Largely will it depend upon him whether her pathway shall be strewn with thorns or roses.

Let your wife understand fully your business. In nearly every case she will be found a most valuable adviser when she understands all your circumstances.

Do not be dictatorial in the family circle. The home is the wife's province. It is her natural field of labor. It is her right to govern and direct its interior management. You would not expect her to come to your shop, your office, your store or your farm, to give orders how your work should be conducted; neither should you interfere with the duties which legitimately belong to her.

If a dispute arises, dismiss the subject with a kind word, and do not seek to carry your point by discussion. It is a glorious achievement to master one's own temper. You may discover that you are in error, and if your wife is wrong, she will gladly, in her cooler moments, acknowledge the fault.

Having confided to the wife all your business affairs, determine with her what your income will be in the coming year. Afterwards ascertain what your household expenses will necessarily be, and then set aside a weekly sum, which should regularly and invariably be paid the wife at a stated time. Let this sum be even more than enough, so that the wife can pay all bills, and have the satisfaction besides of accumulating a fund of her own, with which she can exercise a spirit of independence in the bestowal of charity, the purchase of a gift, or any article she may desire. You may be sure that the wife will very seldom use the money unwisely, if the husband gives her his entire confidence.

Your wife, possibly, is inexperienced; perhaps she is delicate in health, also, and matters that would be of little concern to you may weigh heavily upon her. She needs, therefore, your tenderest approval, your sympathy and gentle advice. When her efforts are crowned with success, be sure that you give her praise. Few husbands realize how happy the wife is made by the knowledge that her efforts and her merits are appreciated. There are times, also, when the wife's variable condition of health will be likely to make her cross and petulant; the husband must overlook all this, even if the wife is at times unreasonable.

Endeavor to so regulate your household affairs that all the faculties of the mind shall have due cultivation. There should be a time for labor, and a time for recreation. There should be cultivation of the social nature, and there should be attention given to the spiritual. The wife should not be required to lead a life of drudgery. Matters should be so regulated that she may early finish her labors of the day; and the good husband will so control his business that he may be able to accompany his wife to various places of amusement and entertainment. Thus the intellectual will be provided for, and the social qualities be kept continually exercised.

The wise husband will provide for the moral and spiritual growth of his family by regular attendance at church; the spiritual faculties of our nature are given for a beneficent purpose; their exercise and cultivation leads up into the higher and the better; one day in seven, at least, should therefore be set apart for the spiritual improvement of the family. Select a church, the religious teaching in which is nearest in accord with the views of yourself and wife, and be regular in your attendance; accompany your wife; give her the pleasure of your escort; see that she is provided with a good seat and all the advantages which the church has to give; enter fully and freely into the religious work of your church, and your family will be blessed in consequence.

Give your wife every advantage which it is possible to bestow. Shut up with her household duties, her range of freedom is necessarily circumscribed, and in her limited sphere she is likely to remain stationary in her intellectual growth. Indeed, oftentimes, if her family be large and her husband's means are limited, in her struggle to care for the family she will sacrifice beauty, accomplishments, health —life, almost— rather than that her husband shall fail. In the meantime, with wide opportunities and intellectual advantages, he will be likely to have better facilities for growth and progression. There is sometimes thus a liability of the husband and wife growing apart, an event which both should take every pains to avert. In avoiding this, much will depend upon the wife. She must resolutely determine to be in every way the equal of her companion. Much also will depend upon the husband. The wife should have every opportunity whereby she may keep even pace with him.

Possibly the wife in social position, intellectual acquirement, and very likely in moral worth, may be superior to her husband. It is equally necessary, therefore, that the husband put forth every effort to make himself worthy of his companion. It is a terrible burden to impose on a wife to compel her to go through life with a man whom she cannot love or respect.

Etiquette of Traveling.

THE reader will call to mind people who always appear at ease when they are traveling. Investigation will prove that these individuals have usually had a wide experience in journeying, and an extensive acquaintance with the world. The experienced traveler has learned the necessity of always being on time, of having baggage checked early, of purchasing a ticket before entering the cars, and of procuring a seat in a good location before the car is full.

The inexperienced traveler is readily known by his flurry and mistakes. He is likely to be behind time, and he is likely to be an hour too early. For want of explicit direction, his baggage often fails to reach the train in time, or does not come at all. His trunks, from lack of strength, are liable to be easily broken. In his general confusion, when he buys a ticket he neglects to place it where it will be secure, and consequently loses it. He forgets a portion of his baggage, and thus in a dozen ways he is likely to be in trouble.

If the person be a lady who is unacquainted with travel, she reveals the fact by a general impatience, restlessness, and absent-mindedness. In her want of self-possession she forgets several things she had intended to bring, and her continual fault-finding at flies, dust, heat, delay and other trials, all betray the fact that she has not heretofore been accustomed to these difficulties.

Fig. 17.   The couple that make themselves appear ridiculous when traveling.

The following suggestions relating to railway traveling may be of service:

Whenever you contemplate a journey, consider carefully what route you want to take, and decide it definitely. Learn accurately what time the train leaves, and provide yourself with a table giving the running time of the road, stations on the way, etc., which will save you the trouble of asking many questions.

If you desire to ride in a sleeping-car, secure your berth a day or two previous to the time of going, in order that you may be in time to take your choice. The most desirable sections are in the center of the car, away from the annoyance of dust, drafts of air and sudden noises resulting from opening and closing doors.

At least a day before you go, consider carefully what baggage you need to take, and have it packed. Take just as little as possible. Have your trunks very secure, and pack all articles of baggage in such a manner that they cannot shake and thus be broken.

Provide among your baggage necessary toilet articles — a linen wrap to exclude the dust from your finer clothing, and a small amount of reading-matter with very coarse type. See that your baggage is perfectly in order, and an hour before you start engage an authorized expressman to take your baggage to the depot. State very distinctly where you want the baggage taken, and for what train. It is also a wise provision to have your trunk labeled with a card bearing your name and destination.

Take the number of the expressman, ascertain his charge, and withhold payment until he has assisted in finding baggage, and has aided in getting it checked at the depot. Be very sure that your watch or clock is perfectly correct with railroad time, and that you, half an hour before the starting time of the train, arrive at the depot, buy a ticket, and take your seat in the car. You are probably early enough to take your choice of location in the seats.

If in the summer time, and the train runs east or west, the north side will probably be most pleasant. Seats midway in the car are easiest to ride in, and the left side is freest from sudden gusts of wind which may come in at the open doors.

Having selected a seat, it is customary to deposit the satchel, umbrella or some article of wearing-apparel in the same, should you not be ready to occupy it; and it is etiquette for anyone finding a seat so occupied to look further.

You should carry just as little baggage into the car as possible, and all separate pieces should have your name plainly written or printed upon them, which will secure their being forwarded to you in case they are left upon the seat.

Having paid for one ticket, you are entitled to only one seat. It shows selfishness, therefore, when the coach is quite full to deposit a large amount of baggage in the surrounding seats and occupy three or four, and engage in reading, while others look in vain for a place to sit down.

It is courtesy for a gentleman when sitting alone to offer the vacant seat beside himself to a lady who may be unattended. He will also give his seat to two ladies, or a lady and gentleman who desire to sit together, and take a seat elsewhere. Such attention will often be a great kindness, while the individual bestowing it may suffer but very little inconvenience.

The true lady or gentleman will always consult the convenience of others when traveling. Thus, care should be exercised that no one be incommoded by your opening doors or windows in a railway coach. If possible, so arrange that the air of a window that you may open shall strike full upon yourself, and not upon those in the rear; certainly not if it is unpleasant to them.

What to Avoid when Traveling.

A lady and gentleman should avoid evidences of undue familiarity in the presence of strangers. Couples who may evince a silly affection by overfondling of each other in public (Fig. 17) make themselves appear extremely ridiculous to all who may see them.

People with weak eyes should avoid reading on the train, and those having weak lungs should avoid much talking, as an undue effort will be required to talk above the noise of the train.

Passengers should avoid eating at irregular times on the journey, and gentlemen should avoid smoking in the presence of those to whom it may be offensive.

Avoid leaving the pockets so open and money so exposed that thieves may steal your effects. In the sleeping-car the valuables should be put in some article of wearing-apparel and placed under the pillow.

Avoid undue haste and excitement when traveling, by forethought. Have a plan matured, and when the time comes to act you will know what to do, and with self-possession you accomplish your work very much better.

Avoid wearing laces, velvets, or any articles that naturally accumulate and hold dust. Excessive finery or a lavish display of jewelry are in bad taste on extended journeys. Before commencing a journey, consider carefully what will be most suitable to wear, and study how little baggage may be taken.

CONDUCT FOR GENTLEMEN

WHEN

TRAVELING WITH LADIES.

If the gentleman is an authorized escort he will, if an old acquaintance, accompany the lady in his charge from her residence to the depot. If the acquaintance is of short duration, it will be sufficient to meet her at the depot in ample time to purchase tickets and see that her baggage is checked, while she remains in the sitting-room at the station.

Arrangements being made, he will secure her a seat upon the train, will find a place for packages, will attend to her wants in adjusting the window, and will aim to put her entirely at ease.

In getting on and off the train, the gentleman will care for all parcels and see that nothing is left. He will assist the lady into the coach or omnibus before getting in himself, and in getting out he will precede her, and afterwards turn and help her carefully down.

If requested by the lady to defray her expenses from her purse, the gentleman may take the same and keep it the entire journey, or he may pay from his own pocket and keep an account of expenses which she will refund at the end of the journey.

He should purchase the needed confections or literature on the train. He should be fruitful in the introduction of topics that will enliven, amuse and instruct the lady, if she is inclined to be reticent; and at her journey's end he should go with her to her home, or the place where she is to stop. He may call next day, and if the acquaintance seems desirable it may be continued. The gentleman should be very careful not to continue his visits unless certain that they are acceptable.

If a hotel be the point of destination, the gentleman will accompany the lady to the parlor. He will then secure for her a room, and leave her in care of a waiter; her desire being probably to proceed to her apartments at once, where she will remove the dust and travel stains of the journey, and meet him again at a concerted hour in the parlor.

Ladies and gentlemen who are strangers, being thrown into the company of each other for a long journey, need not necessarily refuse to speak to each other. While the lady should be guarded, acquaintance may be made with certain reserve.

THE HORSEBACK RIDE,

AND THE

RULES THAT GOVERN IT.

A gentleman who may act as escort for a lady when riding should be very careful that the horse selected for her is entirely reliable and gentle. If he has no horse of his own, and she has none to which she is accustomed, he must understand that there is considerable danger in allowing her to use a horse that has not been tried, no matter what may be the representations of the liverymen or servant.

A trustworthy horse having been secured for the lady, it is the gentleman's duty before mounting to give a very thorough examination of the saddle and bridle, to see that all are secure. It will not do to leave this matter to the stablemen. They are accustomed to such continuous handling of harness that they become careless, and are liable to overlook defects in buckles, girths, etc., that might cause a severe accident.

FIG. 18. THE RIDE ON HORSEBACK.

The gentleman takes his position at the right of the lady.

When all is in readiness, it is the gentleman's province to assist the lady in mounting. To do this, it is well to have some one hold the horse, otherwise he holds the bridle with his left hand. The lady, then, with her skirt in her left hand, will take hold of the pommel of the saddle with her right, her face turned towards the horse's head. The gentleman will stand at the horse's shoulder, facing the lady, and stoop, allowing her to place her left foot in his right hand. She will then spring, while he lifts her gently and steadily into her seat, following which he will place her left foot in the stirrup and arrange her riding habit.

After the lady is in position, the gentleman will still remain with her until she has whip and reins properly in hand and is securely in her seat, when he will mount his horse and take his place (Fig. 18) upon her right, as shown in the accompanying illustration.

Should there be two ladies on horseback, the gentleman should ride to the right of both of them, unless they may need his assistance, in which case he will ride between them.

In dismounting, the gentleman should take the lady's left hand in his right, remove the stirrup and take her foot in his left hand, lowering her gently to the ground.

Etiquette of Carriage-Riding.

PRECAUTIONS AGAINST ACCIDENTS.

THE mode of entering a carriage will depend somewhat upon circumstances. Should the team be very restive, and the gentleman remain in the carriage the better to control his horses, the lady will enter upon the left side, the gentleman assisting her by the hand. While circumstances may sometimes prevent, it is always etiquette for the gentleman to see that the lady enters the carriage first. To aid in entering and alighting from a carriage easily and safely, every residence should be provided with an elevated platform near the walk, beside which the vehicle may be driven, as represented in the illustration.

Of two seats in the carriage facing each other, that in the rear, and facing the horses, is the most desirable; the place of honor being the right side of this seat, which should be given to any elderly person, an honored guest or ladies, during the carriage ride.

The ladies being in place, the gentlemen will take the seat with their backs to the horses, care being observed that dresses and shawls are not shut in the door when it is closed. The

Fig. 19.   Assisting the lady into the carriage.

gentleman last in will sit on the right, and upon him should devolve the giving of orders to the driver, and any other directions which the company may determine upon.

At the close of the ride, the gentlemen will dismount first, and afterwards help the ladies carefully from the carriage, taking care to keep their dresses from being soiled upon the wheels.

The single carriage should be driven as near the curbstone as possible, on the right side. The driver, having the top of the carriage down, should then turn the horses to the left, spreading the wheels on the right side, giving an opportunity for the lady to get into the carriage without soiling her dress upon the wheels. The lady should have both of her hands free to assist herself, while the gentleman (Fig. 19) should aid her, as shown in the illustration. The lady being in her place, her escort will take his seat upon the right side, will spread a lap-robe in front of the lady and himself to ward off dust and mud, and all is in readiness for the ride.

In getting from the carriage, the gentleman should alight first. He should quiet the team, and turn them, that the wheels may spread apart, retaining the reins in his hand, that he may hold the horses in case of

fright. The lady should then place her hands upon the gentleman's shoulders (Fig. 20), while her escort, taking her by the elbows, will assist her carefully to the ground. Being aided thus in safely alighting, a lady will, oftentimes, be saved from severe injury.

The gentleman on the pleasure ride should not drive so fast as to throw mud upon the occupants of the carriage. He should avoid fast driving if the lady is timid, and at the close of the ride he should take the friend to his or her residence.

Horses should not have their heads checked painfully high. They will be less shy if trained and driven without blinds. They should be driven with tight rein, and care should be observed to avoid accidents.

Ladies Unattended.

For the advantage of the unattended lady who may be stopping at a hotel, the following suggestions are made:

Fig. 20.   Assisting the lady when alighting from the carriage.

The lady should enter a hotel by the ladies' entrance. When in the parlor, she should send for the proprietor or clerk, present her card, and state the length of time that she designs to remain.

By requesting the waiter to do so, he will meet the lady at the entrance to the dining-room and conduct her to a seat; thus saving her the necessity of crossing the room without an escort.

Meeting friends at the table, the lady should converse in a voice so low and quiet as not to attract attention from strangers. Particularly should she avoid loud laughter or any conspicuous evidence of commenting upon others.

To make the time spent at the hotel pass agreeably, care should be taken to obtain a pleasant room that will allow the entrance of sunshine and fresh air.

Orders at the table should be given in a low, yet clear, distinct voice. In the interval while waiting to be served, it is allowable to read a paper. Staring about the room, handling of the knife, spoons, or other articles upon the table, should be avoided.

Do not point at a dish wanted. A look in the direction of the article desired, and a request to the waiter that it be passed, will secure the dish without trouble.

The lady in the dining-room, unless accompanied by an escort, should avoid dressing ostentatiously. A very modest dress is in best taste.

Etiquette in Church.

Suggestions Concerning Conduct Appropriate In the House of Worship.

The Stillness, Order and Reverence Due the Place and Occasion.

CHURCH should be entered with a most reverent feeling. The object of attending divine service is to improve the spiritual nature, and hence business and everything of a secular character should be left behind when you enter the church portals.

If a stranger, you will wait in the vestibule until the arrival of the usher, who will conduct you to a seat.

Enter the church quietly, removing the hat, and never replacing it until the door is reached again at the close of the service.

If a stranger and accompanied by a lady, you will precede her, and follow the usher up the aisle until the pew is reached, when you will pause, allow her to pass in, and you will follow, taking seats at the further end if you are first, so that you will not be disturbed by later arrivals. It is no longer a custom, as formerly, for the gentleman to step into the aisle and allow ladies that are strangers to pass to the inside.

The gentleman will place his hat, if possible, under the seat, and while in church the occupant should avoid making a noise, staring around the building, whispering, laughing or nodding to others.

All greetings, recognitions and conversation should be conducted in the vestibule after service. While in church, the passage of a fan or hymn-book to another should be recognized by merely a quiet bow.

Should you see a stranger waiting, you may invite him to enter your pew. No speaking is necessary then, nor when you open the book and point out the service.

If a stranger, it is best to conform to the rules of the service, rising and sitting down with the congregation; and, although the forms may be radically different from what you are accustomed to, you should comport yourself with the utmost attention and reverence.

Avoid making a noise when entering a church after the services have commenced. It is disrespectful to come late, and shows bad manners to leave before the service is through. You should wait until the benediction is pronounced before you commence putting your articles in order for leaving.

It is a breach of etiquette for a number of young men to congregate in the vestibule and there carry forward a conversation, commenting upon the services and various members of the congregation present.

If a member of a church, you should be regular in attendance. While the pastor has put forth, possibly, extra effort to prepare an effective sermon, it is poor encouragement to find members of the congregation absent because of a trivial storm, away upon the pleasure drive, or absorbed in the contents of the Sunday paper.

TREATMENT OF EMPLOYES.

IT TAKES every grade of society to make the complete whole. One class is just as necessary as the other. In carrying forward great enterprises, how plainly do we see this manifested. Take the building of a railroad as an illustration:

A certain grade of mind is essential to prepare the road-bed and lay the track. This class of men must have strong physical natures, and the qualities that give the necessary force and energy to hew down rocks, tunnel mountains and remove all obstructions. Another class will act as foremen of the laborers, another will serve as engineers, another is fitted to act as officers, while still another grade of mind projected the enterprise and furnished the means for carrying it to a successful conclusion.

As in the materials that enter into the erection of the building, the foundation stones that support the superstructure down deep in the earth, while they are never seen, are nevertheless just as essential to the completion of the building as are the ornamental capstones above the windows; so, in associated labor, each grade of mind does its appropriate work. We could not dispense with either, and all should have due praise.

Each class being thus dependent one upon the other, all should labor in harmony together. The workman should guard his employer's interest. He should always be promptly on time and faithful to the last hour. He should make his work a study; he should give it thought, as thereby he renders his services so much the more valuable, and his compensation in the end so much better. Probably, if faithful, he may succeed to the business of his employer; or may enter a separate field. It is certain, at any rate, if he proves himself a competent assistant he is the more likely in time himself to become a manager of others.

The employer, through kind and pleasant manner, may do much toward making the subordinate worthy and competent. The workman should thoroughly understand what the duty is which he is expected to perform, and he should be required pleasantly yet firmly to execute it to the letter. When once there is a definite understanding on his part as to what is explicitly required, it is not necessary that an employer use harsh means or a manner in any way discourteous in order to secure obedience to his commands. A word of encouragement will increase the harmony.

Etiquette in the School.

THE following are the requisites for successful management in the schoolroom:

The teacher must be a good judge of human nature. If so, his knowledge will teach him that no two children are born with precisely the same organization. This difference in mentality will make one child a natural linguist, another will naturally excel in mathematics, another will exhibit a fondness for drawing, and another for philosophy. Understanding and observing this, he will, without anger or impatience, assist the backward student, and will direct the more forward, ever addressing each child in the most respectful manner.

As few rules as possible should be made, and the object and necessity for the rule should be fully explained to the school by the teacher. When a rule has been made obedience to it should be enforced. Firmness, united with gentleness, is one of the most important qualifications which a teacher can possess.

Everything should be in order and the exercises of the day should be carried forward according to an arranged programme. The rooms should be swept, the fires built and the first and second bells rung with exact punctuality. In the same manner each recitation should come at an appointed time throughout the school hours.

The programme of exercises should be so varied as to give each pupil a variety of bodily and mental exercise. Thus, music, recreation, study, recitation, declamation, etc., should be so varied as to develop all the child's powers. Not only should boys and girls store their minds with knowledge, but they should be trained in the best methods of writing and speaking, whereby they may be able to impart the knowledge which they possess.

The teacher should require the strictest order and neatness upon the part of all the students. Clean hands, clean face and neatly combed hair should characterize every pupil, while a mat in the door-

way should remind every boy and girl of the necessity of entering the schoolroom with clean boots and shoes. Habits of neatness and order thus formed will go with the pupils through life.

At least a portion of each day should be set apart by the teacher in which to impart to the pupils a knowledge of etiquette. Students should be trained to enter the room quietly, to always close without noise the door through which they pass, to make introductions gracefully, to bow with ease and dignity, to shake hands properly, to address others courteously, to make a polite reply when spoken to, to sit and stand gracefully, to do the right thing in the right place, and thus, upon all occasions, to appear to advantage.

All the furnishings of the schoolroom should be such as to inspire the holiest, loftiest and noblest ambition in the child. A schoolroom should be handsomely decorated. The aquarium, the trailing vine, the blossom and the specimens of natural history should adorn the teacher's desk and the windows, while handsome pictures should embellish the walls. In short, the pupils should be surrounded with such an array of beauty as will constantly inspire them to higher and nobler achievements.

Boys and girls should be taught that which they will use when they become men and women. In the first place they will talk more than they will do anything else. By every means possible they should be trained to be correct, easy, fluent and pleasant speakers; and next to this they should be trained to be ready writers. To be this, they should be schooled in penmanship, punctuation, capitalization, composition and the writing of every description of forms, from the note of invitation to an agreement, from the epistle to a friend to the promissory note, from the letter of introduction to the report of a meeting.

Above all, the teacher should be thoroughly imbued with the importance of inculcating in the mind of the student a knowledge of general principles. Thus, in the study of geography, the pupil should be taught that the earth is spherical in form; that its outer surface is divided into land and water; that the land is divided into certain grand sections, peopled with different races of human beings who exhibit special characteristics. That civilization is the result of certain causes, and progress in the human race arises from the inevitable law of nature that everything goes from the lower steadily toward the higher. A study of the causes which make difference in climate, difference in animals, difference in intellectual and moral developments among the races—a general study of causes thus will make such an impression upon the child's mind as will never be effaced; while the simple study of facts such as load the mind with names of bays, islands, rivers, etc., is the crowding of the memory with that which is likely in time to be nearly all forgotten.

Thus, in the study of history, dates will be forgotten, while the outlines of the rise and fall of kingdoms, and the causes which produced the same, if rightly impressed by the teacher, will be ever stored in the mind of the pupil.

So should the teacher instruct the student in every branch of study, remembering that facts are liable to be forgotten, but fundamental principles and causes, well understood, will be forever remembered.

It is of the utmost importance, also, that the teacher continuously and persistently keep before the student the importance of temperance, justice and truth; as, without these, however superior the education, the individual is entirely without balance, and is always liable to fall. The teacher should never relax his efforts in this direction.

The good teacher will be a living example in all that he teaches to others. If wise, he will seldom or never resort to the infliction of corporal pain on the pupil, although, if a law or rule be violated, it is of the utmost importance that a just punishment follow the violation, but this should never be such as will destroy the child's self-respect.

Duty of the Pupil.

It should be the aim of the student to be punctual in attendance at school, to be thorough in study, and good in recitation. The boy or girl who would be successful in after-life must lay the foundation of success in youth. They should fully understand the importance of improving their school-days for this purpose.

The student who seeks every opportunity to idle away his time in making sport and amusement for himself and fellow-students will live to regret that he thus wasted his time. The happy, sportive, joyous, laughing boy and girl shed happiness wherever they go if they are careful to control their gayety and allow its flow only in the proper place; but they should never permit the love of the mirthful to infringe on the rules of the schoolroom or the laws of etiquette. On the contrary, true courtesy should teach them to use every endeavor to aid the teacher in his work, as in so doing they are themselves reaping the benefits.

The boy and girl at school foretell the future man and woman. Those who are prompt, punctual and orderly will be so in after-life. Those who are truthful, reliable and honest in childhood, will be trusted in position and place in after-years; and those who store the mind in youth with valuable knowledge will possess that which can never be lost, but on the contrary will always be a means by which they may procure a livelihood; and, if united with energy and perseverance, will be sure to give them reputation, eminence of position, and wealth.

The boy should never take pride in disobedience to the rules of school. To be a truant, to be indolent, to be working mischief, evinces no talent; any rowdy could do this; most worthless men did this when they attended school. It requires effort to be a good scholar; it evinces brain-power to be a good student.

The youth should earnestly resolve to achieve an honorable and noble position in life. With the wide opportunities which open to the ambitious and the enterprising in this age of progression there is no limit to the greatness which the thoroughly earnest student may attain. The idle and dissolute will, naturally, of their own weight drop out by the wayside and sink from sight. The plodder who is content to go the dull, daily round in the same narrow rut will get the reward of his labor, though he never betters his condition. But the earnest, original, aspiring, energetic, intelligent worker can always be sure of new fields to enter, nobler victories to gain, and grander work to be accomplished.

ETIQUETTE IN THE HOME

PARENTS AND CHILDREN.

IN TEMPERAMENT, physical characteristics, mental development and moral inclination, the child is what it has been made by its inheritance and the training it has received since infancy. Born of parents happy in disposition, harmonious in conjugal relation, and pleasant in circumstances, the child will as certainly be as sweet in temper as that sweet fluid which flows from a maple tree. More especially will this be true if the child was welcome, and the days of the mother prior to its birth were full of sunshine and gladness.

If, on the contrary, a badly-developed and unhappy parentage has marked the child, then a correspondingly unfortunate organization of mind and unhappy disposition will present itself for discipline and training.

Fortunate is it for the parent who can understand the cause of the child's predilections thus in the beginning. As with the teacher, when the causes that affect the child's mind are understood, the correct system of government to be pursued is then more easily comprehended. The result of this early appreciation of the case is to teach the parent and teacher that, whatever may be the manifestation of mind with the child, it should never be blamed. This is a fundamental principle necessary to be understood by any person who would be successful in government.

When thoroughly imbued with that understanding, kindness and love will take the place of anger and hatred, and discipline can be commenced aright.

One of the first things that the child should understand is that it must implicitly obey. The parent should, therefore, be very careful to give only such commands as ought to be followed, and then carefully observe that the order is strictly but kindly enforced.

To always secure obedience without trouble, it is of the utmost importance that the parent be firm. For the parent to refuse a request of a child without due consideration, and soon afterward, through the child's importunities, grant the request, is to very soon lose command. The parent should carefully consider the request, and if it be denied the child should feel that the denial is the result of the best judgment, and is not dictated by momentary impatience or petulance. A child soon learns to discriminate between the various moods of the fickle parent, and very soon loses respect for government that is not discreet, careful and just.

If a command is disobeyed, parents should never threaten what they will do if the order is disobeyed again, but at once withhold, quietly, yet firmly and pleasantly, some pleasure from the child in consequence of the disobedience. The punishment should be very seldom, if ever, the infliction of bodily pain. A slight deprivation of some pleasure—it may be very slight, but sufficient to teach the child that it must obey—will be of great service to its future discipline and government by the parent. Commencing thus when the child is very young, treating it always tenderly and kindly, with mild and loving words, it will grow to womanhood or manhood an honor to the parents.

What Parents Should Never Do

Never speak harshly to a child.
Never use disrespectful names.
Never use profane or vulgar words in the presence of a child.
Do not be so cold and austere as to drive your child from you.

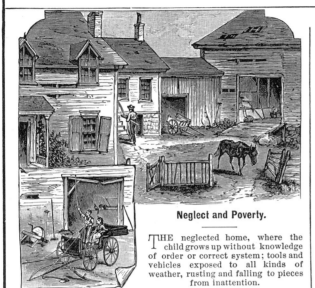

Neglect and Poverty.

THE neglected home, where the child grows up without knowledge of order or correct system; tools and vehicles exposed to all kinds of weather, rusting and falling to pieces from inattention.

Order and Thrift.

THE home of neighbor Thrifty, where the children learn habits of neatness, economy and good management; there being a place for every implement when not in use, and each kept where it belongs.

Never misrepresent. If you falsify the child will learn to deceive also.

Never withhold praise when the child deserves it. Commendation is one of the sweetest pleasures of childhood.

Never waken your children before they have completed their natural slumbers in the morning. See that they retire early, and thus have the requisite time for sleep. Children require more sleep than older persons. The time will come soon enough when care and trouble will compel them to waken in the early morning. Let them sleep while they can.

Do not reproach a child for a mistake which was made with a good motive at the time. Freely forgive, wisely counsel, and the child will thus be taught that there is no danger in telling the truth.

Never give your children money indiscriminately to spend for their own use. However wealthy you may be teach the child the value of money by requiring it to earn it in some manner. Commencing young, let the child perform simple duties requiring labor, which the parent may reward by pennies and very small sums. Let the child thus spend only money of its own earning. The boy who thus early learns by labor the value of a dollar knows how to accumulate the same in after-life, and how to save it.

Never demean yourself by getting angry and whipping a child. The very fact of your punishing in anger arouses the evil nature of the child. Some day the punishment thus inflicted will react upon yourself.

What Parents Should Do.

Always speak in a pleasant voice.

Teach your children how to work; how to obtain a living by their own efforts. Teach them the nobility and the dignity of labor, that they may respect and honor the producer.

Explain the reason why. The child is a little walking interrogation point. To it all is new. Explain the reason. Your boy will some day repay this trouble by teaching some other child.

Teach your children the evil of secret vice, and the consequence of using tobacco and spirituous liquors; teach them to be temperate, orderly, punctual, prompt, truthful, neat, faithful and honest.

Encourage your child to be careful of personal appearance; to return every tool to its place; to always pay debts promptly; to never shirk a duty; to do an equal share, and to always live up to an agreement.

Teach your children to confide in you by conference together. Tell them your plans, and sometimes ask their advice; they will thus open their hearts to you and will ask *your* advice. The girl who tells all her heart to her mother has a shield and a protection about her which can come only with a mother's advice and counsel.

Give your children your confidence in the affairs of your business. They will thus take interest, and become co-workers with you. If you enlist their respect then their sympathy and co-operation, they will quite likely remain to take up your work when you have done and will go ahead perfecting what you have commenced.

If you are a farmer do not overwork your children, and thus by a hard and dreary life drive them off to the cities. Arise at a reasonable hour in the morning, take an hour's rest after meals, and quit at five or six o'clock in the afternoon. Let the young people, in games and other amusements, have a happy time during the remainder of the day. There is no reason why a farmer's family should be deprived of recreation and amusement any more than others.

Teach your child the value of the Sabbath as a day for the spiritual improvement of the mind; that on the Sabbath morn the ordinary work of the week should not be resumed if it is possible to avoid it; that the day should be passed in attendance upon religious service of some kind or exercises that will ennoble and spiritualize the nature. While rest and recreation may be a part of the day's programme, true philosophy dictates that the spiritual faculties of the nature should be cultivated by setting apart a portion of the time for their improvement.

Teach your children those things which they will need when they become men and women. As women they should understand how to cook, how to make a bed, how to preserve cleanliness and order throughout the house, how to ornament their rooms, to renovate and preserve furniture and clothing, how to sing, and play various games, that they may enliven the household. They should be taught how to swim, how to ride, how to drive, how to do business, and how to preserve health. The mother should early intrust money to the girl with which to buy articles for the household that she may learn its value. Think what a man and woman need to know in order to be healthy, happy, prosperous and successful, and teach them that.

Attractive Personal Appearance.

ELEMENTS OF THE BEAUTIFUL.

HE love of beautiful adornment is innate in the human mind, and in reality has a great influence in elevating and refining the race. It is true that the mind may sometimes be too much given to personal decoration, but the instincts which cause us to clothe ourselves beautifully are all refining and elevating in character.

The desire to please and to be beautiful surrounds us on every hand with grace, elegance and refinement.

The person who cares nothing for personal appearance is a sloven. Were all to be thus, the human race would rapidly degenerate toward barbarism. The person who is careless of dress is likely to be equally regardless concerning purity of character.

The little girl that studies her features in the mirror, while she evinces possibly a disposition to be vain, nevertheless in this act shows herself to be possessed of those instincts of grace which, rightly directed, will beautify and embellish all her surroundings through life.

The boy that cares nothing for personal appearance, that does not appreciate beauty in others, is likely to develop into the man who will be slovenly in habits, whose home will quite probably be a hovel, and himself very likely a loafer or a tramp. But the boy—the rolicsome, frolicsome boy, ready to roll in the dirt, possibly—who, under all this, aspires to appear handsome, who desires a clean face, clean hands and a clean shirt, who admires a well-dressed head of hair and a good suit of clothes—that boy possesses the elements which in the man, in an elegant home, will surround him with the artistic and the charming.

The love of the beautiful ever leads to the higher, the grander and the better. Guided by its impulses, we pass out of the hut into the larger and better house; into the charming and elegantly-adorned mansion. Actuated by its influence, we convert the lumbering railway carriage into a palace-car, the swamp into a garden, and the desolate place into a park, in which we wander amid the trees, the streams of limpid water, and the fragrance of beautiful flowers.

All along the world's highway are the evidences, among the most elevated and refined, of the love of the beautiful, which, perhaps more than in any other manner, finds expression in dress.

This love of personal adornment being an inherent, desirable, refining element of character, it does not, therefore, become us to ignore or to suppress it. On the contrary, it should be our duty to cultivate neatness of appearance and artistic arrangement in dress, the whole being accompanied by as much personal beauty as possible.

In the cultivation of beauty in dress, it will become necessary to discriminate between ornament as displayed by the savage, and the science of beauty as observed in a more highly civilized life. Ornament is one thing; beauty is quite another.

To develop beauty, it is necessary to understand that the combination of a few fundamental principles forms the basis in the construction of all that we admire as beautiful. Of these are—

1. CURVED LINES. 2. SYMMETRY. 3. CONTRAST. 4. HARMONY OF COLOR. 5. HARMONY OF ASSOCIATION.

The Curved Line.

A prominent feature of beauty everywhere is the curved line. The winding pathway, the graceful outline of tree, cloud and mountain in the distance, the arched rainbow, the well-trimmed shrub, the finely-featured animal, the rounded form of everything that is beautiful—all illustrate this principle. The delicately, finely rounded face, hands and general features, are essential to the highest forms of beauty in the person, and the same principles apply in the manufacture of dress. Every line and seam should run in curves.

Symmetry of Proportion.

As harmonious proportions always please the eye in every object, so we are pleased with the symmetry displayed in the human form and features. Thus symmetry will give a well-shaped head, a moderate length of neck, a clearly-defined nose, mouth not too large, shoulders of even height, and all parts of the body of proportionate length and size. The clothing should be made to set off the natural features of the body to the best advantage. Thus the coat should be so cut as to make the shoulders of the man look broad. The dress should be so fitted as to cause the shoulders of the woman to appear narrow and sloping.

Long garments will make the individual appear taller. Short garments will cause the person to seem shorter. Lines that run perpendicularly add to the apparent height; horizontal lines shorten it.

Contrast.

Another feature of beauty in personal appearance is contrast, or those qualities which give animated expression and vivacity of manner. Thus the sparkling eye, clear-cut features, a color of hair that contrasts with the skin; happy, lively expression of face; graceful, animated movement of body; interesting conversational powers—all these make the face attractive by variety and contrast.

The lady's dress is relieved by flounce, frill, and various other trimmings, with colors more or less pronounced, according to the complexion of the wearer. The gentleman's dress, as now worn, does not admit of so great variety.

Harmony.

The harmony of colors suitable for various complexions is quite fully detailed elsewhere. Harmony of association will include those principles that derive their beauty chiefly from their association with other objects. Thus the best height and form for man or woman will be the average form of men and women with whom they associate. Anything unusual will detract from this beauty.

Any article of jewelry or dress which may appear out of place for the occasion, or not appropriate with the other articles worn, is also included under this head.

SUGGESTIONS RELATING TO

THE

Selection of Harmonious Colors

IN

Personal Adornment

WITH

Hints on the Care of the Person.

Colors that Befit the Blonde and Colors for the Brunette.

VERY SAFE is it to assume that the reader desires health and beauty, and is willing perhaps to govern habits accordingly. Observe then the following regulations:

Retire sufficiently early to get the necessary rest and sleep, that you may arise early in the morning.

Be sure that plenty of fresh air is admitted to the room throughout the night, by the opening of windows. Avoid feathers. A perfectly clean, moderately hard bed is best for health.

The Bath.

Upon rising, take a complete bath. A simple washing out of the eyes is not sufficient. The complete bathing of the body once each day is of the utmost importance to health and beauty. Not more than a quart of water is necessary. Use the hands the same as you do upon the face. No sponge is required, and water is more agreeable to the skin when applied with the bare hand. Use rainwater; and, for a healthy person, the temperature of that which has been in the room during the night is about right. Use plenty of soap, and wash quickly. Follow by wiping the skin perfectly dry with a soft towel, and afterward give the body and limbs a thorough rubbing. The glow that is diffused throughout the face and body by this exercise is worth more in giving a ruddy, beautiful complexion than all the rouge and powder in the world.

The arrangements for this bath are very simple. There is nothing required but a small amount of soft water, a piece of soap, and a towel. No elaborately-fitted-up bathroom is necessary. We have detailed all the appliances that are essential, and they are so simple that the laboring classes and the poor can have them, and be clean, as well as the rich. Occasionally, warm water, with a sponge, may be necessary to remove completely all the oily exudations from the body, but for the ordinary bath this is not essential.

The sun and air bath is very excellent for health; therefore to leave the body exposed in the sun for a short time previous to dressing is very invigorating.

Before the breakfast hour the lungs should be completely inflated with fresh air. The meals should be partaken of with regularity, while more or less of fruit, oatmeal, rice, cracked wheat, graham bread, etc., will be found necessary as a diet, in order to keep the skin clear.

The Breath.

The breath should be watched, lest it become offensive. Unfortunately, it is one of the troubles which we may not be aware of, as our friends may not feel at liberty to inform us of the difficulty.

Offensive breath may arise from the stomach, the teeth, the lungs, or catarrhal affection of the throat and nose.

Unquestionably the best remedy for bad breath is a system of diet and treatment that shall remove the cause. As a temporary expedient, when offensiveness arises from a peculiar food or drink which has been partaken of, a few grains of coffee, or cassia buds, cloves, cardamom seeds or allspice, may be used; although if the breath is very strong these will not always prove effective. It is better to remove the cause.

The following remedies for offensive breath are commended by those who have had experience in testing the matter:

Powdered sugar, ½ ounce; vanilla, ½ ounce; powdered charcoal, ½ ounce; powdered coffee, 1¼ ounces; gum arabic, ½ ounce. Make into pellets of 18 grains each, and take six a day. Bad breath will disappear.

Disagreeable breath arising from decay or secretions about the teeth may be removed by the following:

Rose-water, 1 ounce, and permanganate of potash, 1 grain. Rinse the mouth every three hours.

To remove catarrh, the following is highly commended:

In pint of water put two tablespoonfuls of common fine table salt. Heat the water in a tin cup. With the aid of a nasal douche, obtained at the drug-store, or even without that, snuff about a teaspoonful of the brine up each nostril, requiring it to pass into the mouth. Use twice a day—morning and night.

For offensive breath arising from foul stomach, the following is recommended:

To a wine-glass of water add 3 grains of chloride of lime. Take a tablespoonful three times a day, before the meal, and eat of simple food which is easily digested.

Another remedy for foul breath is powdered charcoal, half a teaspoonful, spread on a piece of bread, and eaten once a day for two or three days. Another is a drink of pure water, taken twice a day, containing each time 20 grains of bisulphate of soda. The taste is made pleasant by a few drops of peppermint essence.

The following is recommended as beneficial for the teeth, and effective in removing the acidity of the stomach:

Take of gum arabic 5 drachms; vanilla sugar, 3 drachms; chlorate of lime, 7 drachms, and mix with water to a stiff paste. Roll and cut into the ordinary sized lozenge, and eat six each day.

The Skin.

Beware of exterior application of cosmetics for the purpose of beautifying the skin. The greatest beautifiers in existence are plenty of exercise in the fresh air, the keeping of the pores of the skin completely open by bathing, the feeding of the body with a sufficiency of simple, healthy food, and the obtaining of the requisite amount of sleep.

It is true that sometimes a slight touch of art may improve the personal appearance. The very sallow complexion may be improved by a small amount of color applied; the hair, if naturally dry and stiff, may be kept in place by a simple hair preparation, and a white eyebrow may be brought into harmonious color with the hair of the head by a dye; all this being done so adroitly that the external application cannot be detected. But, as a rule, greatest beauty is obtained by a strict observance of the laws of health.

The following preparations, culled from De la Banta's "Advice to Ladies," are recommended for improving the complexion:

Take a teaspoonful of powdered charcoal (kept by druggists) mixed with sweetened water or milk, for three nights successively. This should be followed by a gentle purge afterward, to remove it from the system. Taken once in two or three months, this remedy will prove efficacious in making the complexion clear and transparent.

ANOTHER.

Tincture of balsam of Peru, 2 drachms; tincture of tolu, 2 drachms; tincture of benzoin, 2 drachms. Mix with one gill of distilled water, and take of melted white wax, 1 ounce; spermaceti, ½ ounce; sweet almond oil, 8 drachms, and rose-water, 1 ounce. Mix all the ingredients together, and beat thoroughly, applying to the skin with a sponge.

This may be used with benefit where the skin presents a greasy appearance:

To ½ pint of rose-water add chlorate of potash, 18 grains; glycerine, 1 ounce. Mix carefully, and use in a pure state. Apply with a sponge or linen cloth. Should it irritate the skin dilute with more water. These lotions should be applied with care, and are best used at night.

The greasy skin, inclined to pimples, is benefited by the following preparation:

Bicarbonate of soda, 18 grains; essence of Portugal, 6 drops; distilled water, ½ pint. Mix and bathe the face.

The shiny, polished skin, which is caused by fatty secretions beneath it, may have the difficulty removed by this preparation:

Take 1 quart of camphor water, pure glycerine, 1 ounce, and ½ ounce of powdered borax. Mix and bathe the face. Let it dry and remain a few minutes after applying it, then wash the face thoroughly with soft water.

If the skin is very pallid it is improved by a bath in lukewarm water, followed by brisk rubbing with a coarse towel and exercise in the air and sun. The pale skin is improved also by the sunshine. The rough skin is made smooth by the application of glycerine at night, followed by its removal with water and fine soap in the morning.

The skin may be whitened by the following prescription:

To one pint of water add 1 wineglass of fresh lemon juice and 10 drops of attar of roses. Mix, and keep in a well-corked bottle. Use once a day.

The sallow and muddy skin is improved by this preparation:

To one pint of water add 2 drachms of iodide of potassium and 1 ounce of glycerine. Mix and apply with a sponge once a day.

To keep the skin clear, beware of pork, cheese and other substances containing much grease. Also avoid alcoholic drinks. Keep the bowels loose by fruit and a sufficiency of coarse food. Take exercise sufficient, if possible, to produce a gentle perspiration each day; bathe daily, and get into the sunshine and open air.

The Hand.

Various are the recipes for keeping the hand beautiful. If not engaged in hard manual labor, and it is very desirable to make the hands present an appearance as handsome as possible, there are a few directions necessary to keep them well preserved. Among these is perfect cleanliness, which is produced by a thorough washing, using an abundance of good toilet soap, and frequently a nail-brush.

Should the hands be inclined to chap, they will be relieved of the difficulty by washing them in glycerine before going to bed. In the winter season, to wash them in snow and soap will leave them smooth and soft.

To make the hands very white and delicate, the person is assisted by washing them several times for two or three days in milk and water, and, upon retiring to rest, bathing in palm oil and encasing them in a pair of woolen gloves, cleaning with warm water and soap the next morning. They should be thoroughly rubbed to promote

circulation, and a pair of soft leather gloves should be worn during the day.

Should the hands become sunburned, the tan may be removed by using lime-water and lemon-juice.

Should warts make their appearance, they may be removed by paring them on the top and applying a small amount of acetic acid on the summit of the wart with a camel's hair brush, care being taken that none of the acid gets upon the surrounding skin. To prevent this, wax may be placed upon the finger or hand during the operation, or an old kid glove may be used, the wart being allowed to protrude through.

The nails should be cut about once a week, directly after a bath, and should never be bitten. In rough, hard labor, if it is desired to protect the hands, gloves should be worn.

But however beautiful it may be, the hand should do its full share of work. The hand that is beautiful from idleness is to be despised.

The Feet.

Much care should be taken to keep the feet in good condition. The first important consideration in their management is perfect cleanliness. Some people find it necessary to wash the feet morning and evening. Many find it indispensably necessary to wash them once a day, and no one should fail of washing them at least three times a week, and the stockings should be changed as frequently if much walking be done.

Without washing, the feet are liable to become very offensive to others in a short time. The feet of some persons will become disagreeably so sometimes within a week if they are not washed, more especially if they perspire freely.

A foot-bath, using warm water, followed by wiping the feet completely dry, and afterward putting on clean stockings, is very invigorating after a long walk, or when the feet are damp and cold.

To escape chilblains avoid getting the feet wet. Should they become damp, change shoes and stockings at once. Wear woolen stockings, and do not toast the feet before the fire. The approach of the chilblain is frequently prevented by bathing the feet in a strong solution of alum.

With the first indication of chilblains, as revealed by the itching sensation, it is well to rub them with warm spirits of rosemary, adding to the same a little turpentine. Lint, soaked in camphorated spirits, opodeldoc, or camphor liniment, may be applied and retained when the part is affected.

It is claimed also that chilblains may be cured by bathing the feet in water in which potatoes have been boiled.

Wear boots and shoes amply large for the feet, but not too large, and thus escape corns. A broad heel, half an inch in height, is all that comfort will allow to be worn.

The Hair.

The head should be washed occasionally with soap and water. Follow by wiping perfectly dry, and afterward brush the hair and scalp with a hair-brush of moderate hardness. When the hair is inclined to be harsh and dry, a moderate supply of olive oil, bear's grease or other dressing may be used. With many heads no oil is necessary, and with any over-abundance is to be avoided. Frequent brushing with a perfectly clean brush is of great service in giving a glossy, beautiful appearance to the hair. The brush may be kept clean by washing every day or two in warm water and soda, or in diluted ammonia.

For removing dandruff, glycerine diluted with a little rose-water is recommended. Rosemary in almost any preparation is a very cleansing wash.

The yolk of an egg beaten up in warm water makes an excellent application for cleansing the scalp.

To clip the ends of the hair occasionally is an excellent plan for ladies, as it prevents the hair from splitting.

It is doubtful if a hair-dye is ever advisable, though an eyebrow is sometimes improved by a light application, to bring it into harmonious color with the hair, as is also hair which grows white in patches. There is no objection to the hair growing gray. Indeed the gray is often fully as beautiful as the former color.

Baldness is usually avoided by keeping the head cool. Women seldom have bald heads, but men often do, the baldness commencing upon the head at a point which is covered by the hat. In order to preserve the hair, gentlemen must avoid warm hats and caps, and whatever is worn must be thoroughly ventilated by apertures sufficient in quantity and size to allow all the heated air to escape. The silk hat should have at least twenty holes punched in the top to afford sufficient ventilation.

The beard is nature's badge to indicate manhood. It was an unwise fashion that ordained that the face should be shaved. Gradually men begin to learn that health, comfort and improved appearance come with the full beard, and in later years the beard is acquiring the prestige it held in olden times. Care should be taken to keep the beard and hair so cut and trimmed that they may present a handsome appearance.

The Teeth.

The teeth should be thoroughly cleaned with a toothbrush each morning after breakfast. Some persons clean the teeth after every meal, which is a most excellent habit. By cleaning the teeth regularly, no washes are necessary, though occasionally castile soap will be beneficial. Should tartar collect in such quantity as to be difficult to remove the dentist should be consulted. Should the teeth begin to decay they should be immediately cared for by the dentist. Powdered charcoal easily removes stains and makes the teeth white.

The following also is an excellent wash for the teeth:

Tincture of myrrh, 1 ounce; compound tincture of cinchona, 1 ounce; water, 1 ounce. Put five drops on the toothbrush, dip the brush then in water, and wash the teeth.

Keep the teeth clean. They look badly if not perfectly white and clean.

Ears, Eyes and Nose.

In the daily bath all the crevices of the ear should be thoroughly cleaned, and the earwax carefully removed whenever it shows itself.

Special pains should be taken to keep the eyes clean. It shows filthy habits to see matter gathering in the corners. If dirt accumulates between washings, the eyes should be carefully wiped with a soft handkerchief.

Keep the nasal passages perfectly clear. If there is an inclination for accumulations to stop there, snuff water up the nose, and afterward blow it, placing the thumb on one side while you blow the other. Keep the nose so clear that you can breathe through it with ease, and avoid the coarse habit of picking it.

Regularity of Habits.

It is of the utmost importance, if the individual would enjoy health and possess beauty, that all the personal habits be perfectly regular, and that attention be given to these each twenty-four hours at a regular time.

Do not let visiting, traveling or business interfere with them. You must be regular in sleep, in evacuation of the bowels, in bathing and in eating. Nature will not be cheated. She requires perfect attention to certain duties. If you attempt to violate her requirements you will be certainly punished.

Whenever the person complains of sickness he confesses to a violation, consciously or unconsciously, unavoidably or otherwise, of some of nature's requirements. (See remarks on "Health," in the "Letters of Advice," elsewhere in this volume.)

WHAT COLORS MAY BE WORN.

Nature has her peculiar shades and contrasts, with which she embellishes all her works.

Over the retreating dark gray cloud in the east does the rainbow show itself, strong by contrast, and beautiful in the harmony of its surroundings. Surpassingly lovely are the brilliant rays of the golden sunset, as they lie reflected upon the fleecy clouds at eventide, their charm coming from their surroundings of the gray and azure blue. Dazzlingly bright are the twinkling stars as they smile upon us in their bed of celestial blue; and very beautiful is the rose, as it perfumes the air and charms the eye amid its accompaniments of green.

Nature thus robes all her works with shades that complement and harmonize; the result being to show the object to the best advantage.

In the higher civilization men have donned the conventional suit of black and have abandoned the domain of color to woman, who, with her keenly æsthetic nature can never be induced to forego the pleasure that comes from brilliant and harmonious hues. Alive as woman is, therefore, to the principles that make beauty, it becomes us to investigate the subject of personal appearance as affected by color.

Colors that Suit Different Complexions.

Two distinct types of complexion exist among the white race, namely, the light-haired, fair and ruddy complexions, termed Blondes; and the dark-haired and dark-skinned, called Brunettes.

Between these are several intermediate tints and shades, all requiring much close observation to fully discriminate as to the colors most suitable to be worn to harmonize with the different shades of complexion.

Investigation has proven that the light-haired and rosy-cheeked, with red or golden hair and ruddy complexion, require certain colors in headdress and drapery to harmonize; and the same is true of the dark complexion, with dark hair and eyebrows.

The Shades that Blondes May Wear.

Dark violet, intermixed with lilac and blue, give additional charms to the fair-haired, ruddy blonde. Green, also, with lighter or darker tints, is favorable. With the very ruddy, the blue and green should be darker rather than lighter. An intermixture of white may likewise go with these colors.

The neutral colors are also suitable to the ruddy blondes. Of these are the russet, slate, maroon, and all the hues of brown. Light neutral tints are also pleasing, such as gray, drab, fawn and stone colors.

Transparent and delicate complexions, with light, chestnut or brown hair, should have the same set off by contrast. Thus blue, pale yellow, azure, lilac and black, trimmed with rose or pink, are suitable, as are also the various shades of gray.

Colors that Become the Brunette.

Glossy black becomes the brunette; so do white, scarlet, orange and yellow. The scarlet blossom in the hair, gold-colored ribbon and poppy colors, deftly but not too conspicuously woven about the neck and breast, will display the face to fine advantage. Green also befits the dark complexion.

The sallow complexion is improved by the different shades of dark-green and red. A yellow complexion is made handsomer by the reflection of yellow about it; especially if relieved by poppy colors or black.

The red and yellow face is benefited by coming in contact with blue or orange. The red face is improved by red around it, red and blue tints being developed thereby. Red and blue are relieved by purple, and the blue and yellow by green. White and black become the pale face, but red and blue become it better. Light colors harmonize with and befit the pale skin, while the dark skin is improved by the darker tints.

Colors in Bonnets.

Black Bonnets, with white, pink or red flowers and white feather, become the fair complexion. They also become the black-haired type when trimmed with white, red, orange or yellow.

White Bonnets, made of lace, muslin or crape, suit all complexions, though not so becoming to the rosy complexion as other colors. A white bonnet may be trimmed with white or pink, but with the blonde is handsomest when trimmed with blue flowers. For the brunette, preference should be given to trimmings of red, pink, orange and yellow—never blue.

Blue Bonnets are suitable only for fair or light, rosy complexions. They should never be worn by the brunette.

Yellow and Orange Bonnets suit the brunette, their appropriate trimming being poppy colors, scarlet, white and black, black and scarlet, black, scarlet and yellow.

Light Blue Bonnets are very suitable for those having light hair. They may be trimmed with white flowers, and in many cases with orange and yellow.

Green Bonnets best become the fair and rosy complexion. White flowers will harmonize in the trimming, but pink is preferable.

Colors for Different Seasons.

Red, in its various tints, being a warm color, when worn in dress, has a pleasing effect in winter.

Purple is appropriate in winter, spring and autumn.

Green is becoming in late summer and in autumn, by contrast with the general somber appearance of dead foliage at that season of the year.

White and light tints in clothing give an appearance of coolness and comfort in summer.

Black and dark colors are appropriate at all seasons.

Colors We See First.

Of a variety or color to be seen, the white or light-colored will usually attract attention first and farthest, from the fact that, most objects being of dark shades of color, it is strongest by contrast. Next to white comes the scarlet red, which, close by, is one of the most brilliant and attractive colors. Yellow is one of the most noticeable, succeeded by the orange, crimson, blue and purple.

Colors in Dress Most Beautiful at Night.

A dress of a color that may be beautiful during the day may be lacking in beauty at night, owing to the effect of gaslight; and another, most charming in the evening, may possess little beauty in the daytime. Thus, crimson, which is handsome in the evening, loses its effect upon the complexion in the daytime. So white and yellow, that add beauty at night, are unbecoming by day.

Ill-Fitting and Unbecoming Dress.

ALTHOUGH the dress and costume shown above may be rich, costly and fashionable, it shows the form of the persons on whom it is worn to bad advantage.

The scarlet, orange and the light brown are also most charming at night.

Colors Most Beautiful by Daylight.

Pale yellow, which is handsome by day, is muddy in appearance by gaslight. So purple and orange, that harmonize and are beautiful by daylight, lose their charm at night.

The beauty of rose-color disappears under the gaslight; and all the shades of purple and lilac, the dark-blues and green, lose their brilliancy in artificial light. Ordinarily, the complexion will bear the strongest color at night.

Apparent Size Affected by Color.

The apparent size is affected by colors. As white upon the building will make it appear larger, so a light-colored dress will have the same effect upon the person. Thus the large figure will appear best in close-fitting black, and next best in the sober hues. The smaller figure will show to advantage in the light colors. Black, however, for a person of any size, is the most suitable color for nearly all occasions; and, handsomely made, well-fitted, artistically trimmed, and suitably relieved at throat and bodice with ribbons, lace and flowers corresponding with the complexion, makes always a most beautiful costume.

Persons whose resources are limited and who cannot afford a varied wardrobe should by this fact be guided to a constant preference for black.

Colors that Harmonize.

The object of two or more different tints in dress is to obtain relief by variety, and yet the two shades brought thus in contrast should harmonize, else the beauty of each will be lessened. Thus, a lady with a blue dress would greatly injure its effect by wearing a crimson shawl; as she would also a lilac-colored dress by trimming it with a dark-brown material, no matter how rich.

That the reader may understand the colors that will contrast and yet blend, the following list of harmonizing colors is given:

Blue and gold; blue and orange; blue and salmon-color; blue and drab; blue and stone-color; blue and white; blue and gray; blue and straw-color; blue and maize; blue and chestnut; blue and brown; blue and black; blue and white; blue, brown, crimson and gold.

Black and white; black and orange; black and maize; black and scarlet; black and lilac; black and pink; black and slate-color; black and buff; black, white, yellow and crimson; black, orange, blue and yellow.

Crimson and gold; crimson and orange; crimson and maize; crimson and purple; crimson and black; crimson and drab.

Green and gold; green and yellow; green and orange; green and crimson; green, crimson and yellow; green, scarlet and yellow.

Lilac and gold; lilac and maize; lilac and cherry; lilac and scarlet; lilac and crimson; lilac, scarlet, white and black; lilac, gold and chestnut; lilac, yellow, scarlet and white.

Orange and chestnut; orange and brown; orange, lilac and crimson;

orange, red and green; orange, blue and crimson; orange, purple and scarlet; orange, blue, scarlet, green and white.

Purple and gold; purple and orange; purple and maize; purple, scarlet and gold-color; purple, white and scarlet; purple, orange, blue and scarlet; purple, scarlet, blue, yellow and black.

Red and gold; red, white or gray; red, green and orange; red, black and yellow; red, yellow, black and white.

Scarlet and purple; scarlet and orange; scarlet and blue; scarlet and slate-color; scarlet, black and white; scarlet, white and blue; scarlet, gray and blue; scarlet, yellow and blue; scarlet, blue, yellow and black.

Yellow and red; yellow and brown; yellow and chestnut; yellow and violet; yellow and blue; yellow and crimson; yellow and purple; yellow and black; yellow, purple and crimson; yellow and scarlet.

FASHION---WHY DOES IT CHANGE?

Because change is one of nature's laws. If there was no change there would be no motion; and without motion there would be no life.

Change is ever going forward in nature. To-day it is spring and all nature is waking to new life. A few weeks hence and every tree and shrub will be clothed in a garb of green, sprinkled with blossoms. Later the green of various shades will merge into the autumn tints; and, later still, nature will doff her garb entirely, only to clothe herself in the coming years again with various changes, according to the seasons.

So mankind instinctively change in style of costume, oftentimes for better, and sometimes, it must be admitted, for the worse. But the change ever goes forward, fashion repeating itself within the century, often within a generation, almost as certain as the seasons do within the year.

There is no use, therefore, in issuing a fiat against changes of fashion. Best judgment is shown in accepting of the inevitable and adapting ourselves to circumstances.

Graceful and Refined in Appearance.

WHATEVER may be the fashion, there is such grace and refinement bestowed upon the persons shown above, through properly made dress, as to win our admiration.

Hints to Gentlemen.

It is best to conform to fashion, avoiding extremes.

While it is well to guard against the adoption of a decidedly unwise fashion, it is well also to avoid an oddity in dress.

Well-dressed gentlemen wear dark clothing cut and made to measure. Watch-chain, one ring, shirt-stud and sleeve-buttons, are all the jewelry allowable for the gentleman.

Other colors than black will be appropriate in their season and for various kinds of enjoyment.

Hints to Parents.

Give the boy a good suit of clothes if you wish him to appear manly. An ill-fitting, bad-looking garment destroys a boy's respect for himself.

To require the boy to wear men's cast-off clothing, and go shambling around in a large pair of boots, and then expect him to have good manners, is like giving him the poorest of tools, because he is a boy, and then compelling him to do as fine work with them as a man would with good tools.

Like the man or woman, the boy respects himself, and will do much more honor to his parents, when he is well dressed in a neatly fitting suit of clothes. Even his mother should relinquish her rights and let the barber cut his hair.

As a rule well-dressed children exhibit better conduct than children that are careless in general appearance. While vanity should be guarded against, children should be encouraged to be neat in person and dress.

The mother should strive also to make her boy manly. Possibly, as a pet, her boy has in infancy had his hair curled. Even now, when he is six or eight years of age, the curls look very pretty. But the mother must forego her further pleasure in the curls; for the boy, to take his place along with the others, to run and jump, to grow manly and strong, must wear short hair. His mother can no longer dress it like a girl's. It will be necessary and best to cut off his curls.

Hints to Ladies.

Best taste will dictate an observance of fashion, avoiding extremes. Dress the hair so that it will exhibit variety and relief, without making the forehead look too high.

Have one pronounced color in dress, all other colors harmonizing with that. See "Harmony of Colors."

A dress should fit the form. Well-fitted and judiciously trimmed, a calico dress is handsomer than an ill-fitting silk dress.

To present a handsome appearance, all the appurtenances of the lady's dress should be scrupulously neat and clean. Every article that is designed to be white should be a pure white, and in perfect order.

Much taste may be displayed in dress about the neck, and care should be observed not to use trimmings that will enlarge the appearance of the shoulders. The dress should be close-fitting about the waist and shoulders, though it should not be laced too tightly.

As with the gentleman, quiet colors are usually in best taste. Heavy, rich, dark materials best suit the woman of tall figure; while light, full draperies should be worn only by those of slender proportions. Short persons should beware of wearing flounces, or horizontal trimmings that will break the perpendicular lines as the effect is to make them appear shorter. The pictorial illustrations herewith show how differently people appear with different dress, our opinions of their intellectual capacity, their standing and respectability being largely influenced at first sight by this appearance.

Care should be taken to dress according to the age, the season, the employment and the occasion. As a rule, a woman appears her loveliest when, in a dress of dark color, we see her with the rosy complexion of health, her hair dressed neatly, her throat and neck tastefully cared for, her dress in neither extreme of fashion, while the whole is relieved by a moderate amount of carefully selected jewelry.

We have aimed in this chapter on the toilet to present the scientific principles of dress—principles that can be applied at all times, whatever may be the fashion. It now remains for the reader to study these principles and apply them in accordance with the rules of common sense and the fashions as they may prevail.

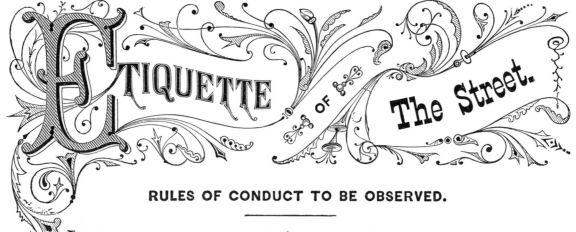

RULES OF CONDUCT TO BE OBSERVED.

LADIES and gentlemen, when meeting on the sidewalk, should always pass to the right. Should the walk be narrow or dangerous, gentlemen will always see that ladies are protected from injury.

Ladies should avoid walking rapidly upon the street, as it is ungraceful and unbecoming.

Running across the street in front of carriages is dangerous, and shows want of dignity.

The gentleman should insist upon carrying any package which the lady may have, when walking with her.

Before recognizing a lady on the street, the gentleman should be certain that his recognition will meet with favor.

No gentleman should stand on the street-corners, steps of hotels, or other public places, and make remarks about ladies passing by.

A gentleman may take two ladies upon his arms, but under no circumstances should the lady take the arms of two gentlemen.

Upon the narrow walk, for her protection, the gentleman should generally give the lady the inside of the walk (Fig. 21), passing behind her when changing at corners.

Allowing a dress to trail on the street is in exceedingly bad taste. Such a street costume simply calls forth criticism and contempt from the more sensible people.

A gentleman walking with a lady should accommodate his step and pace to hers. For the gentleman to be some distance ahead, presents a bad appearance.

Should protection on the street be necessary, it is customary for the gentleman to give his right arm to the lady; but if more convenient, he may give the left.

Fig. 21. The street-promenade. The gentleman gives the lady the inside of the walk. *

It is courtesy to give silent, respectful attention as a funeral procession passes. It shows want of respect to pass between the carriages while the procession is moving.

Staring at people, spitting, looking back after they pass, saluting people across the street, calling out loudly or laughing at people as they go by, are all evidences of ill-breeding.

The gentleman accompanying a lady should hold the door open for the lady to enter first. Should he be near the door when a lady, unattended, is about to enter, he will do the same for her.

In the evening, or whenever safety may require, a gentleman should give a lady his arm. It is not customary in other cases to do so on the street, unless with an elderly lady, or the couple be husband and wife.

A gentleman will assist a lady over a bad crossing, or from an omnibus or carriage, without waiting for the formality of an introduction. When the service is performed, he will raise his hat, bow, and pass on.

In a street car or an omnibus, the passengers who are seated should strive to give seats to those who are standing, rendering such accommodation as they would themselves desire under similar circumstances.

When crossing the pavement, the lady should raise her dress with the right hand, a little above the ankle. To raise the dress with both hands, is vulgar, and can be excused only when the mud is very deep.

No gentleman will smoke when walking with, or standing in the presence of, a lady on the street. He should remove the cigar from her presence entirely, even though permission be granted to continue the smoking.

A gentleman should give his seat to any lady who may be standing in a public conveyance. For this favor she should thank him, which courtesy he should acknowledge by a slight bow. In an omnibus he will pass up the ladies' fares.

A true lady will go quietly and unobtrusively about her business when on the street, never seeking to attract the attention of the opposite sex, at the same time recognizing acquaintances with a courteous bow, and friends with pleasant words of greeting.

Swinging the arms when walking, eating upon the street, sucking the parasol handles, pushing violently through a crowd, very loud and boisterous talking and laughing on the streets, and whispering in public conveyances, are all evidences of ill-breeding in ladies.

A lady should have the escort of a gentleman in the evening. A gentleman at the house where she may call may return with her if she goes unattended; gossip and scandal are best avoided, however, if she have some one from her home call for her at an appointed hour.

On the narrow street-crossing the gentleman will allow the lady to precede him, that he may see that no injury befalls her.

Should a lady stop in the street, when meeting a gentleman, it is courtesy for him to stop also. Should his business be urgent, he will apologize for not continuing the conversation, and ask to be excused. Should it be desirable to lengthen the interview, and the lady resumes her walk in the midst of her conversation, it is courtesy for him to turn and accompany her. Should she desire to end the conversation, a slight bow from her will indicate the fact, when he should bid her "good day" and take his leave.

* Some authorities claim that it is most sensible for the lady to walk always at the right of the gentleman, whether on the street or indoors; her right hand being thus free to hold trail, fan, or parasol.

UNCLASSIFIED

Laws of Etiquette.

N EVER exaggerate.
Never point at another.
Never betray a confidence.
Never wantonly frighten others.
Never leave home with unkind words.
Never neglect to call upon your friends.
Never laugh at the misfortunes of others

Never give a promise that you do not fulfill.

Never speak much of your own performances.

Never fail to be punctual at the appointed time.

Never make yourself the hero of your own story.

Never send a present hoping for one in return.

Never pick the teeth or clean the nails in company.

Never fail to give a polite answer to a civil question.

Never question a servant or a child about family matters.

Never present a gift saying that it is of no use to yourself.

Never read letters which you may find addressed to others.

Never fail, if a gentleman, of being civil and polite to ladies.

Never call attention to the features or form of any one present.

Never refer to a gift you have made or favor you have rendered.

Never associate with bad company. Have good company or none.

Never look over the shoulder of another who is reading or writing.

Never seem to notice a scar, deformity or defect of any one present.

Never arrest the attention of an acquaintance by a touch. Speak to him.

Never punish your child for a fault to which you are addicted yourself.

Never answer questions in general company that have been put to others.

Never, when traveling abroad, be over-boastful in praise of your own country.

Never call a new acquaintance by the Christian name unless requested to do so.

Never lend an article you have borrowed unless you have permission to do so.

Never attempt to draw the attention of the company constantly upon yourself.

Never exhibit anger, impatience or excitement when an accident happens.

Never pass between two persons who are talking together, without an apology.

Never enter a room noisily; never fail to close the door after you, and never slam it.

Never forget that if you are faithful in a few things, you may be ruler over many.

Never exhibit too great familiarity with the new acquaintance; you may give offense.

Never will a gentleman allude to conquests which he may have made with ladies.

Never fail to offer the easiest and best seat in the room to an invalid, an elderly person, or a lady.

Never neglect to perform the commission which the friend intrusted to you. You must not forget.

Never send your guest, who is accustomed to a warm room, off into a cold, damp, spare bed to sleep.

Never enter a room filled with people without a slight bow to the general company when first entering.

Never fail to answer an invitation, either personally or by letter, within a week after the invitation is received.

Never accept of favors and hospitalities without rendering an exchange of civilities when opportunity offers.

Never cross the legs and put out one foot in the street-car or places where it will trouble others when passing by. (*See Illustration.*)

Never fail to tell the truth. If truthful you get your reward. You will get your punishment if you deceive.

Never borrow money and neglect to pay. If you do you will soon be known as a person of no business integrity.

Never write to another asking for information, or a favor of any kind, without inclosing a postage stamp for the reply.

Never compel a woman with an infant in arms to stand while you retain your seat. (*See Illustration.*)

Never fail to say kind and encouraging words to those whom you meet in distress. Your kindness may lift them out of their despair.

Never refuse to receive an apology. You may not revive friendship, but courtesy will require, when an apology is offered, that you accept it.

Never examine the cards in the card-basket. While they may be exposed in the drawing-room, you are not expected to turn them over unless invited to do so.

Never, when walking arm in arm with a lady, be continually changing and going to the other side, because of change of corners. It shows too much attention to form.

Never should the lady accept of expensive gifts at the hands of a gentleman not related or engaged to her. Gifts of flowers, books, music or confectionery may be accepted.

Never insult another by harsh words when applied to for a favor. Kind words do not cost much, and yet they may carry untold happiness to the one to whom they are spoken.

Never fail to speak kindly. If a merchant, and you address your clerk; if an overseer, and you address your workmen; if in any position where you exercise authority, you show yourself to be a gentleman by your pleasant mode of address.

Never attempt to convey the impression that you are a genius by imitating the faults of distinguished men. Because certain great men were poor penmen, wore long hair, or had other peculiarities, it does not follow that you will be great by imitating their eccentricities.

Never give all your pleasant words and smiles to strangers. The kindest words and the sweetest smiles should be reserved for home. Home should be our heaven.

"We have careful thought for the stranger
And smiles for the sometimes guest;
But oft for our own the bitter tone,
Though we love our own the best.
Ah! lips with the curl impatient—
Ah! brow with the shade of scorn,
'Twere a cruel fate were the night too late
To undo the work of the morn."

Etiquette Among Neighbors.

DIVISION FENCES BETWEEN HOUSES.

TO BE kind, and to treat politely the persons with whom we are immediately associated, is not all, nor should civility cease with the casual intercourse between neighbors; it should go beyond. We should regard the rights of the individual. Were all to do so, mankind would take a long stride in advance of the present selfish and thoughtless conduct which too often actuates even those who are reputed to be good and respectable.

This want of regard for the rights of others is shown in many ways. To illustrate:

The individual **who** will conduct a house or an establishment that is unpleasant, injurious to health, or detrimental to the community, evinces a disregard for the courtesy that is due to his neighbors.

The parents who allow children to annoy their neighbors, are always a most undesirable people to have in the vicinity.

The people of a community who will deliberately turn horses, cattle and hogs into the street, entirely disregarding the fact that the animals are liable to do much damage to others, demonstrate a lack of regard for neighbors which is inexcusable, and can only be explained on the ground that the habit is so common that they do not realize the injury they are doing.

The fact that we accosted Mr. Jones politely, and said pleasant things in his presence, was good so far as it went, but the further fact that we turned our cattle into the street, well knowing they were liable to trample Mr. Jones' sidewalk to pieces, and break down his trees, demonstrates that, while we are very agreeable to his face, we care but little what we may do behind his back.

This utter disregard for the wants of others causes people generally to become suspicious of their neighbors. It is true that this suspicion is gradually becoming lessened. The time was when the inhabitants built a castle as nearly as possible impregnable; around that was built a high enclosure, and still outside of that was a canal with a drawbridge. Gradually the fact has dawned that we need not be thus suspi-

cious. We need not build a house of stone, we need not construct a canal, but we still adhere to the high wall or fence, as we are oftentimes compelled to because of the disposition of the neighbor to trample upon our rights by allowing his animals to destroy our property.

The reader has doubtless seen a town in which the people allowed their domestic animals to run at large, the hogs to root the turf to pieces by the roadside, the cattle to destroy sidewalks, to break through fences and to tear down trees. This want of courtesy is not uncommon. In short, it is altogether too common in many towns of the country, and upon the part of the owners of animals it shows a complete disregard of the rights of those who would beautify their homes, and thus correspondingly beautify the town.

The code of etiquette should not alone apply among individuals when directly associated together. It should extend further. It should go out and permeate a neighborhood. It should diffuse itself throughout a town. It should bind together the people of a State—of a nation. It should be a rule of action among all nations. Already the evidences of courtesy among nations begins to manifest itself. The International Congress is based upon this principle. The idea of friendly association of the representatives of nations for mutual adjustment of differences, is the beginning of a recognition of the rights of each other.

FIG. 22. PEOPLE WHO ARE TROUBLED BY THEIR NEIGHBORS.

The above illustration represents a common scene. The neighbors suspect each other, and they destroy the beauty of their grounds in the attempt to shut each other out. Suspicion and selfishness rule. Regardless of the rights of others, animals are allowed to trample to pieces the sidewalks, to destroy shade trees and to despoil the neighbor's yard. Inharmony, disorder, and ill-feeling among the people are characteristics of the neighborhood.

This is evidence of a higher civilization. When we can rise superior to selfishness, when we are willing to consider the rights and the requirements of others, when we are governed by the generous spirit of doing unto others as we would that they should do unto us, then we are directed by a power that will make an entire people, as a whole, what the laws of etiquette determine they shall be individually, in their intercourse with each other.

The illustration (Fig 22) upon this page represents a scene which may be observed in many villages or cities—a group of residences, modern and beautiful in architecture, surrounded and disfigured by high inclosures put up to guard against people who allow their cattle and other animals to destroy their neighbor's property.

Charming, Beautiful Homes.

BARRIERS BETWEEN NEIGHBORS REMOVED.

THE fences shown upon the opposite page, separating houses and lots, often prevent acquaintance with neighbors being made. The result of this non-intercourse is usually a suspicion that the neighbor is unworthy of confidence, an opinion which is never overcome except by interchange of civilities which would show each the worth of the other.

Unacquainted with his neighbors, the resident, ceasing to consider their rights, grows careless of his obligations toward others, and consequently becomes a less worthy citizen.

The illustration upon this page (Fig. 23) represents the scene very much changed. Again we have the same residences, and the same neighbors, who have become acquainted and have learned to value each other. The result of this social intercourse and evident observance of the rights of others has wrought a vast change in the appearance of the homes, which is manifest at a glance.

It is plainly apparent in the scene that a higher civilization pervades the neighborhood. The animals, that broke down the trees and devastated the sidewalks and grounds, have been withdrawn by their owners, and sent to pastures, where they belong. This of itself is evidence of decided advancement.

Examine the scene further. The fences have disappeared, save a low coping that determines the outer edge of the lot. In this alone a heavy item of expense has been removed, while with it has come the enlargement of grounds, which, studded with finely trimmed trees, and intersected with winding pathways, surround every residence with a most elegant park. That this improvement is enjoyed, is shown in the congregating of the neighbors together in the shady nook, the gambols of the children on the lawn, and the promenade of the ladies and gentlemen throughout the beautifully embellished grounds. All delight in the scene, and all are made better by it. While the resident could be coarse and selfish in his own little lot, he is now thrown upon his good behavior as he mingles with others on the beautiful grounds, and thus

all are improved. Even the cat and dog that quarrelled in the former scene are now acquainted with each other, and happily play together.

To maintain pleasant relations among neighbors, there are a few things which the citizen must avoid. Among these are the following:

Never allow children to play upon a neighbor's grounds or premises unless they are invited and made perfectly welcome by the neighbor.

Never allow fowls or animals of any kind, which you have control over, to trespass upon the premises or rights of other people.

Never borrow of neighbors if it be possible to avoid it. It is better to buy what you need than to frequently borrow. There are a few things which a neighbor should never be expected to lend. Among these are fine-edged tools, delicate machinery, and any article liable to easily get out of order. The less business relations among neighbors, the better.

Never fail to return, with thanks, any article borrowed, as soon as you have finished using it, and see that it is in as good or better condition than when you received it.

Articles of provisions which may be borrowed should be very promptly returned in larger quantity, to pay interest, and better in quality if possible. In no way can a neighbor lose character more effectually in business dealing than by the petty meanness of borrowing and failing to pay, or by paying with a poorer quality and in less amount.

Avoid speaking evil of your neighbor. As a rule it is only safe to compliment and praise the absent one.

FIG. 23. THE NEIGHBORHOOD WHERE PEOPLE LIVE IN HARMONY.

This illustration represents a neighborhood where the people evidently do unto others as they wish others to do unto them. They trust each other. The barriers between them are removed. No animal is allowed to do injury. Enjoying peace and beauty they evidently desire that the neighbor shall share the same. This co-operation, kindness and regard for all, give the beauty, the harmony, the peace, and the evident contentment which are here presented.

If any misunderstanding arises between yourself and a neighbor, endeavor to effect a reconciliation by a full explanation. When the matter is fully understood you will very likely be better friends ever afterwards.

Never fail, if the grounds run together, to keep your premises in as good order as your neighbor's. Should you own the house and grounds, and others occupy the same, you will do well to arrange to keep the exterior of the premises in order at your own expense, as tenants have not the same interest. The improvements of grounds among neighbors thus will always be kept up; you will be compensated by securing the best class of tenants, and the neighborhood will be greatly improved.

Kindness to the Erring.

A PLEA FOR THE UNFORTUNATE.

AN officer of the law you may be, and it becomes you to care for the prisoner in your charge. While law should be enforced, for the good of the criminal as well as the protection of society, it does not become you to be unkind. Perhaps investigation may prove that your prisoner is innocent and has been wrongly arrested. But if guilty, at most he is simply unfortunate. He had no power to say what qualities of mind he should inherit, what his temperament should be, or what training he should receive in infancy; all of which are usually determining causes that fix man's destiny in after-life.

He stands before you largely the victim of unfortunate circumstances. He lacks the moral strength which others possess, and hence his weakness and his errors. True, he must pay the penalty of his transgression, but you can temper the administration of your government with such justice as will tend to the improvement and, possibly, the reformation of the criminal. Whatever the conduct of the prisoner, you should always rise superior to the feelings of passion or revenge.

In a thousand ways our paths in life will be crossed by those who commit errors. It will be easy to find fault; it will be natural to blame. But we must never forget that further back, far beyond our sight, lie causes that tended to produce these results.

Well may the mother look with deep anxiety upon the infant, wondering what destiny lies before it. Alas! that a mother's hopes and prayers often do not avail. Drifted away from parental control, the footsteps fall amid temptation, and a life of sorrow is the result.

We should never forget, in our treatment of the erring, that, were the mother present, she would plead with us to deal gently with her child. Very touchingly does the following poem ask that we be lenient for her sake:

Some Mother's Child.

AT home or away, in the alley or street,
Whenever I chance in this wide world to meet
A girl that is thoughtless, or a boy that is wild,
My heart echoes sadly, "'T is some mother's child!"

And when I see those o'er whom long years have rolled,
Whose hearts have grown hardened, whose spirits are cold—
Be it woman all fallen, or man all defiled,
A voice whispers sadly, "Ah! some mother's child!"

No matter how far from the right she hath strayed;
No matter what inroads dishonor hath made;
No matter what element cankered the pearl—
Though tarnished and sullied, she's some mother's girl.

No matter how wayward his footsteps have been;
No matter how deep he is sunken in sin;
No matter how low is his standard of joy—
Though guilty and loathsome, he's some mother's boy.

That head hath been pillowed on tenderest breast;
That form hath been wept o'er, those lips have been pressed;
That soul hath been prayed for in tones sweet and mild;
For her sake deal gently with "some mother's child."

WHILE error must be deplored and virtue ever commended, we should deal carefully and considerately with the erring, ever remembering that a myriad of untoward circumstances are continually weaving a network around the individual, fettering and binding a soul that otherwise would be white and pure.

It is a most fortunate circumstance for the child to be born of an excellent parentage, to be reared amid kindness, and to be guided in youth by wise counsels. Given all these favoring circumstances, and the chances are that the pathway in life will be honorable. Deprived of these advantages, the individual is likely to fall short in excellence in proportion as the circumstances have been unfavorable.

There are those who seemingly have only a smooth pathway in life. They were so fortunate as to be born with an excellently balanced organization of mind. They have no passion unduly in excess. They have no abnormal longings, no eccentricities, no weaknesses. Roses strew their way, and they live a life well rounded out and full of honor.

But while there are those who are apparently exempt from temptation, all are not so fortunate in ability, in strength of purpose and in power of will which may enable them to resist evil. Some are liable to easily err, and it will take, possibly, but a trivial circumstance to carry them aside. In the transgression they will get their punishment—they will suffer sufficiently. It does not become the more fortunate, therefore, to take too much credit to themselves for being more virtuous and free from error. It is vastly more noble and charitable to extend sympathy and compassion. This sentiment is well expressed in the following poem, by Millie C. Pomeroy:

You Had a Smooth Path.

ONE morning, when I went to school,
In the long-vanished Yesterday,
I found the creek had burst its banks,
And spilled its waters o'er my way.
The little path was filled with mud;
I tried to cross it on a log;
My foot slipped, and I, helpless, fell
Into a mass of miry bog.

My clothes were pitiful to see;
My hands and face were covered quite.
The children laughed right heartily,
And jeered me when I came in sight.
Sweet Jessie Brown, in snow-white dress,
Stood, smiling, by the teacher's desk,
The while he, gravely as he might,
Inquired the secret of my plight.

Then Jessie shook her snow-white dress,
And said, "What will you give to me
For coming here so nice and clean?
My very shoes from dirt are free."
The tutor frowned, and answered her,
"You merit no reward to-day;
Your clothes and hands are clean, because
You had a smooth path all the way."

And so, I think, when children grown
Are white in grace or black with sin,
We should not judge until we know
The path fate had them travel in;
For some are led on sunny heights,
Beyond the power of Sin to sway;
While others grope in darksome paths,
And face temptation all the way.

THE SCIENCE OF BEAUTIFUL DRESS ILLUSTRATED.

THE LAW OF PROPORTION —AND— PARALLEL LINES.

CONTRAST BETWEEN STRAIGHT —AND— CURVED LINES.

As Shown in and Drawn from Original Illustrations in Nature.

THE PURPOSE of this chapter is to present the fundamental principles by which dress on human beings may be made beautiful. To favorably impress upon the mind of the reader these truths, various pictorial illustrations are herewith given, which, by the contrasts, clearly convey the idea.

Symmetry and Proportion.

To handsomely adorn the person, the first principle to be understood is that of symmetry, or proportion. To understand these, an examination of the contour of the male and female human body is necessary. In **Figs. 1 and 2** we show the male and female form. The dotted line reveals certain peculiarities in these. In the male it will be seen the shoulders are high and extend considerably outside the line. The shoulder of the female, it is seen, is sloping and much narrower than that of the male, while the lower portion of the form is shown to be considerably broader. Upon this understanding the tailor must work, building the coat, if he would please the eye, high and broad upon the shoulder but narrow upon the hip; while the dressmaker, in order to create the most pleasing effect, must make the lady's dress as small and narrow as comfort will allow, while at the same time she is permitted to arrange tuck and bow and flounce without stint below the waist.

The law is that the dress of man should make him look masculine, while the dress of woman should be made to make her appear effeminate and be in accord with her form.

What Tailors Must Understand.

That the reader may more fully understand this, we present in **Fig. 3** the man somewhat naturally sloping in the shoulder who patronized, at first, a tailor who did not understand, and took no note of his customer's peculiarity of shoulder.

Fig. 1—MALE FIGURE, Broad at Shoulder.

Fig. 2—FEMALE FIGURE, Narrow at Shoulder.

The result was that instead of overcoming this defect by thickening or padding the coat upon the upper part of the body, as shown in **Fig. 4**, the gentleman was allowed to come forth with a coat that made him look woman-like, with a shoulder round and narrow.

Not only was the coat made small across the shoulders, but the tailor allowed another error, and that was the making of side-pockets on the hips, in which the man placed his gloves, mittens and various articles he had to carry in his pockets. Added to this his pants were made large, baggy and rather short. The consequence was he was made to look entirely different from what nature designed him —see **Fig. 5.** Instead of appearing to be the bold, broad-breasted, trim-limbed man that he was, the tailor turned him out a short, broad-hipped, narrow-shouldered individual, apparently possessed of weak lungs, little strength, with nothing of the strong and masculine seemingly about him.

It is not necessary to tell the reader that there is an underlying principle in this, entirely independent of the spring or fall styles, to be observed in order to create a pleasing effect.

What Tailors Cannot Do.

Whatever peculiar cut of garment the tailor might invent, he could never make his customer look well in the suit shown in **Fig. 5.**

The gentleman visits another tailor, who understands the science of dress. The result is the broad shoulder, as shown in **Fig. 4,** and

the trim, manly form that we see in **Fig. 6,** with no pockets on the hips, pants close-fitting and sufficiently long to give length of appearance to the figure.

The reader would hardly suppose that the person shown in **Figs. 5 and 6** was the same individual; yet such is the fact, and that, too, the result of making the garment, in **Fig. 6,** to correspond with the male figure, which, naturally, is broad upon the shoulder, and from that point gradually sloping to the feet, the lower portion of the coat being always close-fitting upon the hips.

Fig. 3--Wrong. Proportion Bad.
Shoulders narrow, coat-collar extends to hair
and no relief from white.

Fig. 4--Right. Proportion Good.
Shoulders broad, suitable contrast and relief
because of white collar above coat.

physical perfection in the male and female form. If the tailor finds his male customer has an exceedingly round or sloping shoulder, has one shoulder lower than the other, or possesses any other physical defect, such peculiarity must, as far as possible, be overcome by cutting the garment accordingly. One means of remedying a defect of the person is shown in **Figs. 7 and 8.** As seen in the illustration, **Fig. 7** presents a very long neck, and the style in which the dress here shown is cut, makes the neck appear even longer than it is. To overcome this peculiarity the neck is dressed higher, as shown at **Fig. 8.**

What Dressmakers Must Do.

If the tailor finds it important to understand these principles, it will be seen to be equally necessary that the dressmaker should also be informed upon this subject. As shown in the female form, in **Fig. 2,** while the lower portion of the body is broad, the shoulder is narrow, and the dressmaker must make her garment to correspond accordingly, if she would produce, in the dress, the best effect.

The violation of this rule is shown in **Fig. 9.** In this we see ornamentation on the dress that has been made to extend over the shoulders in a manner such as to elevate and broaden the shoulders, at the same time the lower part of the dress is made narrow. The whole effect is to make the woman, thus dressed, look masculine and unnatural, assuming, as she does in this, the form of man.

On the contrary, the dress in **Fig. 10** is at once seen to be made in accord with the natural form of woman. The shoulders slope and are narrow, the dress being close-fitting, though not unduly so, upon the upper part of the body to the lower part of the waist, where the robe widens by graceful fold and flounce into pleasing proportions.

No matter what may be the mandates of fashion, the first law to follow, in dressing the person, is that of making the garments in accord with the generally recognized standard of

Fig. 5--Proportions Bad.
Shoulders sloping and narrow. Hips
broad. Pants too short.

Fig. 6--Proportions Correct.
Shoulders broad. Hips narrow. Pants
close-fitting at the bottom.

Effect of Color in Dress.

The apparent size of the person is very materially affected by stripes in clothing, by color, by ornaments, trimming and amplitude. To illustrate: A lady dressed in white will appear larger than if dressed in black. If to white be added stripes running perpendicularly, she will appear taller, the result of the stripes; and if bows, ribbons, flounces and breadth of skirt be added, she will appear much larger in consequence of such trimmings and amplitude of skirt.

On the contrary, the black dress, with little trimming, will make woman look smaller in size, especially if the dress be cut somewhat short and have a close-fitting skirt. Length of skirt adds to apparent height. A short skirt diminishes apparent stature, as do also any lines that run horizontally.

For this reason those persons who desire to add to their apparent height, should avoid those garments that terminate, at their lower edge, near the middle of the person. Thus the gentleman, whose coat comes no lower than his hips, looks shorter than he does in a coat that extends near to the knees. Thus the longer the coat, and the more continuous the perpendicular line, the taller he looks. For this reason the man appears much taller when dressed in woman's costume, and woman is apparently

Fig. 7--Long Neck,
Seems longer from style of
dress.

Fig. 8--Neck Shortened,
Apparently, by trimming of
dress.

much less in height in male attire, because of the horizontal line made by the lower edge of a short garment.

One of the reasons why the bloomer costume never found general favor among the female sex was because its want of long perpendicular lines made woman seem to be much smaller than she appeared to be when robed in a longer dress.

Relief and Variety.

There is another very important principle to be applied in the manufacture of wearing apparel, in order to secure the best effect, and that is the application of that which will give such relief to the garment as will break a monotony of appearance. This is done by a variety of trimming on a dress and a suitable interblending of harmonious colors. The principle applies in household decoration, architecture and landscape gardening. There should be a sufficient variety of object, shape and color as to afford pleasant relief to the eye.

Nature the Teacher.

As we went to nature to consult symmetry and proportion, so we will study the principle of relief as shown in landscape scenes.

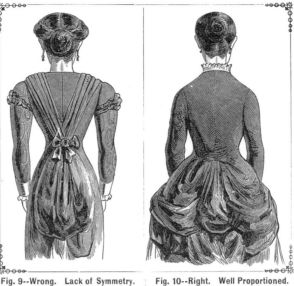

Fig. 9--Wrong. Lack of Symmetry.
Shoulders made to appear too high and broad, and dress narrow below the waist.

Fig. 10--Right. Well Proportioned.
Dress trimmed at neck, made narrow at shoulders; broad and ample below the waist.

leads up to the mountain, that clearly outlines itself against the sky, which is delightfully relieved by the fleecy clouds as they float, in their white, fantastic forms, through the azure blue.

This whole scene is a most charming one to gaze upon, and that, too, because of the continual variety which meets the eye.

As music is beautiful from variety of tone—as the bouquet is more charming from varied color—as oratory is more pleasing from the relief which comes from a sometimes higher, succeeded by a lower tone of voice, interspersed with changing gesture; as the landscape, shown in the picture, is more delightful to the eye when varied by tree, shrub, water, island, hill, mountain and cloud, so dress is more pleasing to the eye when relieved by varied color, suitable trimmings and appropriate ornaments.

Dress for Men.

The severe taste of the more highly cultured does not, at the present time, admit of extended variety on the dress of gentlemen, yet good taste positively demands that there be some relief. This is shown in the contrasting pictures of **Figs. 3 and 4.** In **Fig. 3** the coat-collar, it will be seen, rises into the hair, as does the water into the blue horizon, without relief, as shown in **Fig. 11.** As the view is improved by woodland and mountain coming between water and sky, as seen in **Fig. 12,** so the back of man's head is materially improved by the contrast of a

To illustrate this we present two marine views, one representing but little variety, the other considerable. Thus in **Fig. 11** we see an exceedingly dull and dreary scene, the result of lack of relief in the view. Examination shows that the sandy shore exhibits but little difference from the water, which seems to be merged in the horizon, with little contrast between the water and the sky. In fact were it not for the two or three objects in the shape of man, vessel and rock, which are shown in the view, there would be scarcely any

Fig. 11--Lonely, Cheerless Scene,
Because of no contrast and no variety. Shore is merged in water, water into sky, with no relief between.

Fig. 12--Charming Scene in Nature,
Because of contrast and variety. The view being interspersed with trees, water, island, mountain and cloud.

white collar coming between coat and hair, as represented in **Fig. 4.**

If the upper part of the coat is improved by a strip of white above it, making a clear division between the hair and the coat, so the coat-sleeve is equally benefited, in appearance, by

variety with which to relieve the monotony of this cheerless scene.

We turn to another view shown in **Fig. 12,** which is a most agreeable one to behold because of the pleasant variety which gives relief. A brief study of the picture shows in the foreground a man and horse, the winding roadway and the woody ledge. A little farther away is a sheet of water broken by a miniature island and the white sail of a boat. Beyond is the grove, and further yet is the hill which

the white cuff which clearly determines the length of the sleeve and gives relief between hand and coat, or coat and glove, should the latter be worn. The proof of this is seen in **Fig. 13,** in contrast with **Fig. 14,** the one showing no cuff, consequently no relief, the other being greatly improved in consequence of clear white projecting beyond the sleeve for the space of an inch or less.

Care must be exercised that the cuff and collar do not extend too far from beneath and the coat thus show too much white. As a rule the projection of each should not exceed, in space, an inch.

For the reason that the standing, white collar will usually show itself distinctly above the coat, it gives, when worn by gentlemen, a better appearance than does the turn-down collar, which usually sits so low upon the neck as to be hidden from view under the coat-collar as shown in **Fig. 3.**

Aside from the cuff and collar but little else of white can be shown upon the gentleman's dress, unless it be a portion of the shirt-bosom, which may, and really should, show, for a short space, depending somewhat upon the fashion, below the crevat.

Fig. 13--Hand With No White Cuff,
Consequently no relief between hand and coat.

Fig. 14--Contrast From the White Cuff,
White giving clear contrast between coat and hand.

Relief.

As a land-scape scene is improved by unnumbered variations, so the attire of woman admits of almost endless variety of relief-work, care being duly observed to secure colors suitable for the various complexions and seasons.

As with the gentleman, the upper portion of the lady's dress is seen to better advantage when it terminates with a white collar as shown in **Fig. 10,** and a very clear illustration of this is shown at **Fig. 24,** in contrast with **Fig. 23,** the latter of which reveals the same lady in a dress that shows no relief at collar or wristbands.

As before remarked, the lady's dress admits of endless opportunity for relief of various kinds, but very much care has to be observed that there be not too much trimming, as a confusion of ornamentation, or an excess of variety, resembles a yard too full of trees, shrubbery and flowers.

Our purpose in this is to show that certain fundamental principles underlie the matter of handsomely decorating the person. To properly apply these principles is largely a matter of experience and cultivated taste.

Law of Parallels.

Among the laws of nature which tend to produce beauty is that of parallel lines. An exemplification of the beauty which comes from parallels is shown in a forest in which the trunk of every tree is perfectly straight from the ground upward. A grove of ten thousand such trees, every one of which is straight and consequently parallel to every other, is a beautiful sight which is marred only when a wind-storm or some ill-fate causes certain of them to lean in various directions; hence, when this occurs the eye is immediately pained by the disorder that comes from irregularities in lines.

Fig. 15--Lines Irregular.
Objects all leaning in various directions, consequently disorder and confusion characterize the scene.

Fig. 16--Lines All Parallel.
Objects all point perpendicularly or regularly with others in certain directions. The result is apparent good order.

Thus a field of grain, every stalk of which stands upright, is a beautiful sight. If a breeze sweeps across and all the heads sway together it is then just as charming, because all the stalks bend in the same direction and each is parallel with all the others. But how quickly this beauty is dissipated when the grain, through storm or other cause, is trampled into irregularity!

A field of corn, or an orchard of trees, each row of which is straight, presents a pleasing effect because of regularity. So do we look with pleasure upon parallel rows or lines, wherever we find them.

For the purpose of fully illustrating this idea we present, in **Fig. 15,** a roadway and a goodly number of trees in the scene. Examination

Fig. 17--Disordered Appearance.
Hair irregular in direction and therefore in disorder.

Fig. 18--Hairs Parallel.
Combed, each hair in same direction, the effect is pleasing.

shows that very much disorder reigns throughout, evidently the result of serious neglect. Look-ing closely we see the upright lines of the house out of plumb, the cornice is irregular, the window-frames show want of uniformity, the trellis-lines of the grapery are not straight, the pickets in the fence slant in various ways and the trees lean in all directions.

The scene represents disorder, and is painful to behold. If asked the cause of the ill-look which the neighborhood presents, the reader would attribute it, probably, to neglect, which doubtless may be true; but the actual reason for the

Fig. 19--Lines Irregular,
Consequently dress and hair appear in disorder.

Fig. 20--Lines Parallel.
The result is order, neatness and beauty in the dress.

improved upon his return, and why? Because the wash has removed the dirt that marred one side of his face, making both of his cheeks look alike; and further, in the act of combing, each separate hair has been made to run in the same direction with others; and thus we have a clear exposition of the benefit of parallel lines as an aid to beauty.

This law is yet more fully shown in the succeeding illustration, **Fig. 19,** showing not only disheveled hair, but a badly deranged dress, the result of neglect to observe this law; the whole exhibiting lack of neatness and order.

unpleasant appearance is the want of parallel lines.

There is lack of reg-ularity, the various ob-jects point-ing in a variety of directions.

In **Fig. 16** we see the scene materially changed and all is much more agreeable to the eye.

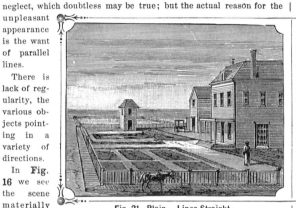

Fig. 21--Plain. Lines Straight.
Home neat and in order, but lacking in curved line which gives the highest order of beauty.

Fig. 22--Charming. Lines Curving.
Home constructed on those principles that give most beautiful effect.

The ben-eficial effect of obeying this princi-ple is seen in **Fig. 20,** uniformity and regu-larity being displayed in hair, paral-lel lines pervading the trim-ming about the neck, and the or-namenta-tion gener-ally upon the dress. The effect conveys the impression of order.

Uniformity, regularity and parallel lines characterize all parts of the dwelling; the trees stand per-pendicular and all point the same way. The rows of straw-berry plants are all straight, the timbers of the grapery all run in parallel lines, as also do the fence-pickets. And thus throughout, all the lines, whether horizontal, perpendic-ular or otherwise, that are de-signed to correspond in shape and form with others, take the same uniform direction.

Johnny's Uncombed Hair.

A clear illustration of the bad appearance resulting from irregularity of lines is pre-sented in Johnny's head, **Fig. 17,** as he appears at break-fast. Being reminded of the importance of arranging his toilet before coming to the table, the lad retires, makes use of water and comb, and soon afterward comes back exhibiting the face we see in **Fig. 18.**

Examination reveals that Johnny's appearance is very considerably

Fig. 23--Straight Lines.
Lady's hair and dress mostly in straight line.

Fig. 24--Curved Lines.
Hair and dress exhibiting an abund-ance of curved line.

Curved Lines.

There is yet another law that constitutes an element of beauty in all nature, and as we have used it elsewhere, in this volume, when illustrating the science of beauty in landscape gardening, in penmanship and household decoration, so we will make use of it here in the construction of handsome dress. We have reference to the curved line.

House With Straight Lines.

There is no object in art that is not improved by the appli-cation of curving outline. To represent this principle clear-ly, we give a pictorial view of a home, located on the level prairie, in which the builder evidently had no thought other than the straight-line: see **Fig. 21.** Examination shows no curve in the windows, none on the porch, nothing of the kind upon or about the house. The paths run straight, the same applies to the fence, the woman's dress hangs straight, the road shows no curve, the clouds extend straight-wise across the horizon, and even the old horse, with its projecting angles, exhibits very little of the curve. The whole scene is inclined to the severely straight.

House With Curved Lines.

We turn the reader's attention now to **Fig. 22**, where we behold a similar house, in size and expense of erection, located on a slight elevation which, of itself, makes a curving surface of the ground. In a study of the picture we find the windows all rounded at the top. The curved line is abundant on the porch, in balustrade, in cresting on the top of the house, on the summer-house in the distance, and on the bridge that leads to it. The lady's dress shows graceful curve; so do flower-vase, roadway, horses, the hill-top in the distance, and the clouds beyond.

It needs no admonition to induce the reader to appreciate the curved line in this. The whole scene portrays its presence and its beauty. The two homes—the one no more expensive than the other—plainly show how the hand of taste and an understanding of this principle will change a solemnly straight monotonous, unattractive home into a bower of beauty and a most charming place of abode.

Dress.

How does this apply in dress? Let us see. In **Fig. 23** we have a lady dressed in a cos-tume composed largely of the straight line. The hair is combed straight; the dress, cut low in the neck, has straight lines and right angles; square buttons adorn the front. A straight band across the waist and others at her wrists exhibit the same absence of curve. Although exceedingly prim in this dress the whole is severely plain and certainly not very attractive.

In **Fig. 24** we have the same lady dressed in a different garb, and, the reader will admit, much more handsomely. Why? Because of the large predominance of the curve. Let us study the picture and see. The Saratoga wave and curving folds of hair, in the beginning, very handsomely become and relieve the face. The oval ear-ring, graceful lace-work about the neck, bouquet, curving outline of form,

curved trimming on the front of the dress, round buttons, curved relief-work about the wrist, and arching line at the lower part of the basque—all create a most lovely and beautiful effect. As the curved line was the principal element of beauty in the residence, with its winding pathways, so the same law has wrought the charm which we find in the lady thus elegantly dressed

Three Ladies.   The Dress of Each Described.

In **Fig. 25** we give the full-length view of a lady dressed very fashionably and expensively in a costume severely stiff, cold and formal in its precision and straight line. This dress is relieved considerably by trimming, and it exhibits order upon the part of the wearer, in the due observance of parallel lines, but symmetry is largely lacking because of the high shoulders, and grace is also wanting because of lack of curved line.

Fig. 26 shows a costume which is certainly not very attractive because of lack of nearly all those requisites that make beauty in dress. We have but to study it to discover its deficiencies, which may be enumerated as follows: *First.* The woman in this cos-tume appears badly proportion-ed. The shoulders are broad and high, while cloak, being close-fitting at the lower part, gives too narrow an appearance to the form below the waist. *Second.* The cos-tume exhibits too much straight line. This is seen in the hat, the

Fig. 25--Very Precise.
The dress being neat, stiff and rich.

Fig. 26--Very Plain.
The dress being without any quality that gives charm.

Fig. 27--Very Graceful.
The dress combining those principles that make beauty.

tume composed largely of the straight line. The hair is combed straight; the dress, cut low in the neck, has straight lines and right angles; square buttons adorn the front. A straight band across the waist and others at her wrists exhibit the same absence of curve. Although exceedingly prim in this dress the whole is severely plain and certainly not very attractive.

edge of the cloak in front, with its straight lower edge, in the lapels of the pockets, in the straight fall of the dress-skirt, with straight edge at the ankles, square buttons, etc.

Third. The dress presents too much irregularity. The trimming about the neck is irregular. The buttons are at irregular distances apart; ear-rings are unmatched, and the lapels on the cloak are not alike in appearance.

Fourth. There is too little relief on the dress throughout. It is too plain to be attractive. The relief about the neck is not sufficient. The cloak is without any trimming which gives variety. No white cuff at the wrist gives contrast at the hand, and the skirt possesses no ornamentation calculated to attract or charm the eye.

The costume seen at **Fig. 27** presents a pleasing combination of the various principles we have enumerated, being all embodied in this dress. The hat gracefully curving, surmounted by a bending plume, is well balanced upon a head rich in abundant, waving hair. The white collar, cuff, handkerchief and trimming of dress, give a fair amount of relief. The garment is so fashioned as to give feminine appearance and symmetry to the form; and throughout the curving line gives a delicate grace which renders the lady pleasingly attractive.

Two Men. How to Dress Most Handsomely.

The application of the laws, or rather lack of application, relating to dress, which we have considered, is very clearly presented in **Fig. 28.** The person here shown is evidently a gentleman of fine manners who only needs a skillful tailor in order to appear to advantage. As he is now dressed it is very evident he has been imposed upon by a dealer in ready-made clothing, and the fact is further clearly proven that he himself lacks an understanding of what constitutes handsome attire, as shown by the suit in which he here presents himself.

From the study we have thus far given of the principles that make beauty in clothing, we now readily enumerate the faults revealed here, and among them we may designate first lack of relief. The face, without beard, mustache or whisker, is too smooth for the highest form of beauty. The coat-collar is too high, allowing, consequently, no relief from the white which should be shown between coat and hair. There is not enough white shown about the cravat, which has but a small, turn-down collar. Added to this deficiency the white cuffs are also lacking. And second, in this suit of clothes the form lacks symmetry, for the following reasons: The shoulders are made to appear very narrow and very sharp in slope. The pockets are placed at the side of the hips, and with lapels and contents, give a width to this portion of the body which makes the person look ungraceful.

The pants are too large and too short. The consequence is the various horizontal lines, those made by the pockets and by the lower edge of the coat at the hips, the other by the pants at the ankles, lessens the apparent stature, so that the gent seems to be considerably shorter than he is, or than he would appear if clothed in a longer garment with no horizontal lines. Apparently he is not as tall as the gentleman in the next illustration, but measurement will find the height to be the same. And third, the pockets at the side of the hips causes the lower portion of the coat to stand out in a position exhibiting straight line so that, as a whole, the figure in this suit of clothing is far from elegant and graceful in appearance.

Gent Elegantly Dressed.

We turn now to **Fig. 29** and study it with a view to ascertaining what may be the law in gentleman's dress that gives handsome appearance to the form as a whole. Examination shows that this figure possesses all the favorable points that we have considered in this chapter, as essential to excellence. Of these we find here perfect symmetry, shoulders high and broad, hips somewhat narrower than the shoulders, no horizontal lines at the hips, made by pockets or a short coat, and pants gradually lessening in size until they reach the feet. The length of coat and pants gives dignity to the form, and the contour of the dress, as a whole, in symmetry and curving line is very pleasing to contemplate. To this is given, also, parallel line, shown in regularity of cuffs which are of even size, buttons at regular distances apart, each side of collar of even height, etc. To this is added all the relief that this style of dress on the gent will admit. The mustache and side-whiskers give variety on the face, the white collar and shirt-bosom give pleasant contrast at the upper part of the body, while the cuffs make a clear distinction between gloves and coat.

Though styles may change somewhat, the coat being longer or shorter, pants larger or smaller, etc., yet in all this, whatever be the style, those principles we have presented in this chapter must be applied if the individual would dress handsomely. For proof of this we present the illustrations in

Fig. 28--Badly Proportioned.	Fig. 29--Elegant Appearance.
Shoulders made to appear too narrow and too sloping. Coat too broad at hip and too short. Pants too large and too short. No relief at wrist.	Shoulders broad and high. Coat slim and narrow at hip. Pants gracefully long. White collar and cuff handsomely relieve neck and wrist.

contrast, thus giving our readers the opportunity to study and determine for themselves.

From the foregoing it will be seen that, in order to dress handsomely always with certainty, it will be necessary to apply the following: *First.* The dress must bring out the most perfect natural form. *Second.* Wherever there is opportunity for parallel lines, such must be used. *Third.* A certain amount of variety should pervade the dress in order to prevent a monotony of appearance. *Fourth.* Care must be taken to have every part of the garment present a curving outline.

When thus a dress is made, which presents the person in fine proportion, curving in outline, orderly in appearance, with relief sufficient to please the eye, the wearer is certainly handsomely dressed.

OU have thoughts that you wish to communicate to another through the medium of a letter. Possibly you have a favor to bestow. Quite as likely you have a favor to ask.

In either case you wish to write that letter in a manner such as to secure the respect and consideration of the person with whom you correspond.

The rules for the mechanical execution of a letter are few; understanding and observing the rules already considered for composition, the writer has only to study perfect naturalness of expression, to write a letter well.

Style and Manner.

The *expression* of language should, as nearly as possible, be the same as the writer would speak. A letter is but a talk on paper. The *style* of writing will depend upon the terms of intimacy existing between the parties. If to a superior, it should be respectful: to inferiors, courteous; to friends, familiar; to relatives, affectionate.

Originality.

Do not be guilty of using that stereotyped phrase,

Dear Friend:
    I now take my pen in hand to let you know that I am well, and hope you are enjoying the same great blessing.

Be original. You are not exactly like any one else. Your letter should be a representative of yourself, not of anybody else. The world is full of imitators in literature, who pass on, leaving no reputation behind them. Occasionally originals come up, and fame and fortune are ready to do them service. The distinguished writers of the past and present have gone aside from the beaten paths. Letter writing affords a fine opportunity for the display of originality. In your letter be yourself; write as you would talk.

* In the preparation of this chapter the author gathered many valuable suggestions from " Frost's Original Letter-Writer," and other works on epistolary correspondence, published by Dick & Fitzgerald, New York.

Position while Writing.

AN object early to be attained, is to acquire an easy, graceful and healthful position of body while sitting or standing, when writing. To obtain this, the writer should sit with the right side to the desk, using a table so high as to compel the body to sit erect.

Rest the arm lightly upon the elbow and fore-arm, and the hand upon the two lower fingers, the wrist being free from the desk. Allow the body and head to incline sufficiently to see the writing, but no more.

Maintain a position such as will give a free expansion of the lungs, as such posture is absolutely indispensable to the preservation of health.

A desk or table, with a perfectly level surface, is best for writing. Where a decided preference is manifested for sitting with the left side, or square, to the desk, such position may be taken. If the desk slopes considerably, the left side is preferable.

Avoid dropping the body down into an awkward, tiresome position. If wearied with continued sitting, cease writing. Lay down the pen, step forth into the fresh air, throw back the arms, expand the chest, inflate the lungs, and take exercise. When work is again resumed, maintain the same erect position, until the habit becomes thoroughly fixed of sitting gracefully and easily, while engaged in this exercise.

Business Letters.

 N letters of business, use as few words as possible.

2. Business letters should be promptly answered.

3. Use a clear, distinct writing, avoiding all flourish of penmanship or language.

4. Come at once to your subject, and state it so clearly that it will not be necessary to guess your meaning.

5. Give town, county, State and date explicitly. It is frequently of great importance to know *when* a letter was written.

6. Read your letter carefully when finished, to see that you have made no omissions and no mistakes. Also carefully examine your envelope, to see that it is rightly directed, with postage-stamp affixed.

7. Copy all business letters, of your own, by hand, or with the copying-press made for the purpose.

8. Send money by Draft, P. O. Money-Order, or Express, taking a receipt therefor; thus you have something to show for money, guarantying you against loss. Always state in your letter the amount of money you send, and by what means sent.

9. Write date, and by whom sent, across the end of each letter received, and file for future reference, fastening the letters together with rubber bands, or binding in a letter-file adapted to the purpose. The possession of a letter sometimes prevents litigation and serious misunderstanding.

Ordering Goods.

In ordering goods, state very explicitly the amount, kind, quality, color, shape, size, etc., and on what terms wanted. Whether you wish the same sent by freight or express, and *what* express. Much inconvenience is experienced among business men because of a neglect to designate explicitly what is wanted.

Should the writer wish to make suggestions, ask questions, or add other matter to the letter, which is foreign to the subject, such words should be placed entirely separate from the order. Of fifty or a hundred letters received to-day by the merchant, that one which is mixed up with complaints, enquiries, etc., will probably be laid over till to-morrow, or until time can be spared to read it through. Had the order been explicitly stated, and the suggestions placed elsewhere, the goods would have been forwarded immediately. It is, in fact, better to write the order on a separate sheet from the other matter.

Send your order, also, early enough to give yourself plenty of time in which to receive the goods before they are needed.

Books, being a common article ordered, may be taken as an example showing the importance of giving a careful description of the goods wanted. To illustrate: be explicit in giving name of book, name of author, by whom published, style of binding, price at which it is advertised, etc. Thus, a careless person, ordering of Harper & Brothers a United States History, will say, "Send me a United States History." Of course the first query of the shipping-clerk is, "*Whose* history?" There are many histories of the United States, published by as many different authors, and the clerk is liable to send the one not wanted; in which case the person ordering is very likely to unjustly blame Harper & Brothers.

If the writer should say, "Send me a copy of Willard's History of the United States, by Emma Willard, published by A. S. Barnes & Co., bound in cloth," there would be no liability to mistake. The following will serve as sample forms:

Form of Letter Ordering Books.

ROCKFORD, ILL., March 1, 18—.
MESSRS. JANSEN, MCCLURG & CO.,
    Chicago, Ill.
    Dear Sirs:
        Enclosed find draft for $48.75, for which please send, by American Express,

10 Tennyson's Poems.	Published by Harper & Bros.	$1.25	$12.50
10 Thirty Years in the Harem.	" " " "	1.50	15.00
10 Literature and Art, by M. Fuller.	" Fowler & Wells.	1.00	10.00
5 Getting on in the World, Mathews.	S. C. Griggs & Co.	2.25	11.25
			$48.75

Thanking you for the promptitude with which you have filled my orders heretofore, I am,
        Very Respectfully,
            CASH DOWN.

Form of an Order to a Dry-Goods Merchant.

April 5, 18—.
MESSRS. A. T. STEWART & CO.,
    New York.
    Dear Sirs:
        Enclosed find Post Office Order for $25, for which please send, by American Express, the following goods:

2 Lancaster Table Spreads ($3.50),	$ 7.00
4 prs. Alexandre Kid Gloves ($2.50), No. 6½, Brown, Green, Yellow, Black,	10.00
8 yds. Calico, Brown, with small figure (25c.),	2.00
12 " " White, " " pink dot "	3.00
2 Linen Handkerchiefs (50c.),	1.00
4 prs. Ladies' Cotton Hose (50c.), No. 9,	2.00
	$25.00

Direct to
        MRS. MARY WILSON,
          ELKHART, IND.

From a Young Man Commencing Business, to a Wholesale House, with Order.

RACINE, WIS., Aug. 10, 18—.
MESSRS. FIELD, LEITER & CO.,
    Chicago, Ill.
    Dear Sirs:
        Having recently commenced business for myself, with fair prospects of success, I shall be pleased to open an account with your house, and trust it will be to our mutual advantage. Should you think favorably of the matter, you will please fill the accompanying order with the least possible delay, and on your best terms.

For testimonials, I refer you to Carson, Pirie, Scott & Co., of your city, by whom I have been, until recently, employed; but, as this is my first transaction with your house, upon forwarding me an invoice of goods, and deducting your usual discount for cash, I will remit a sight draft on the First National Bank of your city, for the amount, by return mail. Expecting your usual prompt attention, I am,
        Yours Respectfully,
           HENRY MAYNARD.

Reply from Wholesale House, with Invoice.

CHICAGO, Aug. 12, 18—.
MR. HENRY MAYNARD,
    Racine, Wis.
    Dear Sir:
        We take pleasure in sending this day, by your order, the enclosed invoice of goods, amounting to $1,400, subject to 5 per cent discount for prompt cash.

Your references being entirely satisfactory, we have no hesitation in opening an account and allowing you our best terms. Trusting that the goods, which are shipped by express, will arrive safely and meet your favor, we are,
        Yours Truly,
           FIELD, LEITER & CO.

Requesting Information Concerning the Opening of a Store.

BOSTON, MASS., Sept. 18, 18—.
CHAS. H. WILLIAMS, ESQ.,
    Bennington, Vt.
    Dear Sir:
        My partner and myself being desirous of establishing a branch store in the clothing trade, I take the privilege of a friend in asking you to send me the number of clothing stores already in your village, and such other information as may be necessary, concerning the feasibility of establishing our business in your place. An early reply will greatly oblige,
        Yours, Very Truly,
           WM. B. HOPKINS.

Answer to the Foregoing.

BENNINGTON, VT., Sept. 20, 18—.
MR. WM. B. HOPKINS,
    Boston, Mass.
    Dear Sir:
        I have taken occasion to enquire in relation to the extent and number of clothing stores in this place, and am happy to inform you that, while that department of trade is very fairly represented, there seems to be a good opening for a first-class store, such as your house would undoubtedly establish.

There is also a large store just vacated, in the center of the village, one of the best locations in the town, which can be had at reasonable rent. Hoping that you may carry out your design of locating here, and trusting that you may realize your expectations, I am,
        Yours Truly,
           CHAS. H. WILLIAMS.

Enquiry Concerning Real Estate.

SPRINGLAKE, MICH., Sept. 4, 18—.

MESSRS. S. TOWN & SON,
    Aurora, Ill.,
        Dear Sirs:
            Having heard much said in praise of your beautiful city, particularly concerning railroad privileges, church and educational advantages, I have concluded to make your town my permanent place of abode, if I can locate myself aright, inasmuch as I have a large family of children to educate, and the numerous lines of railway radiating from your city will afford me the desired accommodations in my traveling agency.

My object in writing you at present is to learn your best terms for a residence containing not less than ten rooms, having from six to ten acres of land attached, situated not over a mile from the postoffice.

An immediate answer will oblige,
            Your Obedient Servant,
                HARVEY B. WILCOX.

Superintendent's Resignation.

GALESBURG, ILL., Sept. 1, 1878.

TO THE GENERAL SUPERINTENDENT OF THE C., B. & Q. R. R.,
    Chicago, Ill.,
        Dear Sir:
            I herewith tender my resignation as local superintendent of the railroad repair works in this city, my labors in behalf of your company to cease October 1, 1878.
            Respectfully Yours,
                D. B. LAWSON.

Short Form of Resignation.

PITTSBURGH, PA., Dec. 2, 1879.

TO THE DIRECTORS OF THE PITTSBURGH GLASS WORKS,
    Pittsburgh, Pa.,
        Dear Sirs:
            Please accept my immediate resignation as business manager of your manufactory.
            Yours Respectfully,
                WM. D. WEBSTER.

Clergyman's Resignation.

TO THE TRUSTEES OF FIRST BAPTIST CHURCH,
    Pittsfield, Mass.,
        Gentlemen:
            It has now been seven years since the commencement of my pastoral connection with the First Baptist Church of this city. During this time the church society has grown in numbers, the sabbath school has been continually blessed by a large attendance, and the relations between pastor and congregation have always been of a most pleasant character. For these and other reasons it would be agreeable to continue my connection with the society longer; but other fields of labor affording wider and better opportunities, I feel it but just that I accept the privileges offered.

Thanking the congregation to whom I have ministered for their kind and unwavering support, and praying for your continued prosperity, I desire you to accept my resignation as pastor of your society, to take effect January 15, 1878.   Yours Very Respectfully,
                CHAS. B. HANFORD.

Letter Complaining of Error in a Bill.

TROY, N. Y., June 10, 18—.

MESSRS. H. B. CLAFLIN & CO.,
    New York,
        Dear Sirs:
            Upon examining bill accompanying your last lot of goods, I find that I am charged with four dozen pairs of cotton hose which I never ordered nor received. I enclose the bill and copy of the invoice of goods, that the error may be corrected. I am, gentlemen,
            Yours Very Respectfully,
                H. B. MOORE.

Answer to the Foregoing.

NEW YORK, June 11, 18—.

MR. H. B. MOORE,
    Troy, N. Y.,
        Dear Sir:
            We regret that you were put to any trouble by the carelessness of a clerk, who, having proved himself incompetent, has left our service. We enclose the correct bill to you, and offer apologies for the error.   Truly Yours,
                H. B. CLAFLIN & CO.

An Application for a Situation on a Railway.

DAVENPORT, IA., Jan. 15, 18—.

HON. B. C. SMITH,
    Dear Sir:
            Understanding that you are a shareholder in some of the principal railways, and on intimate terms with several of the directors, I venture to solicit your kind interest in behalf of my eldest son, William, now in his twentieth year. His education has been varied and useful, and his character, so far as I know, is above reproach.

For several years he has expressed a desire to enter the employ of a railroad company, and under the circumstances I venture to write to you, in the hope that, should you have it in your power to oblige me, you will kindly intercede in his favor. By doing so you will confer a lasting obligation both on him and me. I remain, sir,
            Your Ob'd't Servant,

Recommending a Successor in Business.

MILWAUKEE, WIS., Dec. 24, 18—.

MESSRS. BELL & HARDY,
    Dear Sirs:
            We flatter ourselves that there are many friends among our connection who will regret that we are on the point of relinquishing business. In doing so our premises and stock of goods will be transferred to the hands of Messrs. Williams & Co., who will in future carry on the business on the same approved system and extensive scale as ourselves, provided they can rely upon receiving the patronage of our connection; in the hope of which, it is our pleasure and duty to present these gentlemen to your notice. We cannot speak too highly of the confidence we feel in their liberal mode of conducting mercantile transactions; and, in the hope that they may be honored with the same countenance received by ourselves from your respected firm, we beg to sign ourselves
            Your Most Obedient Servants,
                HOPE, GOOD & CO.

Notice of Having Forwarded Goods.

SOUTH HAVEN, MICH., Sept. 1, 18—.

MESSRS. HAGER, SPIES & CO.,
    Chicago, Ill.,
        Dear Sirs:
            According to your order, I have shipped you this day, per Steamer Morning Star,
            200 baskets Peaches,   (Marked H., S. & Co.)
            10 bbls. Sweet Potatoes,   "   "   "
            12 " Apples,   "   "   "
Trusting that these will prove as satisfactory as those heretofore sent, and bring as good a price, I am
            Respectfully Yours,
                A. M. GOODFELLOW.

Requesting a Friend to Make Purchases.

KANKAKEE, ILL., Jan. 1, 18—.

DEAR MARY:
            I am going to trespass on your kindness by asking you to make a few purchases for me. Enclosed find twenty dollars and a memorandum of what I want.

My household duties, combined with the objection I have to leaving my children at this season of the year in the care of servants, very closely confine me to my home, and are my excuse for troubling you.

We are in usual health, and I hope this note will find your family all well. With kind regards to Mr. Webster and love to children, I remain,

Your Sincere Friend,
HELEN D. WELLS.

To Mrs. May Benson,
— Michigan Ave., Chicago.

Requesting Settlement of Account.

MEMPHIS, TENN., Oct. 9, 18—

Hiram Baxter, Esq.,
Nashville, Tenn.
Sir:
I enclose your account. I shall feel obliged by your settlement at an early date, as I have several heavy payments to make. Trusting that you will excuse my troubling you, I am,

Yours Respectfully,
DELOS HARTWELL.

Reply to the Preceding.

NASHVILLE, TENN., Oct. 12, 18—.

Delos Hartwell, Esq.,
Memphis, Tenn.
Sir:
As I am unable to send you the money for settlement of our account, without inconvenience, I enclose my acceptance for thirty days, which I trust you will be able to use.

Yours Truly,
HIRAM BAXTER.

Urging Payment of Rent.

COLUMBUS, O., March 11, 18—.

Mr. D. P. Hoyt.
Dear Sir:
I have waited patiently for your convenience in the payment of rent for the house you are at present occupying. As, however, you have now been my tenant for four months without meeting any of the payments, which were to be made monthly, I feel obliged to remind you of the fact that there are now $80 due to me.

Trusting that you will give the subject your immediate attention, I am,

Yours Truly,
WEBSTER GREEN.

Letter to a Pioneer Settler in the West.

TOLEDO, OHIO, July 9, 18—.

Mr. Martin Fuller.
Dear Sir:
I take the liberty, though a stranger, of addressing you a few lines relative to the inducements for new settlers in your section of the country, having been recommended to do so through our mutual friend, Artemas Carter.

As I have sold out my business in this city for ten thousand dollars, I am anxious to invest the proceeds in a large farm in a young State, feeling satisfied that a new country, like that you are now in, offers attractions for young and energetic men not found in the old cities.

You will much oblige me by giving information concerning climate, soil, water, timber, and other inducements for settling in your vicinity. Trusting that doing so will not seriously trouble you, and that I may hear from you soon, I remain,

Yours, Very Respectfully,
CHAS. W. CANFIELD.

Answer to the Foregoing.

BIG STRANGER, KANSAS, Aug. 15, 18—.

Mr. Chas. W. Canfield,
Toledo, Ohio.
Dear Sir:
Your welcome letter was received yesterday. I can assure you that I will be only too happy to furnish you all the information you desire relative to the prospects in this portion of Uncle Sam's domains.

I have now been two years in this place, and I can truly say that these years have been the happiest of my life. True, we have endured some hardships incident to pioneer life; but the glorious freedom from the frivolities of fashion and the formalities of aristocratic life, common to the old towns in the East, together with the pleasure one takes in making new improvements, all have combined to render our family perfectly delighted with the country.

For a quarter of the money in your possession, you can purchase all the land you will desire to cultivate; the remainder you can loan hereabouts, on bond and mortgage, at good interest.

The climate here is healthy and invigorating; the soil good, with running streams in sufficient abundance to water most of the farms. Plenty of building material and fuel can be had in the timber skirting the streams; and the prospect for the ultimate opening of the land in this section to a ready market, through several lines of railway now in contemplation, is very flattering. At present, however, the nearest station to my farm, on the stage route, is Chesterfield, thirty-four miles distant, at which place I will take great pleasure in meeting you, with my team, at any time you may appoint.

A very excellent farm, adjoining mine, can be bought for five dollars ($5) per acre. One corner of the land is crossed by a never-failing stream, with considerable timber along the same.

You will have to rough it for a little while after you arrive; but the neighbors will all turn out to aid in getting up your log house, after which you will be at home "under your own vine and fig-tree."

We have two rooms in our house, and, till your house is completed, we will give one of them to your family. It will seem a little odd, at first, for a fashionable family of six or eight persons to occupy one room, with wolf and deer skins for quilts and coverlets; but, by-and-by, when the young ladies find they are in just as good style as anybody else, they will dismiss their fastidiousness, and think it jolly fun. These privations that we at first endure are necessary, perhaps, to enable us to appreciate the fine homes which we all expect to have in the good time coming. Hoping to have the pleasure of welcoming yourself and family as neighbors, I am,

Yours, Very Truly,
MARTIN FULLER.

# Applications for Situations.

Letters Answering Advertisements.

THE following advertisements, taken from metropolitan papers, are but samples of hundreds of such to be seen every day in the advertising columns of the leading daily newspapers in the great cities; showing that abundant opportunities constantly offer for obtaining employment, the positions to be secured, however, by letters making application for them.

WANTED.

Miscellaneous.

WANTED—AN EDITORIAL ASSISTANT ON A literary paper. A thoroughly competent lady preferred. Address D 71, Herald office, New York.

WANTED—IN A GRAIN COMMISSION HOUSE, a smart lad for office work; must be a good penman. Address, in own handwriting, stating age and salary expected, W 32, Ledger office.

WANTED—A YOUNG LADY CLERK IN A DRY goods store. Must be accustomed to the business. Address, with reference, B 80, Picayune office.

WANTED—AN ASSISTANT BOOKKEEPER, one who writes neatly and rapidly; willing to work for a moderate salary, and who can bring A No. 1 recommendations. Address, stating experience and particulars, X. Y. Z., Bulletin office.

WANTED—AN EXPERIENCED BOOKKEEPER in a bank. Address, with reference, Z 61, Journal office.

WANTED—LADY COPYIST, ABLE TO WRITE A bold, distinct hand. Salary good. Address, in applicant's own handwriting, COPY, Republican office.

WANTED—A COMPETENT SALESMAN TO sell pianos — one who has experience and good references. Address, stating salary expected, PIANOS, Tribune office.

WANTED—AN ACCOMPLISHED, EDUCATED young lady as a companion, to travel for six months in Europe, with a gentleman, wife, and daughter. Must be a ready writer, a good conversationalist, and possess vivacity and pleasing manners. Wardrobe furnished, and money to pay all expenses. Address Z. B M., Commercial office, stating where an interview can be had.

As a hundred different persons will sometimes make application for one position, which will be given to the individual writing the best letter, everything else being equal, this illustrates in a striking manner the importance of being able to write a letter elegantly and correctly.

Answer to an Advertisement for an Assistant Editor.

Maplewood, Mass., April 1, 18—.

Dear Sir:

Observing the enclosed advertisement in this morning's "Herald," I improve the opportunity by writing you an application for the place, as I am at present disengaged.

I graduated four years ago at Mrs. Willard's Seminary, Troy, N. Y., since which time I conducted the literary department of Frank Leslie's "Magazine of Fashion" up to October last, when failing health, resulting from too much close confinement, compelled me to travel abroad, from which journey, principally through England and France, I have just returned, with health completely restored.

I beg to refer you to Mr. Leslie for testimonials. Being exceedingly fond of literary pursuits, I shall be happy to occupy the position you offer, if mutually agreeable.

Yours, Most Respectfully,

Harriet Sibley. (May Myrtle.)

General Directions.

Letters in reply to advertisements should be written immediately, else you may be too late.

Paste the advertisement at the head of your letter; thus it will be known exactly what your communication has reference to.

It is not necessary to speak much in praise of yourself, but you may state your reference, your experience, and qualifications fitting you for the position, the whole being told as briefly as possible.

Write your application yourself, your hand-writing and the manner of expressing yourself being the test by which the advertiser judges you. If you have written testimonials, copy the same, marking them as such, and enclose the copy.

From a Boy Applying for a Clerkship.

879 Market Street, PHILADELPHIA, PA., Nov. 4, 18—.
DEAR SIR:

I notice in this morning's "Ledger" your advertisement of "a boy wanted in a grain commission house," which position I take the first opportunity to apply for.

I am fourteen years old, have been at school most of the time, winters, for the past seven years, and understand bookkeeping and conducting correspondence pretty well, having assisted my father much of the time while he was in the coal trade, which was about three years.

I am perfectly willing and ready to take my coat off and go right to work at handling grain or anything else in your line.

I refer you to Mr. Ira Belden, coal dealer, at 56 Benton street, who has always known me.

I will board at home, and will try to earn for you five dollars a week.
Very Respectfully Yours,
JOHN CLANCY.

From a Young Lady Applying for a Clerkship in a Store.

182 Murray St., BUFFALO, N. Y., May 19, 18—.
DEAR SIR:

I take the earliest opportunity of replying to the enclosed advertisement.

I have been for the past two years in the employ of Bennett & Hawley, dry-goods dealers, 492 Camden street, until the dissolution of their firm, about four weeks ago. I beg to refer you, for testimonials, to Mr. Chas. H. Bennett, of the firm of Snow, Williams & Bennett, 178 Harvard street, should you entertain my application.
Your Very Obedient Servant,
MARY H. BENSON.

Answering an Advertisement for a Bookkeeper.

1184 Longworth St., CINCINNATI, O., May 1, 18—.
DEAR SIR:

In reply to your advertisement in to-day's "Commercial" for a clerk or assistant bookkeeper, I beg to offer my services to your firm.

I have been in the employ of Mr. Wm. H. Wilson for the past four years, until he sold out his business a few days ago, having kept the books of his house during the time.

He permits me to refer to him for any testimonial of character or ability which you may require.

Should my application meet your views, it will be my earnest endeavor to faithfully and punctually fulfill the duties required. I have the honor to remain,
Yours, Very Respectfully,
HOMER BUXTON.

Answering an Advertisement for a Cook.

48 Wentworth Ave., PITTSBURGH, PA.,
March 17, 1873.
MRS. D. N. HASKINS.
Respected Madam:

Seeing an advertisement in this morning's "Press" for a good plain and fancy cook, I take the opportunity to apply for the situation.

I have been with my present mistress, Mrs. Burton, for three years, and only leave because she has rented her house for the summer, to make an extended visit among her relatives in New England.

I shall remain here until Tuesday next, unless I find a place sooner, and Mrs Burton will give you any information you may desire regarding my capacity.
I Remain, Very Respectfully,
SARAH E. WESTON.

Answer to an Advertisement for a Chambermaid.

(Advertisement pasted in.)

No. —— St., NASHVILLE, TENN.,
Feb. 14, 18—.
DEAR MADAM:

In answer to the above advertisement, I beg to state that I am about to leave my present situation, as Mrs. Harrington, with whom I have been for the past six years, is about breaking up housekeeping; and I take the opportunity to apply for the position you offer.

Mrs. Harrington assures me that she will take pleasure in recommending me to any person who may apply to her concerning my industry and trustworthiness.
MARGARET BALLENTINE.

Application for a Situation as Gardener.

No. —— 7th St., NEW YORK,
June 10, 18—.
DEAR SIR:

Understanding that you want a gardener, I beg to offer myself as a candidate to fill the place. I have had constant experience for ten years, both in nursery grounds and private gardens, and am thoroughly acquainted with the management of the greenhouse and hothouse.

The enclosed testimonials, from gentlemen for whom I have worked, will, I trust, prove satisfactory. My last employer, Mr. Snow, I would like to have you see personally concerning my fitness for the position.

I am a married man, thirty-three years of age. If favorable to my application, please address as above, and oblige,
Your Obedient Servant,
JAMES H. HARPER.

Application for a Situation as Coachman.

178 —— St., BOSTON,
April 10, 18—.

MR. JOHN H. WILLIAMS.

Dear Sir:

Having been informed that you are in want of a coachman, I take the liberty of enclosing you the accompanying testimonials, to which I ask your attention. Though reared in Deerfield, I have been in Boston for the past fourteen years, having constantly had charge of horses during that time, as I did on the farm before leaving home.

As further evidence of my ability, I may mention that I had chief charge of the Tremont Street Livery Stable until the death of the owner, Mr. Paxton, after which the stock was sold and the stable closed.

Should my application meet your favor, I shall be glad to engage as your coachman, and will do all in my power to merit your approval.

Yours Respectfully,
HIRAM WILDER.

Application from a Governess Answering an Advertisement.

(*Advertisement pasted in.*)

No. 784 —— St., TROY, N. Y.,
July 18, 18—.

MRS. C. B. WILLIAMS.

Dear Madam:

In answer to the above, I would say that I am seeking such a situation as you offer. My present term of teaching will close August 15th, at which time I would be ready to enter upon the work of superintending the education of your daughters.

I have, for several years, taught the higher English studies, besides German, Latin and drawing. For testimonials, I beg to refer you to the principal of my school, Rev. H. B. Watson.

Hoping that I may hear from you soon, and that we may make an arrangement mutually satisfactory, I remain,

Very Respectfully Yours,
HELEN B. CHANDLER.

Requesting the Character of a Governess.

No. 84 —— St., TROY, N. Y.,
July 19, 18—.

REV. H. B. WATSON,
Principal, Glenhaven Seminary.

My Dear Sir:

Having inserted an advertisement in the papers requiring the services of a governess competent to instruct my two daughters, I will esteem it a great favor if you will inform me concerning the ability of Miss Chandler to give instructions in the higher English studies, German and drawing, she having referred me to you.

I am especially desirous of securing the services of a young lady whose moral influence will guard my children from danger — one whose amiability of character will make her a pleasant companion as well as teacher. I am much pleased with the appearance of Miss Chandler, and, if your report is favorable, I shall not hesitate to perfect an engagement with her at once.

Yours, Very Respectfully,
CLARA B. WILLIAMS.

Favorable Reply to the Foregoing.

GLENHAVEN SEMINARY, N. Y.
July 21, 18—.

MRS. CLARA B. WILLIAMS.

Dear Madam:

Your letter of enquiry in regard to Miss Chandler is before me, in reply to which it affords me much pleasure to bear testimony to the high moral character, and superior intellectual culture, of which she is possessed. During five years' residence in our family she has ever been as one of our own household, and I can thus speak understandingly of her merits. She is thoroughly conversant with the higher English branches, and is quite fluent in Latin and German. Should you complete an engagement with her, I feel confident you will have every reason for being pleased with having done so.

Very Truly Yours,
HARVEY B. WATSON.

Unfavorable Reply to the Foregoing.

GLENHAVEN SEMINARY, N. Y.,
July 21, 18—.

MRS. CLARA B. WILLIAMS.

Dear Madam:

In reply to your polite inquiries, I am sorry to say that the educational acquirements of Miss Chandler, I fear, will not be up to the standard you require. While she has taught the higher English for some years, knowing, as I do, the proficiency of your daughters, I doubt if she is capable of advancing them in their studies. Another very unfortunate fault of which she is possessed, which causes me to dispense with her services at the close of the present term, is her failure to sufficiently command her temper. In other respects I have nothing to say to her prejudice.

Regretting that I cannot give a more favorable reply to your letter, I remain, Your Most Obedient Servant,
HARVEY B. WATSON.

Answering an Advertisement for an Apprentice to a Dressmaker.

(*Advertisement pasted in.*)

MRS. HARRIET MUNSON.   CHICAGO, ILL., Aug. 1, 18—.

Dear Madam:

In answer to the above, I respectfully apply for the situation. Though I never took up the business as a trade, I have long been in the habit of doing all the dressmaking for our family, and feel myself competent to do all plainer kinds of sewing neatly and rapidly.

Having recently, by the death of an only brother, been thrown upon my own resources, I am thus induced to seek a position which I think I will enjoy.

Hoping that you will accept my services, I remain,

Very Respectfully Yours,
PAMELIA HARRISON.

Answer to an Advertisement for a Music-Teacher.

WALNUT GROVE ACADEMY, MASS.,
June 9, 18—.

COL. H. B. DARLING.

Dear Sir:

Seeing your advertisement in to-day's "Journal," I write to offer my services as music-teacher in your family.

I am a graduate of Music Vale Seminary, and have taught a music-class in this institution for the past three terms. My training has been with special reference to teaching the piano, the guitar, and vocal music.

I am permitted by Professor Weston, the teacher of music in the Academy, to refer to him for any testimonial of ability. I am,

Yours, Very Respectfully,
AMELIA D. PORTER.

Answering an Advertisement for an Apprentice to a Printer.

TROY GROVE, ILL.,
Feb. 4, 18—.

MR. A. B. COOK.

Dear Sir:

Having seen your advertisement in the last *Eagle,* I would respectfully apply for the position for my son Henry, who is anxious to learn printing. He is well versed in the common English branches, having been regular in attendance at the public school for the past seven years. He is now fifteen.

I would like to have you take him on trial for a few weeks, and, if he pleases you, will arrange to have him remain until he masters the trade. Respectfully Yours,
Z. K. HENDERSON.

Letters of Recommendation.

 KNOWLEDGE of persons recommended, of their fitness and capacity for the work they engage in, is always essential, before they can be conscientiously commended to others.

A letter of recommendation should be written in a plain hand, in as few words as can be used to express the idea distinctly.

A recommendation, after considering the moral character of the individual, should relate directly to the work of which the person makes a specialty.

An individual giving a recommendation is, in a certain sense, responsible for the character and ability of the person recommended; hence, certificates of character should be given with caution and care.

Recommending a Salesman.

SYRACUSE, N. Y., April 10, 18—.
MESSRS. DUTTON & BROWN.
   Dear Sirs:
         Your favor of the 4th inst., relative to the ability of Mr. Benjamin Walker, is received. We take great pleasure in testifying to his high moral worth and his business capacity. He was in our employ for four years, as a salesman, during which time his affability and uniform courtesy to customers, coupled with his truthful representations in regard to goods, made him a universal favorite.

Accurate in accounts, ready and graceful as a penman, attentive and kind to all, he is a most useful man in the counting-room; and the firm securing his services may be congratulated on their good fortune.
            Very Truly Yours,
                 SMITH & PAXTON.

Recommending a Schoolmistress.

GLEN DALE SEMINARY,
            March 1, 18—.
GEN. A. B. COTTRELL.
   Dear Sir:
         It gives me pleasure, in reply to your note of the 24th ult., to most cordially recommend Miss Fannie Chapman to the position of teacher of your village school.

As a graduate of this Seminary, and subsequently as a teacher, much of the time conducting the various classes alone, she has proven herself thoroughly competent to conduct a school under almost any circumstances.

Though very amiable, she is a strict disciplinarian, and thoroughly conversant with the ordinary branches of an English education.
            Yours Respectfully,
                 DELOS SIMPSON,
                 Principal Glen Dale Seminary.

Recommending a Bookkeeper.

WHITEHALL, N. Y., Sept. 10, 18—.
Mr. Ransom Fellows having been in my employ for the past two years as a bookkeeper, it gives me great pleasure to testify to his ability. He is an upright, conscientious, exemplary young man, a good penman and accountant, and a most faithful clerk. He leaves my employ voluntarily, with my best wishes.
                 MARTIN BIGELOW.

Recommending a Waiter.

TREMONT HOUSE, CHICAGO,
            Aug. 11, 18—.
Arthur Brooks, who has been in my employ for two years, has given entire satisfaction, both to myself and guests, as a table-waiter. Honest, obliging and neat, it affords me pleasure, as he now leaves my employ, to commend him as a first-class hotel waiter.
                 BROWN PORTER,
                 Steward, Tremont House.

Recommending a Cook.

HARRISBURG, PA., Dec. 20, 18—.
This is to certify that Catherine Miller did the cooking for my family some ten months, to my entire satisfaction, serving me both as a plain and fancy cook. She is very attentive to her work, and strictly honest and reliable.
                 MYRA D. ROWE.

Recommending a Washerwoman.

NEW ORLEANS, LA., May 7, 18—.
This certifies that Hannah Webber, who has been employed in my laundry for the past year, is an excellent washer and ironer, understanding fine starching, crimping, polishing, etc.
                 HELEN MAYDWELL.

Recommending a Porter.

CHARLESTON, S. C., Sept. 18, 18—.
Donald Kennedy, the bearer of this, has been in my employ, as a porter, for the last eighteen months. He is a strong, honest, reliable man, and always very punctual, careful, and faithful in the discharge of his duty.
                 JOHN H. BLISS.

Declining to Recommend a Cook.

SAVANNAH, GA., Oct. 10, 18—.
MRS. BALLARD:
         In reply to your note of enquiry, I decline to recommend Bridget Mallory. She is both dishonest and addicted to intemperance.
                 HENRIETTA SANFORD.

Letters of Congratulation.

LETTERS of Congratulation are very properly written upon receiving intelligence of the sudden prosperity of a near and intimate friend.

They should be written as soon as possible after the occasion that calls them forth.

These letters will admit of an abundance of good-natured merriment.

Do not indulge in over-praise, or too much flowery exaggeration, lest your friend may doubt your sincerity.

No envy or discontent should show itself in such a letter. Nor should the same be marred by advice, bad news, the expression of any doubt, or any unfavorable prediction calculated to throw a cloud over the happiness of your friend.

Form of Letter Congratulating a Friend upon Election to Office.

Troy, N. Y., Feb. 1, 18—.

My Dear Friend Callie:

My newspaper informs me that the people of your County have shown their good judgment by selecting you to represent them as Superintendent of Public Schools. It affords me unfeigned pleasure to hear of the choice falling upon yourself. I am confident that no person in your district could fill the place more worthily.

Accept my congratulations.

Yours Truly,

S. D. Willing.

To Miss Callie M. Spencer,
Cedar Grove, Ill.

Congratulating a Friend upon Receiving a Legacy.

APPLETON, WIS., Jan. 1, 18—.

FRIEND GEORGE:
I have learned to-day, through our friend Charlie Goodwin, of your good fortune in receiving a very material addition to your worldly possessions. Good! I congratulate you. I know of no one who more justly deserves good fortune, and of no person who will use it more worthily. You would be ever the same to me, whether good or ill success should attend your pathway. As it is, I take a friend's delight in congratulating you upon your fortune.

Your Friend,
DANIEL TEMPLETON.

Congratulating a Gentleman upon his Marriage.

KINGSTON, CANADA, April 4, 18—.

DEAR WILL:
I have just received a little missive, which informs me of two happy hearts made one. I wish you much joy. You have my earnest congratulations on the event, and good wishes for a long and serenely happy married life. May each succeeding year find you happier than the one before.

God bless you and yours, and surround you ever with his choicest blessings.

Your Friend,
JOHN K. BUEL.

Congratulating a Friend upon the Birth of a Son.

GRACELAND, FLA., Jan. 3, 18—.

DEAR CLARK:
Accept my warmest congratulations upon the birth of your son. May his years be long in the land which the Lord giveth him. May he honor his father and his mother, and be the blessing and support of their declining years. I anticipate holding the young gentleman on my knee, and will be over to see you in a few days.

My kindest regards to Mrs. Henry. I remain,

Faithfully Your Friend,
DEB. HARTWELL.

Congratulating a Friend upon the Twenty-fifth Anniversary of his Wedding Day.

DARTMOUTH, N. H., March 5, 18—.

MY DEAR MR. BANCROFT:
I acknowledge the receipt of a kind invitation to be present at the celebration of the twenty-fifth anniversary of your marriage. I have since learned that large numbers of your friends were present on the occasion, presenting you with an abundant and varied collection of silver, and other elegant and appropriate gifts.

I congratulate you and your good wife upon passing the signal-station indicating a quarter of a century of blissful wedded life. That you may both live to allow your friends to celebrate your golden and diamond weddings, is the hope of,

Your Sincere Friend,
PERRY OLMSTED.

Congratulating a Lady upon her Approaching Marriage.

BANGOR, ME., Dec. 2, 18—.

DEAR CATHERINE:
Two beautiful cards on my table advise me of your approaching nuptials. Allow me to congratulate you upon the choice of such a noble man, to whom you are to entrust your life's happiness. That the mid-day and evening of your married life may be as cloudless and beautiful as the morning, is the earnest wish of,

Your Loving Friend,
NELLIE GRANT.

Congratulating a Friend on Passing a Successful School Examination.

UTICA, N. Y., April 6, 18—.

DEAR HELEN:
I was greatly pleased to hear, through our friend Mary, that you had, through diligent application, passed through the prescribed course of study in the Aurora public schools, and had graduated with honors. Knowing how deeply interested your parents and relatives have been in your success, it is particularly gratifying to have you reward them by the achievement of such rapid progress. Accept my best wishes for your future success.

Your Friend,
DELLA MAYNARD.

Congratulating an Author upon the Success of his Book.

MARENGO, VA., May 7, 18—.

FRIEND KEMPLE:
I have just finished an attentive examination of your most valuable book, and cannot wonder, after a careful reading, that it is meeting so large a sale. The world is greatly indebted to you for presenting in such an attractive form the amount of useful information you have collected within its pages.

Thanking you for the benefit I have obtained from its perusal, I remain, Yours Truly,
SILAS ACKLEY.

Congratulating a Friend upon Obtaining a Business Situation.

ASHBURY, PA., June 8, 18—.

FRIEND JOHN:
I am greatly pleased to learn that, notwithstanding the general dullness of business, you have succeeded in obtaining a clerkship. I doubt not your firm will regard themselves fortunate in securing your services. In the meantime, accept my congratulations upon your success.

Hoping that your stay may be permanent and prosperous, I am,

Yours Truly,
CHARLES BELSHAW.

JOHN BELDEN.

Letters of Introduction.

ETTERS of Introduction should be written very plainly, and should be brief, as the person introduced is compelled to wait while the letter is being read.

In introducing a person in a business capacity, state distinctly what is his business; if a professional man, his profession, and your knowledge or information of his ability.

The letter of introduction should be left unsealed. It would be a great discourtesy to prevent the bearer from seeing what you have written.

As in letters of recommendation, the person giving a letter of introduction is, in a measure, responsible for the character and ability of the person introduced. Hence, such letters should be guardedly written, or given with full knowledge of the person they introduce.

That the person receiving such a letter may know at a glance its character, the letter should, on the envelope, be addressed thus:

Chas. D. Kingsbury, Esq.,
478 Broadway,
Introducing
New York,
Wm. H. Brown,
of Cleveland, O.

Presenting the letter of introduction at the private house, send it by the servant to the person addressed, accompanied with your card.

At the business house, send the letter to the counting-room, accompanied by your card.

Introducing one Gentleman to Another.

NORWAY, MAINE, July 9, 18—.
FRIEND WILLIAM.

The bearer of this, Mr. Sterling Hepworth, is a dry-goods merchant in our town, who visits your city for the purpose of making purchases for his fall trade. Mr. H. is a heavy dealer in his line, pays cash for all he buys, and expects the discount accompanying cash payment. Any favor you can render him by introduction to your leading wholesale houses, or otherwise, will be appreciated by Mr. Hepworth, and acknowledged by,

Your Friend,
WALTER KIMBALL.

WILLIAM DARLING.

Introducing one Lady to Another.

ROME, GA., Aug. 10, 18—.
DEAR ANNABEL:

I take this occasion to introduce to you the bearer of this letter, Mrs. Pemberton, who is on a visit to her relatives in your city. Mrs. P. is my very dear friend, of whom you have often heard me speak. Believing that your acquaintance with each other would be mutually agreeable, I have urged her to call upon you during her stay. Any attention you may bestow upon her, during her visit, will be highly appreciated by,

Your Friend,
DELIA MAYBORNE.

Introducing a Young Musician to a Lady Friend.

SALEM, MASS., Sept. 12, 18—.
MRS. STEPHEN HAWKINS.
Dear Friend:

The bearer, Miss Serena Snow, visits your city for the purpose of pursuing a musical education, being as yet undetermined whom she will choose as an instructor. Any advice and assistance you may render will be highly appreciated by her, and duly acknowledged by her parents, who have great confidence in your judgment in matters pertaining to music.

Trusting that you will find it agreeable to aid my young friend, I remain,

Yours Sincerely,
MARY A. BARNET.

Introducing an Officer to a Brother-Officer.

HOLYOKE, MASS., Sept. 17, 18—.
DEAR CAPTAIN:

My old-time comrade, Capt. H. M. Benson, visits your town for the purpose of attending the Army Reunion on the 27th. As he will remain some little time, I commend him to your brotherly care. Believing that your acquaintance will be mutually agreeable, I remain,

Fraternally Yours,
T. M. SEYMOUR.

CAPT. A. M. BELLOWS.

Introducing a Gentleman Seeking a Clerkship.

DENVER, COL., Oct. 13, 18—.

FRIEND PATTERSON:

This letter will introduce to you my young friend, Morgan Hatfield, who has been in my employ as a clerk for the past eighteen months, and whom I would still retain, had not the disposing of a portion of my business rendered his services, with those of others of my clerks, unnecessary.

Believing that your wide influence would very materially aid him in securing a good position in the dry-goods trade in your city, I presume upon the acquaintance of an old friend in thus writing you. For reference you can use my name.

Believing that you will not afterwards regret any assistance you render the young man, I am,

Your Friend,
HERBERT HOPKINS.

A. B. PATTERSON, ESQ.

Introducing a Sister to a Schoolmate.

SALEM, OREGON, Nov. 14, 18—.

DEAR FRIEND:

This will be brought you by my sister Callie, of whom you have heard me talk so much. No words of mine are necessary in introducing you. I have told you both so much of each other that you are already acquainted. I bid you love each other as well as I love you both.

Affectionately Yours,
JENNIE.

MISS LIZZIE BRAYTON.

Introducing a Clerk to an Old Fellow-Clerk.

SILVER CITY, NEW MEXICO, Dec. 18, 18—.

DEAR HAL.:

My friend and fellow-clerk, Wm. Bell, will spend a week in your city, and wants to look at the desk where you and I stood, side by side, so long. You will find him a genial, friendly fellow, and will most assuredly not regret my sending him to you.

Ever Your Friend,
CON. BALDWIN.

HALBERT STEBBINS.

Introducing a Student to the Writer's Mother.

SAN FRANCISCO, CAL., Feb. 2, 18—.

DEAR MOTHER:

The bearer of this is my college chum, Harry Worthington. Being about to visit his parents at San Jose, I have persuaded him to stop over one train to see you and sister Kate. Harry is in the same class with myself, and is, I can assure you, a splendid fellow. Of course, you and Kate will treat him so finely as to make him, perhaps, stay longer than one day. He will tell you all the news.

Your Ever Affectionate Son,
SAMMY DOBBIN.

Introducing a Friend to a Member of Congress.

DOVER, DEL., Mar. 3, 18—.

HON. D. B. GRAHAM.

Respected Sir:

The bearer, Mr. D. H. Harmon, is the son of Mrs. Lieut. W. H. Harmon, of this town, whose husband was killed at the battle of Iuka, bravely defending the flag. This young man has just graduated from one of our best schools, and at my suggestion visits Washington, thinking to acquaint himself with the condition of things at the Capitol, and, if the same could be obtained, would gladly occupy a clerkship for a time. Should it be in your power to grant him such a favor, it will be warmly appreciated by his mother and myself. I remain,

Yours Respectfully,
V. H. MARTIN.

Introducing a Literary Lady to a Publisher.

BATON ROUGE, LA., March 4, 18—.

MR. WARREN H. WEBSTER.

Dear Sir:

The bearer, Mrs. Lydia Huntington, visits New York for the purpose of conferring with some publisher relative to introducing her first book to the public. She is a lady of well-known reputation and acknowledged talent throughout the South, and will, I feel sure, assume prominent rank ere long in the literary world. I take the liberty of an old friend to ask of you a consideration of her claims.

Yours, Very Respectfully,
B. H. CAMPBELL.

Introducing a Daughter About to Make a Visit.

CHARLESTON, S. C., May 6, 18—.

MY DEAR MRS. HAMILTON:

In compliance with your oft-repeated request, I send my daughter to spend a few weeks of her vacation in your delightful country home, trusting that her visit may be as delightful for her and yourself as mine was a year ago. Anticipating a visit from you all, ere the close of the present summer, I remain,

As Ever, Your Devoted Friend,
MARY DAVENPORT.

Letters of Advice.

"OUR life has been a success," said an individual to an old and prosperous business man. "To what do you attribute your success?" "To an admonition given me by my father, when a boy, which was this:

"First, to attend strictly to my own business. Second, to let other people's business alone. Observing this, I incurred no ill will by inter-meddling with others, and I saved my time for the development and improvement of my own business."

Be very sparing of letters of advice. As a rule, you will have enough to do to attend to your own affairs; and, as a general thing, advice even when solicited is liable to give offence.

If, however, you are asked to give an opinion, you may plainly state it. Do not give it, however, as a law, nor feel offended if your advice is disregarded.

Beware of giving advice from selfishness. Sooner or later your motive will be discovered. Let your admonition be alone for the interest and welfare of your friend. If you expect, however, to be benefited by the course which you advise the person to pursue, you may frankly state the fact.

Advising a Young Lady to Refuse Gifts from Gentlemen.

Monroeville, O., Feb. 2, 18—.

My Dear Caroline:

Your letter of the 28th ult. is before me. I regret to learn that you accepted of a bracelet at the hands of Wm. Spencer. By all means return it. In its acceptance you place yourself under obligation to him, as you would to any one from whom you accept presents, unless you render an equivalent.

Nothing will more surely injure a young lady's reputation than the acceptance of many presents from different young men. When married, the gifts of your husband will come hallowed with his affection. Until then, refuse gifts from all gentlemen.

I am,

Your Sincere Friend,

Harriet McInhill.

Letter Advising a Young Man to Beware of Bad Company.

WASHINGTON, D. C., Jan. 1, 18—.

MY DEAR YOUNG FRIEND:

I observe, by the tone of your last letter, that you are becoming very intimate with Henry Hubbard and Barney McIntosh. I need not tell you that your letter has given me much uneasiness. These young men are bad characters, and you cannot continue your association with them, without contaminating your morals.

I am an old man, and I write this, my boy, with a most earnest desire for your happiness. You have acquired a fine education, and have entered upon your profession with every prospect of success. You have a widowed mother to support, and an orphaned sister looking to you for guidance. It becomes you, therefore, to maintain a reputation unsullied, and obtain a good credit, which, to a young man in the commencement of a business career, is equal to a large capital of itself.

Association with these young men will certainly carry you downward. They are both without employment, they drive fast horses, they wear flash jewelry, they frequent gambling-houses, they both use intoxicating drink, chew tobacco, and talk profane language. What would you think of another that might be seen in their company? People will judge you as you would judge any one else. There is much truth in the old proverb, "A man is known by the company he keeps," and I would have your company such as will reflect the highest honor upon yourself.

I have written this letter earnestly and strongly, for I believe your good judgment will take it kindly; and I trust, when you sincerely reflect upon the matter, you will at once dismiss that class of associates from your company.

Your Earnest Well-Wisher
and Sincere Friend,
DAVID CLINE.

Advising a Young Man Against a Hurried Marriage.

RUTLAND, VT., April 5, 18—.

FRIEND CHARLES:

You ask me if you will not act the wiser part by marrying Miss Manchester at once, and settling yourself permanently; and yet you inform me that it has been but three weeks since you first made her acquaintance. You may possibly be in jest, and perhaps in earnest; in either case, as you ask my advice, I can but give it.

The choosing of a life-companion, dear Charles, is a too serious matter to be so hastily decided. The selection of a partner for a dance or a ride may be of little moment; the choice of an associate for business may be determined in a short time; but the acceptance of a partner for life requires the most serious deliberation. You should take ample time for the study of the character, temperament, disposition and accomplishments of the lady whom you choose to be the sharer of your labors, joys, sorrows, reverses and prosperity.

Upon this step hangs a large share of your happiness in life. Do not act too hastily. Trusting, however, that I will some day see you happily married and settled, I am, as ever,

Your Most Sincere Friend,
GEORGE BATCHELDER.

Advice to a Gentleman on the Subject of Health.

BOSTON, MASS., May 6, 18—.

MY DEAR FRIEND:

Yours of the 2d inst. is before me. I am pleased with the prospect that you report in your business, but regret that you should be discouraged about your health. You ask me what you had better do; I will answer.

The first great secret of good health is good habits; and the next is *regularity* of habits. They are briefly summed up in the following rules:

1.—*Sleep.* Give yourself the necessary amount of sleep. Some men require five hours of the twenty-four; others need eight. Avoid feather beds. Sleep in a garment not worn during the day. To maintain robust health, sleep with a person as healthy as yourself, or no one.

2.—*Dress.* In cold weather, dress warmly with underclothing. Remove muffler, overcoat, overshoes, etc., when remaining any considerable length of time in a warm room. Keep your feet warm and dry. Wash them, in warm water, two or three times a week. Wear warm stockings, large boots, and overshoes when in the snow or wet. Wear a light covering on the head, always keeping it cool.

3.—*Cleanliness.* Have always a pint or quart of water in the sleeping room. In the morning, after washing and wiping hands and face, then wet, with the hands, every part of the body. Cold water will not be disagreeable when applying it with the bare hands. Wipe immediately; follow by brisk rubbing over the body. The whole operation need not take over five minutes. The result of this wash is, the blood is brought to the surface of the skin, and made to circulate evenly throughout the body. You have opened the pores of the skin, allowing impurities in the body to pass off, and have given yourself in the operation a good, vigorous morning exercise. Pursue this habit regularly, and you will seldom take cold.

4.—*Inflation of the Lungs.* Five minutes spent in the open air, after dressing, inflating the lungs by inhaling as full a breath as possible, and pounding the breast during the inflation, will greatly enlarge the chest, strengthen the lung power, and very effectually ward off consumption.

5.—*Diet.* If inclined to be dyspeptic, avoid mince pie, sausage and other highly seasoned food. Beware of eating too freely of soups; better to eat food dry enough to employ the natural saliva of the mouth in moistening it. If inclined to over-eat, partake freely of rice, cracked wheat, and other articles that are easily digested.

Eat freely of ripe fruit, and avoid excessive use of meats. Eat at regular hours, and lightly near the hour of going to bed. Eat slowly. Thoroughly masticate the food. Do not wash it down with continual drink while eating. Tell your funniest stories while at the table and for an hour afterwards. Do not engage in severe mental labor directly after hearty eating.

6.—*Exercise.* Exercise, not too violent, but sufficient to produce a gentle perspiration, should be had each day in the open air.

7.—*Condition of Mind.* The condition of the mind has much to do with health. Be hopeful and joyous. To be so, avoid business entanglements that may cause perplexity and anxiety. Keep out of debt. Live within your income. Attend church. Walk, ride, mix in jovial company. Do as nearly right as you know how. Thus, conscience will always be at ease. If occasionally disappointed, remember that there is no rose without a thorn, and that the darkest clouds have a silver lining; that sunshine follows storm, and beautiful spring follows the dreary winter. Do your duty, and leave the rest to God, who doeth all things well.

Hoping to hear of your continued prosperity and recovery of health, I am,

Your Very Sincere Friend,
SIBLEY JOHNSON, M. D.

ALLEN MATLOCK.

Advice to an Orphan Boy.

ARLINGTON, N. C., June 7, 18—.

MY DEAR CHARLIE:

I received your letter last evening. I was greatly pleased to hear that you have secured a position with Colby, Henderson & Co., and that your sisters are comfortably situated in their new homes. You ask me for advice as to what you shall do to maintain the good opinion of your employers, and thus ultimately prosperously establish yourself.

This desire that you evince to please is one of the very best evidences that you *will* please. Your question is very commendable. How can you succeed? That should be the great question with all young men. It is best answered, perhaps, by the reply of the wealthy and honored old man, who gave this advice to his grandson:

"My boy, take the admonition of an old man who has seen every phase of human life.

"If I could give you but one precept to follow, it would be, *Keep good company*. But, adding more, I will say:

"Be truthful; you thus always have the confidence of others.

"Be temperate; thus doing, you preserve health and money.

"Be industrious; you will then be constantly adding to your acquisitions.

"Be economical; thus, you will be saving for the rainy day.

"Be cautious; you are not then so liable to lose the work of years.

"Be polite and kind; scattering words of kindness, they are reflected back upon yourself, continually adding to your happiness."

Observe these directions, and you will prosper. With many wishes for your success, remember I am always,

Your Friend,
ABEL MATTOCK.

Letters of Excuse.

ETTERS of Excuse should be written as promptly as may be.

Any damage that may have been caused by yourself, you should, if possible, repair immediately, with interest.

In apologizing for misconduct, failing to meet an engagement, or for lack of punctuality, always state the reason why.

By fulfilling every engagement promptly, discharging every obligation when due, and always being punctual, you thereby entirely avoid the necessity for an excuse.

Any article borrowed by measure, be certain to return in larger quantity and better quality, to make up the interest. To fail to make good that which has been borrowed is the certain loss of credit and business reputation in the neighborhood where you live. No letter of apology can make amends for neglecting to pay your debts.

Apologizing for a Broken Engagement.

FREDERICK, MD., July 13, 18—.

MY DEAR MISS MERTON:

I fear that you will feel injured at my failure to keep my appointment this evening. You will, however, I know, forgive me when I explain. When about to proceed to your residence, my horse, being very restive, became so frightened at an object by the roadside as to cause his runaway, throwing me violently to the ground, breaking an arm, and completely demolishing my carriage. Regretting my failure to keep my engagement, I am yet rejoiced that the accident occurred before you had entered the carriage.

Trusting that my excuse is a sufficient apology, I remain,

Your Faithful Friend,
ALBERT BIGBEE.

Apologizing for Failure to Pay Money Promptly.

DANBY, N. Y., July 11, 18—.

MR. D. B. FRISBIE.

Dear Sir:

I very much regret that the failure of H. Cole & Son will prevent my payment of your note on the 20th instant, without serious inconvenience to myself. I shall be able to pay it, however, promptly on the 25th. Should the five days' delay seriously incommode you, please write me at once, and I will aim to procure the money from another source.

Your Obedient Servant,
DANIEL FRAZIER.

Excuse to a Teacher for Non-Attendance of Child at School.

WEDNESDAY MORNING, Sept. 4, 18—.

MISS BLAKE:

You will please excuse Gertrude for non-attendance at school yesterday afternoon, she being detained in consequence of a severe headache.

Very Respectfully,
MARCIA BARROWS.

Apology for Breaking a Business Engagement.

MONTICELLO, ILL., Oct. 15, 18—.

MR. PAUL D. WARREN,
Kensington.

Dear Sir:

I very much regret being compelled to apologize for not meeting you at the railroad meeting in Salem last Saturday, as I agreed to do. The cause of my detention was the sudden and severe illness of my youngest child, whose life for a time we despaired of. Please write me the result of the meeting. Hoping that the arrangements we anticipated were perfected, I am,

Yours Truly,
SOLOMON KING.

Apology for Delay in Returning a Book.

KENTLAND, IND., Nov. 19, 18—.

MY DEAR AMY:

You must excuse my long delay in returning your book. The truth is, it has been the rounds for several to read, though it has not been out of our house. When I had nearly finished its reading, Aunt Mary became interested in its contents and read it through. Her glowing description of the character of the work caused mother to peruse it; so that we have kept it from you several weeks. We feel very grateful to you, however, for furnishing us such an intellectual feast, and hope to have the pleasure of doing you a like favor.

Truly Your Friend,
LIZZIE BRAINARD.

Letters Asking Favors.

 T is to be hoped that you will not often be compelled to write a letter asking a favor.

Do not urge your claims too strongly. Should you be refused, you will feel the more deeply humiliated.

In conferring a favor, avoid conveying the impression that the recipient is greatly under obligation to you. Rather imply that the granting and accepting of the favor is mutually a pleasure.

Letters refusing a favor should be very kindly worded, and, while expressing regret at your inability to comply with the request, state the reason why.

Requesting the Loan of a Book.

WEDNESDAY MORNING, JAN. 1, 18—.

DEAR BERTHA:

Will you be so kind as to loan me, for a few days, "How I Found Livingstone?" By so doing, you will greatly oblige,

Your Friend,

NANNIE WHITE.

Reply Granting the Favor.

WEDNESDAY MORNING, Jan. 1, 18—.

DEAR NANNIE:

I send you the book with pleasure, and hope you will enjoy its perusal as much as I did. I shall be over to see you next Thursday afternoon.

Affectionately Yours,

BERTHA.

Requesting a Loan of Money.

LISBON, ILL., Feb. 2, 18—.

FRIEND BAKER:

Will you do me the kindness to loan me one hundred dollars until Wednesday of next week. Having several large collections to make during the next three days, I may return the loan before then.

Yours Truly,

GEORGE HASKINS.

Answer Refusing the Request.

LISBON, ILL., Feb. 2, 18—.

FRIEND HASKINS:

I regret that all the money I have at liberty I am compelled to use this afternoon; else I would comply with your request with pleasure.

Respectfully,

JOHN BAKER.

Requesting a Letter of Introduction.

SPRINGFIELD, MASS., March 4, 18—.

FRIEND RICH:

I start for Boston to-morrow, to make arrangements for our excursion. I shall arrange to have the journey extend as far as the Holy Land. Be so kind, if you please, as to give me a letter of introduction to Prof. Wm. Kidder, whom I hope, also, to enlist in the scheme.

With warmest regards to your family, I remain,

Very Truly Yours,

HENRY FRENCH.

Reply Granting the Request.

SPARTA, R. I., March 6, 18—.

DEAR FRENCH:

I enclose, with pleasure, the letter to Prof. Kidder, who, I think, will be pleased to join us. Wishing you much success, I am,

Yours Truly,

BARTON RICH.

Requesting the Loan of an Opera Glass.

THURSDAY AFTERNOON, April 7, 18—.

DEAR MABEL:

Accompanied by cousin Fred and Jennie Masters, I am going to the theater to-night, and in behalf of Fred I wish you would loan me your opera-glass for the evening.

BECKIE HOWELL.

Answer Refusing the Request.

THURSDAY, April 7, 18—.

DEAR BECKIE:

Charlie Hackney called and borrowed my glass about an hour since; otherwise, I would take the greatest pleasure in granting your request. Wishing you a delightful evening, I am,

Your Devoted Friend,

MABEL GALE.

Requesting the Loan of a Pistol.

FRIDAY MORN., MAY 8, 18—.

FRIEND GODARD:

Please loan me your pistol this forenoon, and oblige

JOHN OGDON.

Reply Granting the Request.

FRIDAY, May 8, 18—.

FRIEND JOHN:

Accept the pistol. Beware that you do not get hurt. I shall want it to-morrow.

Truly Yours,

BEN GODARD.

Letters Accompanying Gifts.

U SUALLY, in sending gifts, it is customary to accompany the same with a prettily written note. Such letters, with their answers, are very brief, and are usually written in the third person, unless among relatives or very intimate friends.

Though a reply should be given immediately, no haste need be made in repaying the gift, else it would seem that you feel the obligation, and will experience relief by paying the debt.

———◦⟡◦———

Accompanying a Betrothal Gift of a Ring.

No. 84 ELDRIDGE COURT, Jan. 1, 18—.
DEAR ANNIE:
Will you accept the accompanying ring, and wear it as a pledge of the undying affection of,
Yours Constantly,
WILLIAM.

———◦⟡◦———

Reply to the Foregoing.

No. 8 ——— ST., Jan. 2, 18—.
DEAR WILLIAM:
Your beautiful gift is on my finger, where it will be ever worn as a token of your love.
Yours Truly,
ANNIE.

Form of Letter Accompanying Photographs.

Rockland, Va., Oct. 20, 18—.
Dear Helen:
Will you accept the accompanying photographs of husband, May, Jennie, and your humble servant, in lieu of the visit that we anticipated making you this month?

We want the photos of all your family to make our album complete, and I shall watch the mail, expecting to get them. Hoping to hear from you soon, I remain,
Your Friend,
Emily Gerry.

Answer to the Foregoing.

JACKSON, MISS., Oct. 25, 18—.

DEAR EMILY:

I regret that we are not to have the anticipated visit from you this spring. We are very thankful for the photographs, however, if we can do no better. We regard them very life-like in expression, and truthful in representation. When baby is a few weeks older, we will group ourselves together, and you shall see us as we are.

Our love to all your family, and remember me as,

Your Constant Friend,
HELEN STANFORD.

Accompanying a Book Sent by the Author.

SPRINGDALE, N. J., June 1, 18—.

Miss Harmon will please accept the accompanying volume as a token of the high esteem and regard of the Author,

ARTHUR WELLS.

MISS MARTHA HARMON.

Answer to the Foregoing.

No. 9 —— —— ST., Aug. 2, 18—.

Miss Harmon presents her regards to Mr. Wells, and accepts with much gratification his highly esteemed and valuable gift.

ARTHUR WELLS, ESQ.

Accompanying a Bouquet to a Lady.

Will Miss Beveridge honor Mr. Haines by carrying the accompanying flowers to the concert this evening?

Answer to the Foregoing.

Miss Beveridge's compliments and thanks to Mr. Haines. His beautiful and fragrant gift will be a welcome addition to her toilet for this evening.

Accompanying a Birthday Gift.

BELVIDERE, ILL., Dec. 10, 18—.

FRIEND DAVID:

Sixty years ago, to-day, you and I exchanged birthday greetings, then in our twentieth year. How the years have flown by since then, sprinkling our heads with snow, and finally covering them with white! You will please accept this staff as an evidence that time cannot dim the unchanging friendship of,

Your Friend,
JOSEPH BARLOW.

Answer to the Foregoing.

FREEPORT, ILL., Dec. 10, 18—.

MY FRIEND JOSEPH:

Your very valuable and welcome gift came to-day. I lean on it, and look back. The noonday of our life has passed. Gradually we are descending the slope towards the going-down of our life's sun. It is appointed for all to reach life's meridian, stand there for a little while, and go down on the other side. Youth may not be recovered here, but I doubt not that we may be young again, in that bourne towards which we are fast passing. During my remaining years I will cherish your gift. Accept my warmest thanks, and remember me as,

Your Constant Friend,
DAVID BINNINGER.

Accompanying a Donation to a Clergyman.

To THE REV. WASHINGTON SMITH,
Pastor of the —th St. M. E. Church.

Dear Sir:

Will you confer upon us the great pleasure of appropriating to your own use the accompanying check? It is presented by your many friends in your congregation, as a slight token of the very high esteem in which you are held by the people, as a Christian gentleman and a most eloquent and instructive preacher.

Trusting that its acceptance will afford you as much pleasure as is given us in the presentation, we are,

Very Respectfully,
MARTIN FULLER, }
WM. B. KING, } Com. of Presentation.
CHAS. H. SNOW. }

Answer to the Foregoing.

ST. LOUIS, Mo., Jan. 1, 18—.

MESSRS. MARTIN FULLER, WM. B. KING, AND CHAS. H. SNOW.

Gentlemen:

Your very kind and courteous letter, accompanied by your valuable testimonial, is received, for which please accept my grateful acknowledgments. The gift itself, however, is not more valued than the golden words of sympathy and encouragement that accompany its presentation. Trusting that, through God's blessing, I may be able to serve the generous donors as acceptably in the future as your testimonial leads me to suppose I have in the past, I am,

Your Very Obedient Servant,
WASHINGTON SMITH.

Accompanying a Gift to a Superintendent upon Retirement.

CHICAGO, ILL., Feb. 2, 18—.

MR. ARTHUR P. STEPHENS.

Dear Sir:

The undersigned, employes of the Northwestern Sheet Lead and Zinc Works, deeply regretting your departure from among us, desire your acceptance of the accompanying memorial, in testimony of our affection and respect for you as a gentleman and a mechanic, and as a faint expression of our appeciation of your kindly efforts to render our connection with this manufactory not only pleasant and agreeable to ourselves, but profitable to the company.

Deeply regretting that our connection must be severed, we shall gratefully remember our association in the past, and hope always to be held in pleasurable remembrance by you.

(SIGNED BY THE EMPLOYES.)

Answer to the Foregoing.

CHICAGO, ILL., Feb. 3, 18—.

To THE EMPLOYES OF THE NORTHWESTERN SHEET LEAD AND ZINC WORKS.

Gentlemen:

I am in receipt of your kind letter and testimonial. Wherever fortune may cast my lot, I shall never cease to remember the pleasant associations of the past few years, and the many kind attentions I have received at your hands. If our relations and labors have been pleasant, I do not forget that they were largely made so by your always generous efforts and willing coöperation.

I will ever cherish your beautiful gift as a memorial of our pleasant years together, and can only wish that each of you, when occupying positions of trust, may be as warmly supported and as ably assisted by those in your charge as I have been since my connection with yourselves. Thanking you for this testimonial and your generous words of approval, I remain,

Your Friend,
ARTHUR P. STEPHENS.

LETTERS OF FRIENDSHIP AND RELATIONSHIP.

WRITE letters to friends and relatives very often. As a rule, the more frequent such letters, the more minute they are in giving particulars; and the longer you make them, the better.

The absent husband should write a letter at least once a week. Some husbands make it a rule to write a brief letter home at the close of every day.

The absent child need not ask, "Do they miss me at home?" Be sure that they do. Write those relatives a long letter, often, descriptive of your journeys and the scenes with which you are becoming familiar. And, if the missive from the absent one is dearly cherished, let the relatives at home remember that doubly dear is the letter from the hallowed hearthstone of the home fireside, where the dearest recollections of the heart lie garnered. Do not fail to write very promptly to the one that is away. Give all the news. Go into all the little particulars, just as you would talk. After you have written up matters of general moment, come down to little personal gossip that is of particular interest. Give the details fully about Sallie Williams marrying John Hunt, and her parents being opposed to the match. Be explicit about the new minister, how many sociables you have a month, and the general condition of affairs among your intimate acquaintances.

Don't forget to be very minute about things at home. Be particular to tell of "bub," and "sis," and the baby. Even "Major," the dog, should have a mention. The little tid-bits that are tucked in around, on the edge of the letter, are all devoured, and are often the sweetest morsels of the feast.

Let the young, more especially, keep up a continual correspondence with their friends. The ties of friendship are thus riveted the stronger, and the fires of love and kind feeling, on the altar of the heart, are thus kept continually burning bright.

From a Husband, Absent on Business, to his Wife.

DETROIT, MICH., Feb. 1, 18—.

MY DEAR HENRIETTA:

I have been to the end of my journey, and am now homeward bound. Another week, and I hope to kiss my wife and babies, and tell them that this is my last journey of the winter. One or two journeys next spring, and then I am done traveling away from home. What better news can I write you than this? Yes, perhaps I have better news yet, which is, that I have completed such arrangements, during my absence from you this time, as will greatly increase my income without it being necessary for me to travel.

Isn't that pleasant? How I long to get home and tell you all about it. At present, when not closely engaged in business, I am busy thinking of many improvements that we will make around our home next summer, being the very changes that you have so long desired, but which our means hitherto have not permitted us to make.

Kiss Sammie and Tillie for me, and accept many kisses for yourself. I will write you from Cleveland, if not before. Good night.

Your Loving Husband,
WM. TILDEN.

From a Young Lady to a Schoolmate just Married.

GALVA, ILL., DEC. 26, 18—.

DEAR MINNIE:

I have just heard, through our mutual friend and former schoolmate, Nellie Crandall, that you are the first of our school-girl circle who has taken upon herself the cares and duties of married life.

Thus, one by one, I expect, our little band of joyous, happy girls, so short a time ago together, will drop away into happy homes, which, if they do not make them, they will at least adorn.

And so you are married. Well, I had some intimation, months ago, that such an event might sometime take place, but really I did not think you would change your name so soon. Mrs. Charles Blackwell!—well, that *does* sound a little odd, I confess, but then it is a pretty name, nevertheless. I assure you I am impatient to meet you, and witness how you dignify the name.

Accept my most sincere good wishes for your future happiness, and tell your husband that he must be prepared to feel an interest in the welfare of all your old friends, especially,

Your Friend,
CALLIE BROWN.

From a Young Girl, at Boarding-School, to her Mother.

Hopeville Female Seminary,
Oct. 1, 18——.

Dear Mother:

I want you to write me a letter at once, asking me to come home and see you. O dear! I am so homesick! You know, mother, this is the first time I was ever away from you so long. You must let me come right home, or I will certainly die of homesickness.

Your Miserable Child,
Ella Bennett.

To Mrs. D. C. Bennett.

Answer of the Mother.

NEW YORK, Oct. 3, 18—.

MY DEAR CHILD:

I am sorry that you should urge me to grant you such an unreasonable request. Of course, nothing could please me better than to have my darling little Ella sitting on my lap at this very moment; but think how seriously the absence from your school, now, would derange all your recitations for this term. You must not think of it; recollect that all your brothers and sisters have been away at school, and always remained until the vacations. It is true that you, being the youngest, have been petted more than the rest, but it would be very unfortunate to have my indulgence interfere with your studies. You know that you are the idol of our hearts; for that very reason you should endeavor to become proficient in those branches of study that will render you an accomplished lady.

Believe me, my dear child, you will find school more pleasant every day, as you get better acquainted with your schoolmates; and, through improvement in your studies, you will steadily grow in favor with your teachers.

I will write Mrs. Mayhew to render your tasks as light as possible at first, and I have no doubt she will do all in her power to aid you.

Only a few weeks, remember, and you will be home for a long vacation, which will be all the more delightful for the privation you are at present undergoing. Your father, brothers and sisters all unite with me in sending you their love.

I remain, my dear child,
Your Affectionate Mother,
NANCY BENNETT.

To ELLA BENNETT,
Hopeville Female Seminary.

From an Absent Wife to her Husband.

ARGYLE, N. Y., March 2, 18—.

DEAREST LOVE:

I am at last safely under uncle's roof, having arrived here last evening, baby and myself both well, but really very tired. We had no delay, except about two hours at Buffalo. Uncle met me at the depot with his carriage, and, in fifteen minutes from the time of my arrival, I was cosily seated in my room, which was all in readiness for me.

Uncle and aunt seem greatly pleased with my coming, and both are loud in their praise of the baby. They very much regret that you could not have come with me, and say they intend to prevail on you to make them a visit when I am ready to go home.

Baby looks into my eyes once in a while and says, solemnly, "Papa, papa!" I do actually believe he is thinking about home, and wants to keep up a talk about you. Everybody thinks he looks like his papa.

By day after to-morrow I will write a long letter. I want you to get this by the first mail, so I make it short. With dearest love, I am,
Your Wife,
CAROLINE.

Answer to the Foregoing.

MICHIGAN CITY, IND., March 7.

DEAR WIFE:

I was indeed rejoiced to hear of your safe arrival, having felt no little anxiety for you, which is relieved by the receipt of your letter.

I miss you very much, the house looks so dreary without your loved presence; but I am, nevertheless, glad that you are making your visit, as the journey, I trust, will be beneficial to your health.

Kiss baby for me. Only by his absence do I know how much I have enjoyed my play with our little Charlie.

Don't take any concern about me. Enjoy your visit to the utmost extent. In one of my next letters I will write whether I can go East and return with you.

Remember me to uncle and aunt.
Your Ever-Faithful Husband,
ARCHIBALD.

From a Servant in the City, to her Parents in the Country.

NEW YORK, June 1, 18—.

MY DEAR PARENTS:

I take the first opportunity, since I arrived in the city, to write to you. It was a sore trial, I assure you, to leave home, but since coming here I have been quite contented, and I am getting so well accustomed to my work that I begin to like my place very much.

Mr. and Mrs. Benedict are both very kind to me. The family consists of father, mother and three children, the youngest being a little boy three years old—a beautiful little fellow, that always reminds me of brother James. Eliza, the oldest girl, is thirteen, and Martha is eleven. They are both very kind to me, and do so much about the house that it helps me very considerably.

Mr. Benedict is a clothing merchant in the city, and, I judge, is in very good circumstances. The girls are attending school at present. All the family are very regular in their attendance at church.

For the first few days here, everything seemed very strange. I hardly knew what to make of so much noise and so many people on the streets. I have now, however, become accustomed to the multitudes, and would, I presume, consider my native village very dull indeed, compared with the bustle and activity of the city.

I realize every day, dear parents, the worth of your good advice to me, which I never knew the value of so much before; thanking you for the same, I will always endeavor to follow it.

Give my love to Johnny, Mary, Jimmy and all inquiring friends. I shall anxiously look for a letter from you. Write me in the care of Solon Benedict, No.——Thirteenth Street.
Your Dutiful and Affectionate Daughter,
BETSEY ANN FAIRBANKS.

To MR. AND MRS. H. K. FAIRBANKS,
Swallow Hill, Pa.

The Mother's Reply.

SWALLOW HILL, PA., June 7, 18—.

DEAR BETSEY:

Your letter, which has been received, affords great pleasure and satisfaction to your father and myself. Nothing could give our hearts greater happiness than to know of your enjoyment and firm purpose to do right. Now that you are removed from all parental restraint, it is of the most vital importance that you implicitly rely upon the religious precepts which have been instilled into your mind, and that you daily pray to God for guidance and mercy.

We are greatly pleased that you are well situated with Mr. and Mrs. Benedict; in return for their kindness you must be honest, industrious, kind and obliging, always doing your duty faithfully, which will be a real satisfaction to yourself as well as to your employers.

Several of the neighbors, who have called, have wished to be remembered to you; Mary and Jimmy unite with your father and myself in sending you love.

We shall constantly pray for your continued protection and prosperity. I remain, dear Betsey,
Your Affectionate Mother,
HARRIET FAIRBANKS.

Letter from a Father, Remonstrating with his Son.

DANBURY, CONN., July 7, 18—.

MY DEAR SON:

I am sorry to learn that you are not inclined to be as strict in your line of duty as you should be. Remember, my son, that a down-hill road is before you, unless you rouse yourself and shake off immediately the habits of dissipation that are fastening themselves upon you. Be sure, dear boy, that nothing but sorrow and shame can come of bad company, late hours, neglect of duty, and inattention to the obligations of morality. I am willing to think that you have not given this matter sufficient thought heretofore; that your actions are the result of thoughtlessness, rather than a disposition to do wrong.

But be forewarned in time. You must change your course of action immediately, or incur my severe displeasure.

I urge this, my boy, for your sake. Remember that my happiness is bound in your own, and that nothing could give me greater pleasure than your prosperity. I trust that it will not be necessary for me to use more severe language than this.

Your Anxious Father,

RUDOLF MATHEWS.

The Son's Reply.

BOSTON, MASS., June 9, 18—.

DEAR FATHER:

I·realize that I need the good advice contained in your letter. I am aware, as I stop to think of my conduct, that I have given you reason for anxiety, but I intend, by attention to my business hereafter, and a complete reformation of my habits, to give you no occasion for concern about me in the future. Believe me, I love and respect you too much to intentionally wound your feelings, or to bring down your gray hairs with sorrow.

Excuse me, dear father, for having given you this uneasiness, and trust me as,

Your Affectionate and Repentant Son,

CHARLES MATHEWS.

From a Married Man to a Friend About to Marry.

ATLANTA, GA., Aug. 20, 18—.

FRIEND BATCHELDER:

Can it be possible? Am I right, or am I dreaming? Has it come to this at last? You, Batchelder Button — you cynic, railer against women, the unalterable, unchangeable bachelor, — is it possible that you have at last been captured, and have surrendered all your ordnance, heavy guns and small arms to the enemy?

What a defeat! That large, strong heart of yours all crumbling to pieces, and surrendering to Cupid's battery!

Well, now, seriously, my friend, from my point of view, I think you have done a very sensible thing. The man who goes the journey alone through life, lives but half a life. If you have found the woman fitted by temperament and accomplishments to render your pathway through life the joyous one that the married state should be, you are certainly to be congratulated for awakening to a true sense of your condition, though rather late in the day.

Though but slightly acquainted with Miss Howell, I have formed a very favorable idea of her intelligence and worth, which opinion, I believe, is generally shared by those who know her best. I doubt not, with her your married life will be a continually happy one.

Your Friend,

HERBERT TRACEY.

From a Young Man Who Has Recently Entered College.

HARVARD COLLEGE, MASS., May 18, 18—.

DEAR FATHER:

I am happy to inform you that I passed my examination with credit, if I am to believe the commendation bestowed upon me by Dr. H——.

I was very agreeably surprised, soon after my arrival, to meet my former schoolmate, Hartley Montague, who is one of the most respected and influential in his class, with whom I am, as formerly, on quite intimate terms. Many things are quite new to me here. The society is very much mixed, and I cannot tell just where my level is; but I trust I shall be able to follow the good advice of my parents, and always do credit to myself and my relatives, who have labored so assiduously to advance me to this position.

I thank you for the check you so kindly sent me, which was fully adequate to cover all expenses of entrance, and leave me a surplus sufficient for the rest of the term.

Love to dear mother and sisters. Hoping to meet you all at our forthcoming commencement, I am,

Your Affectionate Son,

BARFORD D. CLAY.

Descriptive Letter
From a Young Man at the "Old Home," to his Parents in the West.

CAMBRIDGE, N. Y., June 18, 1873.

DEAR PARENTS:

Agreeable to your request, I take the first opportunity, after my visit to the "old home" and a hurried call upon our relatives, to write you how I found the people and scenes that you knew so well in the days lang syne, and that I remember as a boy.

I arrived at Cambridge after a ninety minutes' ride from Troy. What a great change in traveling! When last I was here, it was a day's journey from Troy, by stage-coach. To-day, New York, in time, is nearer to our old home than Troy was then; and Troy, after traveling among the thriving, driving cities of the great West, seems like a wayside village, instead of the great metropolis that it once seemed to be; though it is a beautiful, growing, wealthy manufacturing city to-day, nevertheless. It is not that the villages and cities that we once knew grow less, but by observation and comparison we class them where they belong.

At Cambridge I secured a livery team for a three days' sojourn among the scenes of my boyhood. Up the Battenkill. Could it be that this was the great river in which my parents were in such constant fear of their boy being drowned? Was this the Mississippi of my childhood? Alas! that I had floated down the Ohio River to the real Mississippi, that I had been up the Missouri, two thousand miles from its mouth, and that I had navigated the Father of Waters from its fountain-head to its outlet in the Gulf of Mexico.

Had the Battenkill been drying up? Not at all. Though a brook, comparatively, there are the same milldams, the same trout-holes, and the same bending willows by its side; and the first to meet me among our old neighbors was uncle Nat., the same old jolly fisherman, returning from his daily piscatorial excursion, with a small string of trout. Uncle Nat. complains bitterly of the scarcity of fish at present in the river, caused, he says, by "them city chaps" from Troy, New York and Albany, who are in the habit of sojourning during the summer months in the hotels among the mountains hereabouts.

Stopping first at uncle Henry's, I visited the old homestead towards evening on the day of my arrival. Whatever may be said about the village and rivers growing smaller, it must certainly be admitted that the mountains, hills and rocks hold their own. Up there, on the hillside, was "the old house at home," which I had not seen for fifteen years. I went up the walk. There were the maples that I assisted father in planting, twenty years ago — great, spreading trees now. There was the same rosebush that mother and I cared for sixteen years ago. No other evidence of the flowers and shrubbery that mother so much delighted in remained about the premises.

I had learned that the place had passed into the hands of an Irishman named Sweeny, so I rapped at the front door, and was met by Mrs. S., from whom I obtained permission to stroll around the place. "Oh, yes," said the kind-hearted woman, "go all about, and when Mr. Swainy comes, he'll go wid ye."

So I strolled in the quiet evening hour, alone, among the scenes of my childhood, where we boys picked stones and played ball in the summer, and slid down hill and chopped firewood in the winter. The barn was the same old barn. I clambered to its old girtbeam, and sat looking down on the haymow where I had jumped, hundreds of times, into the hay below. I climbed to the box, close under the rafters, where we boys used to keep doves. The same box is there yet. I went down into the stables, where we hunted hens' eggs. Apparently, the same speckled hens are there now. And down around the barn are the same old maples, and willows beside the brook.

I went out to the fields. What immense tracts of land I thought these ten-acre fields, when I was a boy! The same orchards are there. The old Jones sweet-apple tree is dead, however, and none of the trees are looking thrifty. I took a drink from the upper spring, in the Barnes lot, which tasted just as cool as ever, and getting down on my hands and knees to drink seemed like old times. I saw a woodchuck and several squirrels, in my walk, and heard the same old caw, caw, of the crows, which brought back the past the most vividly of anything I had heard.

Returning, and looking through the house, I found almost every-thing changed. Two American and three Irish families had occupied it since we left, and they, evidently thinking that they would soon leave, did not pretend to make any improvements for their successors to enjoy. To sum up the description of the house — it has never been painted since we left; the dooryard fence is gone; the woodhouse has been removed; the outdoor cellar has caved in; the wagon-house leans so badly it is liable to fall over at any time; the house itself, in a few years, will go the way of the fences; and most of the outbuildings are already gone. Nearly every American family that once lived here has gone West; the population of the vicinity, at the present time, being largely made up of Irish. Another generation, and, it is probable, scarcely an American will be left to tell the tale. Though sorrowing to see the wreck of our old home, I am greatly enjoying the visit. The scenery is truly beautiful; though, unfortu-nately, the people here know nothing of its beauties, and it takes us some years on the level plains of the West to learn to appreciate it.

One thing must be said of the people here, however, especially the Americans that are left — they take their full measure of enjoyment. With continuous snow four months in the year, the winter is made up of sleighriding to parties and festal occasions; the sunshine of spring is the signal for maple-sugar-making, and sugaring-off parties; the hard work of summer is broken up by fishing, berrying, and fre-quent excursions to various parts of the country; the fall is charac-terized by apple-parings and corn-huskings; so that, with their maple sugar, berries, cream, trout, honey and pumpkin pies, they are about the best livers and happiest people I ever met. I never knew, till I returned, that they enjoyed themselves so well.

I will continue the record of my visit in my next.

Yours Affectionately,
ALFRED T. WEEKS.

Descriptive Letter.
From a Young Lady Visiting Chicago, to her Parents in the East.

CHICAGO, ILL., June 1, 1873.

DEAR PARENTS:

Having been the rounds among our relatives here, I seat myself to give you something of an idea of this wonderful city — in many respects one of the most remarkable on the face of the earth, having a population to-day of over 300,000.

You have heard so much of the city that I must give you a brief sketch of its history.

The first white man ever known to have set foot on the spot where Chicago now stands, was a French Missionary, from Canada, named Pierre Jacques Marquette, who, with two others, having been on a missionary tour in the southern part of Illinois, when homeward bound was detained at this place in the fall of 1673, in consequence of the severe cold, until the following spring. That was two hun-dred years ago.

The first settler that came here was Point-au-Sable, a St. Domingo negro, who, in 1796, commenced a few improvements — seventy-seven years since. Au-Sable soon afterwards removed to Peoria, Ill., his im-provements passing into the hands of one Le Mai, a Frenchman, who traded considerably with the Indians. The first permanent settler here was John Kinzie, who came over from St. Joseph, Michigan, and com-menced his improvements in 1804 — sixty-nine years ago. Mr. Kinzie was, indeed, what Romulus was to Rome, the founder of the city. There was a fort built that year, a blockhouse made of logs, a few rods southwest of what is now known as Rush street bridge. Mr. Kinzie had a house near the south end of the bridge, which bridge, of course, had no existence in those days. An employe of Mr. Kinzie, named Ouilmette, a Frenchman, had a cabin a little west of Mr. Kinzie; and a little further west was the log cottage of one Burns, a discharged soldier. South of the fort, on the South Side, a Mr. Lee had a farm, in the low swamp lands, where now stands the heart of the business center of the city, and his cabin was a half mile or so down the river.

For a quarter of a century the growth of the village was remarkably slow, as shown by the fact that in 1830 there were but twelve houses in the village, with three suburban residences on Madison street, the entire population, whites, half-breeds and negroes, making about one hundred. That was forty years ago.

I should have told you that Chicago has a river, which is doubtless the cause of the wonderful commercial growth of the place of late years, which, at the time of its discovery, was two hundred feet wide, and twenty feet deep, with banks so steep that vessels could come up to the water's edge and receive their lading. A half mile or more from the mouth of the river, the stream divides: that portion north of the stream being known as the North Side; that between the forks, the West Side; and that south of the river, the South Side.

At that time, the North Side was covered with a dense forest of black walnut and other trees, in which were bears, wolves, foxes, wild cats, deer and other game in great abundance; while the South Side, now the business center, was a low, swampy piece of ground, being the resort of wild geese and ducks. Where the court house stands, was a pond, which was navigable for small boats. On the banks of the river, among the sedgy grass, grew a wild onion, which the Indians called Chikago, and hence the name of the city.

On a summer day, in 1831, the first vessel unloaded goods at the mouth of the river. In 1832, the first frame house was built, by Geo. W. Dole, and stood on the southeast corner of Dearborn and South Water streets. At an election for township trustees in 1833, — just forty-one years since — there were twenty-eight voters. In 1840, there were less than 5,000 people in the place. Thus you see this city, now the fifth in the order of the population in the United States, has grown from 5,000 to 300,000 in thirty-three years.

It is needless for me to describe the wonderfully rapid up-building of the city since the fire. You have heard all about it. What I want to tell you more especially is concerning our relatives. Uncles John, William and James, you recollect perhaps, all came here in 1836. They worked that summer for different parties, and until the next spring, when, in the summer of 1837, each of the men they had labored for failed. Uncle John had due him $150. Fortunately, as he thought, he was able to settle the claim at fifty cents on the dollar, and with $75 he left the place in disgust, and went to work for a farmer in Dupage County, a little distance west of Chicago. Uncle William could not get a cent. He even proposed to take $50 for the $175 that were due him, but cash could not possibly be obtained. He finally settled his claim by taking six acres of swampy land on the South Side, which he vainly tried to sell for several years that he might leave the city; but, unable to do so, he continued to work in Chicago. Uncle James took fifteen acres in the settlement of his claim, which he also found it impossible to sell, his experience being about the same as that of uncle William. Well, now the luck begins to come in. Uncle William got independent of his land by and by, but at last sold an acre for money enough to put up one of the most elegant residences you ever beheld. He sold afterwards another acre for money with which he bought a farm three miles from the court house, that is now worth $500,000. With two acres more, he got money enough to put up five business blocks, from which he gets a revenue, each year, sufficient to buy several farms.

Uncle James' experience is almost exactly similar to uncle William's. He has sold small portions of his land at various times, re-investing his money in real estate, until he is worth to-day about $2,000,000. Uncle William is said to be worth about the same amount. Uncle John came in from the country a few years ago, and, in various capacities, is working for his brothers around the city, being to-day a poor man; but will, I presume, be just as rich in eternity as uncles James and William.

All have interesting families of intelligent children, among whom I have almost terminated one of the most delightful visits I ever made. Such in brief is the history of Chicago, and a sketch of two of its sample rich men, who were made wealthy in spite of themselves.

In my next I will describe the parks and boulevards about the city. Till then, adieu.

Your Affectionate Daughter,
AMELIA SPARLAND.

Letters of Love.

 F all letters, the love-letter should be the most carefully prepared. Among the written missives, they are the most thoroughly read and re-read, the longest preserved, and the most likely to be regretted in after life.

IMPORTANCE OF CARE.

They should be written with the utmost regard for perfection. An ungrammatical expression, or word improperly spelled, may seriously interfere with the writer's prospects, by being turned to ridicule. For any person, however, to make sport of a respectful, confidential letter, because of some error in the writing, is in the highest degree unladylike and ungentlemanly.

NECESSITY OF CAUTION.

As a rule, the love-letter should be very guardedly written. Ladies, especially, should be very careful to maintain their dignity when writing them. When, possibly, in after time the feelings entirely change, you will regret that you wrote the letter at all. If the love remains unchanged, no harm will certainly be done, if you wrote with judgment and care.

AT WHAT AGE TO WRITE LOVE-LETTERS.

The love-letter is the prelude to marriage — a state that, if the husband and wife be fitted for each other, is the most natural and serenely happy; a state, however, that none should enter upon, until, in judgment and physical development, both parties have completely matured. Many a life has been wrecked by a blind, impulsive marriage, simply resulting from a youthful passion. As a physiological law, man should be twenty-five, and woman twenty-three, before marrying.

APPROVAL OF PARENTS.

While there may be exceptional cases, as a rule, correspondence should be conducted only with the assent and approval of the parents. If it is not so, parents are themselves generally to blame. If children are properly trained, they will implicitly confide in the father and mother, who will retain their love until they are sufficiently matured to choose a companion for life. If parents neglect to retain this love and confidence, the child, in the yearning for affection, will place the love elsewhere, frequently much too early in life.

TIMES FOR COURTSHIP.

Ladies should not allow courtship to be conducted at unseasonable hours. The evening entertainment, the walk, the ride, are all favorable for the study of each other's tastes and feelings. For the gentleman to protract his visit at the lady's residence until a late hour, is almost sure to give offence to the lady's parents, and is extremely ungentlemanly.

HONESTY.

The love-letter should be honest. It should say what the writer means, and no more. For the lady or gentleman to play the part of a coquette, studying to see how many lovers he or she may secure, is very disreputable, and bears in its train a long list of sorrows, frequently wrecking the domestic happiness for a life-time. The parties should be honest, also, in the statement of their actual prospects and means of support. Neither should hold out to the other wealth or other inducements that will not be realized, as disappointment and disgust will be the only result.

MARRYING FOR A HOME.

Let no lady commence and continue a correspondence with a view to marriage, for fear that she may never have another opportunity. It is the mark of judgment and rare good sense to go through life without wedlock, if she cannot marry from love. Somewhere in eternity, the poet tells us, our true mate will be found. Do not be afraid of being an "old maid." The disgrace attached to that term has long since passed away. Unmarried ladies of mature years are proverbially among the most intelligent, accomplished and independent to be found in society. The sphere of woman's action and work is so widening that she can to-day, if she desires, handsomely and independently support herself. She need not, therefore, marry for a home.

INTEMPERATE MEN.

Above all, no lady should allow herself to correspond with an intemperate man, with a view to matrimony. She may reform him, but the chances are that her life's happiness will be completely destroyed by such a union. Better, a thousand times, the single, free and independent maidenhood, than for a woman to trail her life in the dust, and bring poverty, shame and disgrace on her children, by marrying a man addicted to dissipated habits.

MARRYING WEALTH.

Let no man make it an ultimate object in life to marry a rich wife. It is not the possession, but the *acquisition*, of wealth, that gives happiness. It is a generally conceded fact that the inheritance of great wealth is a positive mental and moral injury to young men, completely destroying the stimulus to advancement. So, as a rule, no man is permanently made happier by a marriage of wealth; while he is quite likely to

be given to understand, by his wife and others, from time to time, that, whatever consequence he may attain, it is all the result of his wife's money. Most independent men prefer to start, as all our wealthiest and greatest men have done, at the foot of the ladder, and earn their independence. Where, however, a man can bring extraordinary talent or distinguished reputation, as a balance for his wife's wealth, the conditions are more nearly equalized. Observation shows that those marriages prove most serenely happy where husband and wife, at the time of marriage, stand, socially, intellectually and pecuniarily, very nearly equal. For the chances of successful advancement and happiness in after life, let a man wed a woman poorer than himself rather than one that is richer.

POVERTY.

Let no couple hesitate to marry because they are poor. It will cost them less to live after marriage than before — one light, one fire, etc., answering the purpose for both. Having an object to live for, also, they will commence their accumulations after marriage as never before. The young woman that demands a certain amount of costly style, beyond the income of her betrothed, no young man should ever wed. As a general thing, however, women have common sense, and, if husbands will perfectly confide in their wives, telling them exactly their pecuniary condition, the wife will live within the husband's income. In the majority of cases where men fail in business, the failure being attributed to the wife's extravagance, the wife has been kept in entire ignorance of her husband's pecuniary resources. The man who would be successful in business, should not only marry a woman who is worthy of his confidence, but he should at all times advise with her. She is more interested in his prosperity than anybody else, and will be found his best counselor and friend.

CONFIDENCE AND HONOR.

The love correspondence of another should be held sacred, the rule of conduct being, to do to others as you wish them to do to you. No woman, who is a lady, will be guilty of making light of the sentiments that are expressed to her in a letter. No man, who is a gentleman, will boast of his love conquests, among boon companions, or reveal to others the correspondence between himself and a lady. If an engagement is mutually broken off, all the love-letters should be returned. To retain them is dishonorable. They were written under circumstances that no longer exist. It is better for both parties to wash out every recollection of the past, by returning to the giver every memento of the dead love.

HOW TO BEGIN A LOVE CORRESPONDENCE.

Some gentlemen, being very favorably impressed with a lady at first sight, and having no immediate opportunity for introduction, make bold, after learning her name, to write her at once, seeking an interview, the form of which letter will be found hereafter. A gentleman in doing so, however, runs considerable risk of receiving a rebuff from the lady, though not always. It is better to take a little more time, learn thoroughly who the lady is, and obtain an introduction through a mutual acquaintance. Much less embarrassment attends such a meeting; and, having learned the lady's antecedents, subjects are easily introduced in which she is interested, and thus the first interview can be made quite agreeable.

The way is now paved for the opening of a correspondence, which may be done by a note inviting her company to any entertainment supposed to be agreeable to her, or the further pleasure of her acquaintance by correspondence, as follows:

148 —— ST., July 2, 18—.
MISS MYRA BRONSON:
Having greatly enjoyed our brief meeting at the residence of Mrs. Powell last Thursday evening, I venture to write to request permission to call on you at your own residence. Though myself almost entirely a stranger in the city, your father remembers, he told me the other evening, Mr. Williams of Syracuse, who is my uncle. Trusting that you will pardon this liberty, and place me on your list of gentleman acquaintances, I am,
Yours, Very Respectfully,
HARMON WILLIAMS.

Favorable Reply.

944 —— ST., July 8, 18—.
MR. HARMON WILLIAMS.
Dear Sir:
It will give me much pleasure to see you at our residence next Wednesday evening. My father desires me to state that he retains a very favorable recollection of your uncle, in consequence of which he will be pleased to continue your acquaintance.
Yours Truly,
MYRA BRONSON.

Unfavorable Reply.

944 —— ST., July 2, 18—.
Miss Myra Bronson, making it a rule to receive no gentleman visitors upon such brief acquaintance, begs to decline the honor of Mr. Williams' visits.
HARMON WILLIAMS, ESQ.

An Invitation to a Place of Public Amusement.

462 —— ST., April 4, 18—.
MISS FARRINGTON:
May I request the very great pleasure of escorting you to Barnum's Museum, at any time which may suit your convenience? To grant this favor will give me very much pleasure. No pains will be spared by myself to have you enjoy the occasion, and I will consult your wishes in every particular as to time of calling for you and returning. Waiting an early reply to this, I remain,
Most Sincerely,
CHAS. STEVENSON.

Reply Accepting.

876 —— ST., April 7, 18—.
MR. STEVENSON.
Dear Sir: I thank you for your very kind invitation, which I am happy to accept. I will appoint next Monday evening, at which time, if you will call for me at our house, I will accompany you.
Yours Sincerely,
CLARA FARRINGTON.

Reply Refusing.

876 —— ST., April 4, 18—.
MR. STEVENSON.
Dear Sir: I am grateful to you for your very polite invitation, but, as I should go only with my own family were I to attend any place of amusement, I am unable to avail myself of your kindness. Thanking you, I remain,
Yours Truly,
CLARA FARRINGTON.

Reply with Conditions.

876 —— ST., April 4, 18—.
MR. STEVENSON.
Dear Sir: I shall be most happy to visit Barnum's Museum with you, but will prefer being one of a company in which yourself is included, such also being the wish of my mother, who sends her kind regards. A visit from you at our house, next Tuesday evening, will enable us to decide upon the time of going.
Very Sincerely,
CLARA FARRINGTON.

Love at First Sight.

96 —— St., June 1, 18—.

DEAR MISS HAWLEY:

You will, I trust, forgive this abrupt and plainly spoken letter. Although I have been in your company but once, I cannot forbear writing to you in defiance of all rules of etiquette. Affection is sometimes of slow growth, but sometimes it springs up in a moment. I left you last night with my heart no longer my own. I cannot, of course, hope that I have created any interest in you, but will you do me the great favor to allow me to cultivate your acquaintance? Hoping that you may regard me favorably, I shall await with much anxiety your reply. I remain,

Yours Devotedly,

BENSON GOODRICH.

Unfavorable Reply.

694 —— St., June 1, 18—.

MR. GOODRICH.

Sir: Your note was a surprise to me, considering that we had never met until last evening, and that then our conversation had been only on commonplace subjects. Your conduct is indeed quite strange. You will please be so kind as to oblige me by not repeating the request, allowing this note to close our correspondence.

MARION HAWLEY.

Favorable Reply.

694 —— St., June 1, 18—.

MR. GOODRICH.

Dear Sir: Undoubtedly I ought to call you severely to account for your declaration of love at first sight, but I really cannot find it in my heart to do so, as I must confess that, after our brief interview last evening, I have thought much more of you than I should have been willing to have acknowledged had you not come to the confession first. Seriously speaking, we know but very little of each other yet, and we must be very careful not to exchange our hearts in the dark. I shall be happy to receive you here, as a friend, with a view to our further acquaintance. I remain, dear sir,

MARION HAWLEY.

A Lover's Good-bye Before Starting on a Journey.

104 —— St., May 10, 18—.

MY DARLING MINNIE:

I go west, to-morrow, on business, leaving my heart in your gentle keeping. You need be at no expense in placing a guard around it, for I assure you that, as surely as the needle points towards the pole, so surely my love is all yours. I shall go, dearest, by the first train, hoping thereby to return just one train sooner, which means that not an hour, not a minute longer will I be absent from you, than is imperatively necessary. Like the angler, I shall "drop a line" frequently, and shall expect a very prompt response, letter for letter. No credit given in this case; business is business — I must have prompt returns.

Ever Faithfully Yours,

WINFIELD BAKER.

Reply to the Foregoing.

814 —— St., May 10, 18—.

DEAR WINFIELD:

I have had my cry over your letter — a long, hard cry. Of course, I know that does not help the matter any. I suppose you must go, but I shall be *so* lonely while you are gone. However, you promise that you will return at the earliest moment, and that is one little ray of sunshine that lines the cloud. Shall we be enough happier after your return to pay for this separation? Thinking that we may be, I will let that thought sustain me. In the meantime, from this moment until your return I will think of you, *just once* — a long-drawn-out thought.

Yours Affectionately,

MINNIE LA SURE.

Letter Asking an Introduction through a Mutual Friend.

912 —— St., April 2, 18—.

FRIEND HENRY:

I am very desirous of making the acquaintance of Miss Benjamin, with whom you are on terms of intimate friendship. Will you be so kind as to give me a letter of introduction to her? I am aware that it may be a delicate letter for you to write, but you will be free, of course, to make all needed explanations in your letter to her. I will send her your letter, instead of personally calling upon her myself, thus saving her from any embarrassment that may result from my so doing. By granting this favor, you will much oblige,

Yours, Very Respectfully,

WM. H. TYLER.

Reply.

117 —— St., April 2, 18—.

FRIEND TYLER:

Enclosed, find the note you wish. As you will observe, I have acted upon your suggestion of giving her sufficient explanation to justify my letter. Your desire to please the lady, coupled with your good judgment, will, I doubt not, make the matter agreeable.

Truly Yours,

HENRY PARSONS.

LETTER OF INTRODUCTION.

DEAR MISS BENJAMIN: This will introduce to you my friend Wm. Tyler, who is very desirous of making your acquaintance, and, having no other means of doing so, asks of me the favor of writing this note of introduction, which he will send you, instead of calling himself, thus leaving you free to grant him an interview or not. Mr. Tyler is a gentleman I very highly respect, and whose acquaintance, I think, you would not have occasion to regret. Nevertheless, you may not regard this a proper method of introduction, in which case, allow me to assure you, I will entertain the same respect for yourself, if you will frankly state so, though it would be gratifying to Mr. Tyler and myself to have it otherwise. With sincere respect, I am,

Very Respectfully,

HENRY PARSONS.

To the Father of the Lady.

BURLINGTON, IOWA, Jan. 1, 18—.

RESPECTED SIR:

I take this means of consulting you on a subject that deeply interests myself, while it indirectly concerns you; and I trust that my presentation of the matter will meet with your approval.

For several months your daughter Mary and myself have been on intimate terms of friendship, which has ripened into affection on my part, and I have reason to think that my attentions are not indifferent to her. My business and prospects are such that I flatter myself I can provide for her future, with the same comfort that has surrounded her under the parental roof. Of my character and qualifications, I have nothing to say; I trust they are sufficiently known to you to give confidence in the prospect of your child's happiness.

Believing that the parents have such an interest in the welfare of the daughter as makes it obligatory upon the lover to consult their desires, before taking her from their home, I am thus induced to request you to express your wishes upon this subject.

I shall anxiously await your answer.

Your Very Obedient Servant,

DANIEL HARRISON.

To WM. FRANKLIN, ESQ.,
184 —— St.

Favorable Reply.

184 —— St., Jan. 1, 18—.

My Dear Mr. Harrison:

I very highly appreciate the manly and honorable way in which you have addressed me in reference to my daughter Mary.

Believing you to be honest, industrious, ambitious to do well, and possessed of an excellent moral character, I unite with Mrs. Franklin in the belief that our darling child may very safely trust her happiness to your protecting care.

If agreeable and convenient to you, we shall be happy to have you dine with us to-morrow.

Very Sincerely Yours,
WM. FRANKLIN.

To Mr. Daniel Harrison.

Unfavorable Reply.

184 —— St.

Dear Sir:

Highly appreciating the straightforward and gentlemanly manner in which you have written me concerning a subject that every parent has an interest in, I am compelled to inform you that, though my daughter has treated you with much friendliness, as she is accustomed to with all her friends, she will be unable to continue with you a love acquaintance with a view to marriage, owing to a prior engagement with a gentleman of worth and respectability, which contract she has no occasion to regret.

Fully sensible of your most excellent qualities, and the compliment paid in your selection of her, my daughter unites with me in the wish that you may meet with a companion in every way calculated to ensure your happiness.

Yours, Very Respectfully,
WM. FRANKLIN.

To Mr. Daniel Harrison.

Reply to a Young Man that Uses Tobacco.

662 —— St., July 18, 18—.

Mr. Bannister.

Dear Sir:

I am in receipt of your courteous letter, containing a declaration of love. I will be frank enough with you to admit that, while I have been sensible of your affectionate regard for me for some months, I have also cherished a growing interest in you. In truth, to make a candid confession, I most sincerely love you. I should, perhaps, say no more, but I feel it due to you, as well as to myself, to be strictly honest in my expression, lest we foster this growing love, which, under present conditions, must be broken off.

I have always admired your natural ability; I appreciate you for your industry; I respect you for your filial conduct towards your parents. In fact, I consider you quite a model young man, were it not for one habit, which has always been, heretofore, a very delicate subject for me to speak of, fearing that it might give you offense. But believing it best that I be true to my convictions and state my objections plainly, I thus freely write them.

I have reference to the use of tobacco. Apparently, this is a little thing. I am aware that ladies generally consider it beneath their notice; but so thoroughly convinced am I that it is one of the most destructive habits, sapping the morality and vigor of our young men, that I could never consent to wed a man addicted to its use, my reasons being as follows:

It would impoverish my home. Only ten cents a day expended for a cigar, in a lifetime of forty years, with its accumulations of interest, amounts to over four thousand dollars! The little sum of eleven cents per day, saved from being squandered on tobacco, and properly put at interest, amounts in that time to $5,160! No wonder so many homes, the heads of which use tobacco, are without the comforts of life.

It might wreck my happiness. It is a well-known physological fact that the use of tobacco deadens the sense of taste; that water and all common drinks become insipid and tasteless when tobacco is used, so that the person using the same involuntarily craves strong drink, in order to *taste* it. Therein lies the foundation of a large share of the drunkenness of the country. Observation proves that, while many men use tobacco that are not drunkards, almost every drunkard is a user of tobacco, having nearly always formed the habit from the use of this narcotic weed.

It would surround me with filth. To say nothing of the great drain on the physical health by the constant expectoration of saliva, thus ruining the health of many robust constitutions, I could not endure the fetid breath of the tobacco-user. I sicken at the sight of the brown saliva exuding from between the lips; physiology proving that, with tobacco-chewers, nearly all the waste fluids from the body pass through the mouth. I am immediately faint at the thought of dragging my skirts through spittle in a railway car, or any place where it is thrown upon the floor; I turn with disgust at the atmosphere — God's pure, fresh air — that is tainted with the stench of tobacco smoke.

It would corrupt my husband's morals. All the associations of tobacco are bad. It is true that many good men use tobacco. It is also a truth that nearly every man that is bad is addicted to its use. To smoke in peace, the man must resort to the place where others smoke. In that room are profanity, obscene language and every species of vulgarity. There may be occasionally an exception. The fact is patent, however, that, in the room in which vulgarity and obscenity prevail, there is always tobacco smoke in the air, and the vile spittle on the floor.

You will forgive me for speaking thus plainly. I love you too well to disguise my feelings on the subject. I could not possibly constantly love a tobacco-user, for the reasons that I have given.

While I devotedly love you, I cannot consent that you should bestow your affections upon a person that would instinctively repel you. Believing, therefore, under the circumstances, that our further correspondence should cease, I remain,

Your Friend and Well-Wisher,
MARIETTA WILCOX.

Letter to an Entire Stranger.

478 —— St., Jan. 1, 18—.

Miss Henderson:

I beg to apologize for addressing you thus, being an entire stranger; but having the misfortune to be unknown to you is my excuse for this strange proceeding, which, I am well aware, is entirely at variance with the rules of etiquette. I have for two sabbaths seen you at church, and I am frank to confess that your appearance has made so deep an impression upon me as to make me extremely desirous of forming your acquaintance. I am, at present, a clerk in the ribbon department at Smith & Brown's store. Will you do me the great favor of allowing this to commence a friendship, which, I trust, will never be regretted by yourself. Please deign to give me at least a single line in reply to this, and oblige,

Your Sincere Admirer,
WESLEY BARNUM.

Unfavorable Reply.

Mr. Barnum.

Dear Sir:

I considerably question whether it is due to propriety to answer your note at all. But as you might fear that your letter had miscarried, and thus be induced to write again, it is best, probably, for me to make an immediate reply, and thus settle the affair entirely, and relieve you, possibly, of further suspense. It will be impossible for me to recognize you, or to think under any circumstances of permitting an acquaintance to be commenced by such an introduction as you seem to deem sufficient. More especially should I regret allowing a friendship to be formed by recognitions in the hours of divine service in church, while the mind should be employed in religious observances. You will, therefore, please understand that I am not favorable to further recognition, nor to a continuance of correspondence.

AMELIA HENDERSON.

Reply More Favorable.

355 —— St., June 10, 18—.

Mr. Barnum.
Dear Sir:

I am in receipt of your note, and must confess that I am surprised at your request. I am entirely opposed to commencing, on general principles, an acquaintance with such an introduction, and consider it very improper, especially to allow it to originate in church during the hours of divine service. Were it not that I think your meaning kind and your intentions good, I would return your letter unanswered. As it is, I will take your request under consideration, and, if I think best to grant it, you may know of the fact by my recognition at the close of the service in the Sabbath School.

Respectfully,
AMELIA HENDERSON.

An Advertisement in a Morning Paper.

PERSONAL.—Will the lady who rode up Broadway last Thursday afternoon, about two o'clock, in an omnibus, getting out at Stewart's, accompanied by a little girl dressed in blue suit, please send her address to D. B. M., Herald office?

REMARKS.

It is useless to advise people never to reply to a personal advertisement like the above. To do so is like totally refusing young people the privilege of dancing. People will dance, and they will answer personal advertisements. The best course, therefore, is to properly direct the dancers, and caution the writers in their answers to newspaper personals. If the eye of the young lady referred to meets the above advertisement, she will possibly be indignant at first, and will, perhaps, resolve to pay no attention to it. It will continue to occupy her attention so much, however, and curiosity will become so great, that, in order to ease her mind, she will at last give her address; in which case she makes a very serious mistake, as any lady replying to a communication of such a character, giving her name and residence to a stranger, places herself at a great disadvantage. Should her communication never be answered, she will feel mortified ever afterwards that she committed the indiscretion of replying to the advertisement at all; and, should the person she addresses prove to be some worthless fellow who may presume to press an acquaintance upon the strength of her reply, it may cause her very serious perplexity and embarrassment.

It is clearly evident, therefore, that she should not give her name and address as requested; and yet, as the advertisement may refer to a business matter of importance, or bring about an acquaintance that she will not regret, she may relieve her curiosity on the subject by writing the following note in reply:

THE REPLY.

(Advertisement pasted in.)

D. B. M.:

I find the above advertisement in the "Herald" of this morning. I suppose myself to be the person referred to. You will please state your object in addressing me, with references.

Address,   A. L. K., Herald Office.

It is probable that the advertiser, if a gentleman, will reply, giving his reasons for requesting the lady's address, with references, upon receiving which, the lady will do as she may choose relative to continuing the correspondence; in either case, it will be seen that she has in no wise compromised her dignity, and she retains the advantage of knowing the motive and object that prompted the advertisement, while she is yet unknown to the advertiser.

Great caution should be exercised in answering personals. The supposition is, if the advertiser be a gentleman, that he will honorably seek an interview with a lady, and pay court as gentlemen ordinarily do. Still, an occasion may happen to a man, who is in the highest sense a gentleman, wherein he sees the lady that he very greatly admires, and can learn her address in no other way without rendering himself offensive and impertinent; hence, the apparent necessity of the above personal advertisement.

Instances have also occurred where gentlemen, driven with business, and having but little time to mingle in female society, or no opportunity, being strangers comparatively, desirous of forming the acquaintance of ladies, have honestly advertised for correspondence, been honestly answered, and marriage was the result.

Those advertisements, however, wherein Sammy Brown and Coney Smith advertise for correspondence with any number of young ladies, for fun, mutual improvement, "and what may grow out of it, photographs exchanged," etc., young ladies should be very wary of answering. Instances have been known where scores of young ladies, having answered such an advertisement, could they have looked in upon those young men, a week afterwards, would have seen them with a pile of photographs and letters, exhibiting them to their companions, and making fun of the girls who had been so foolish as to answer their advertisement.

It is true that no one but the meanest kind of a rascal would be guilty of such a disgraceful act as to advertise for and expose correspondence thus, and it is equally true that the young lady who gives the advertiser the opportunity to ridicule her shows herself to be very foolish.

Personal Advertisement.

PERSONAL.—A gentleman, a new comer in the city, having a sufficiency of this world's goods to comfortably support himself and wife, is desirous of making the acquaintance of a lady of middle years, with a view to matrimony. Address, in the strictest confidence, giving name, residence and photograph, H. A. B., Station H, Postoffice.

THE REPLY.

To H. A. B.

Sir:

I am led to suppose, from the reading of the above, that it is dictated in sincerity, by a desire to meet with a lady who would be treated with candor and respect. I have at present no acquaintance to whom I am inclined to give a very decided preference, nor have I ever had any very distinct ideas on the subject of marriage. I am free, however, to confess that, should circumstances favor my acquaintance with a gentleman whom I could honor and respect, I might seriously think of a proposal. Believing that you wish, as you intimate, this letter in confidence, I will say that I am — years old, am in receipt of —— annually, from property that is leased. I have been told that I was handsome, though others, probably, have a different opinion. Of that fact, you must be the judge. I am entirely free to select whomsoever I may choose. My social standing, I trust, would be satisfactory, and my accomplishments have not been neglected. It is not necessary that I should write more. I shall be happy to correspond with you with a view to better acquaintance, when, if mutually agreeable, an introduction may take place. You desire me to send name, address and photograph, which, I trust you will perceive, would be improper for me to do. It is due to myself, and, under certain circumstances, to you, that I should be very guarded as to the manner of my introduction. A letter addressed to M. A. L., Station A, Postoffice, will reach me.

I sign a fictitious name, for obvious reasons.

Respectfully,
NANCY HILLIS.

A Gentleman Makes a Frank Acknowledgment. — Gushing with Sentiment, and Running Over with Poetry.

WHITE MOUNTAINS, N. H., Oct. 1, 18—.

MY DEAR MARY:

One by one the brown leaves are falling, reminding us that the golden summer that we have so delightfully loitered through approaches its close. How thickly our pathway has been strewn with roses; how fragrant have been the million blossoms; how sweetly the birds have sung; how beautiful have been the sunny days; how joyous have been the starry nights! Dear M., I do not need to tell you that this delightful summer has been to me one grand Elysian scene. I have gazed on and dreamed of thy beauty. I have been fed by thy sparkling repartee and merriment; I have drank at the fountain of thy intellectuality; but the feast is ended, and gradually the curtain is falling. Dear, beautiful summer; so beautiful to me because of thy loved presence. And standing now on the threshold of a scene all changed, I take a last, fond, long, lingering look on the beautiful picture that will return to me no more; and yet, who knows, but on in that great eternity we may live again these Eden hours.

"Like a foundling in slumber, the summer day lay
    On the crimsoning threshold of even,
And I thought that the glow through the azure-arched way
    Was a glimpse of the coming of Heaven.
There together we sat by the beautiful stream;
    We had nothing to do but to love and to dream
In the days that have gone on before.
    These are not the same days, though they bear the same name,
With the ones I shall welcome no more.

"But it may be the angels are culling them o'er,
    For a Sabbath and Summer forever,
When the years shall forget the Decembers they wore,
    And the shroud shall be woven, no, never!
In a twilight like that, darling M. for a bride—
    Oh! what more of the world could one wish beside,
As we gazed on the river unroll'd
    Till we heard, or we fancied, its musical tide,
Where it flowed through the Gateway of Gold?"

Dearest, you must forgive my ardent expressions in this letter. With a temperament gushing to the brim and overflowing with sentiment and rhapsody, I have passed the fleeting summer in thy charming presence in one continual dream of poesy. I cannot now turn back to the solemn duties before me, without telling you what trembled on my tongue a thousand times, as we gathered flowers together and wove our chaplets in the sunny days gone by. Dear, darling Mary, *I love you, I adore you.* How often in the beautiful moonlight nights, as we strolled among the lilacs and the primroses, have I been on the verge of clasping your jeweled hand and telling you all my heart. But, oh! I did not quite dare; the hours were so delightful, even as they were. Fearing that I might be repulsed, I chose to accept the joy even that there was, rather than run the risk of losing it all.

How many a morning have I arisen and firmly resolved that, ere another day, I would know my fate! But, ah! the twilight would fall, and the evening hour would pass by, and I never completely dared to risk the result of a declaration. The morrow I knew would be joyous if I bridled my impulse; it might not be if I made a mistake. But the dream has passed by. To-morrow, I bid adieu to these silvan groves, the quiet meadows and the gurgling brooks, to go back to the prose duties of business. And now, at the close of this festal season, as I am upon the verge of going, having nothing to lose and everything to gain, I have told you my heart. I have not the slightest idea what your reply will be. You have been to me one continual puzzle. If your answer is adverse, I can only entertain the highest respect for you ever in the future; and memory shall keep alive the recollection of the most blissful summer I have ever known. If your reply is favorable—dearest, may I fondly hope that it will be?—then opens before me a great volume of happiness, of which this joyous summer has been but the opening chapter.

Dear M., may I come again and see you, and address you henceforth as a lover? The messenger who brings you this will return again in an hour for your answer. I need not tell you what an hour of suspense this will be to me. Upon your reply hangs my future. If your reply is favorable, I shall tarry another day; and will you grant me a long interview, as I have much to talk over with you? If unfavorable, please return this letter with your note. Accept my warmest thanks for the entertainment which I, in common with others, have received at your hand in the past; and, if I may not sign myself your devoted lover, I shall at least, I trust, have ever the pleasure of subscribing myself,

Your Sincere Friend,
CLARENCE HARRINGTON.

Favorable Reply.

DEAR CLARENCE:

I shall not attempt in this to answer your missive with the same poetic fervor that colors your letter from beginning to end. While it is given you to tread the emerald pavements of an imaginative Eden, in my plainer nature I can only walk the common earth.

I fully agree with you in your opinion of the beautiful summer just passed. Though in seasons heretofore many people have been here from the cities, I have never known a summer so delightful. Yes, Clarence, these three months have been joyous, because—shall I confess it?—because *you* have been here. I need not write more. You have agreed to stay another day; I shall be at home this afternoon, at two o'clock, and will be happy to see you.

Yours Very Truly,
MARY SINGLETON.

To a Lady, from a Gentleman Confessing Change of Sentiment.

844—ST., April 2, 18—.

MISS MARION THORNTON:

Your note accusing me of coldness is before me. After spending several hours in a consideration of this subject, to determine what is my duty, I have concluded that it is decidedly best for me to be perfectly frank with you, and give my reasons for a change of sentiment.

I do not think we could live happily together if we were married, because, from disparaging remarks I have heard you make concerning people that are not wealthy, I think you would be entirely dissatisfied with my circumstances; and the further fact that you allow your mother to do all the drudgery of the household, you sitting in the parlor entertaining gentlemen, and affecting to have no knowledge of housekeeping, is proof that our tastes would not accord in home matters. I consider it just as honorable, and just as important, that young ladies should do something to support themselves, as that young men should. If the opportunities are not as great for them to go abroad, they can, at least while at home, learn to be good in sewing, cooking and housekeeping, and thus be prepared when opportunities offer, to make prudent, economical, tidy housewives. I do not under-value the importance of being proficient in the lighter accomplishments which go to make a lady at ease in society; but I vastly more prize

the lady who knows how to get an excellent breakfast early in the morning, who is not only a model of neatness herself, but relieves her mother in household duties, keeping her younger brothers and sisters clean and orderly.

I have admired and loved you for your musical talent and your fine conversational powers, but, as I could not keep the necessary servants to enable you constantly to gratify those talents to the exclusion of the more substantial duties, I feel that our marriage would be a mistake for us both.

You asked my reason for my changing love; I have reluctantly, yet plainly, stated it. Hoping, however, that you may always be happy in life, I am,

Your Friend,
CLINTON HOLMES.

Reply to a Young Man Addicted to Intemperance.

669——— St., Nov. 7, 18——

Mr. Spellman.

Dear Sir:

Your kind invitation to accompany you to the opera, to-morrow evening, is received. Under ordinary circumstances, I would be delighted to go with you, believing you at heart to be really a most excellent gentleman. I regret to add, however, that I have undoubted evidence of the fact that you are becoming addicted to the use of the wine-cup. I regard it entirely unsafe for any young lady to continue an intimacy with a young man upon whom is growing the habit of intemperance. With an earnest prayer for your reformation, ere it be too late, I beg you to consider our intimacy at an end.

Respectfully,
Helen Sanford.

One Way of Breaking the Ice.

584 —— St., July 1, 18—.

My Dear Friend Caroline:

I returned yesterday from a brief trip into Canada, my journey being most agreeable; only one little episode breaking the monotony, as I neared home, which was this: in the next seat behind me in the car sat a young couple, who were evidently regretting that their ride was so near an end. Though buried in my reading, I could not avoid hearing much that they said. One question asked by the young man made a striking impression on my mind. "Maggie," said he, "we have now been acquainted a good while; you know me, and I know you. I do not need to tell you that I love you with all my heart; now, do you love me?"

I knew the young fellow had taken that occasion, when the cars were thundering along, so that he might not be knocked down by the beating of his own heart. I confess to have been guilty of eavesdropping, then. I listened intently for the lady's answer, but just at that moment, as my ill luck would have it, another train came thundering by us, and her voice was drowned in the noise. I got to thinking like this: suppose you and I were riding thus, and I should ask precisely the same question; what would be your reply? I am very curious to know what your answer would be, and shall await a letter from you, with much anxiety.

Most Truly Yours,

ROLAND MILLS.

An Offer of Marriage.

248 —— St., Dec. 10, 18—.

Dearest Bertha:

I have intended, oh, how many times! when we have been together, to put the simple question which I intend this note shall ask; but, although apparently a very easy matter to ask the hand in marriage of one I so deeply love as yourself, it is no easy task. I therefore write what I have never found courage in my heart to speak. Dearest, will you bestow upon me the great happiness of permitting me to call you mine? If I have spoken this too boldly, you will forgive; but I fondly hope that you will not be indifferent to my appeal. I trust, if you answer this in the affirmative, that you will never regret doing so. Anxiously awaiting your answer, I remain,

Yours Affectionately,

HARLAN DEMPSTER.

Favorable Reply.

367 —— St., Dec. 10, 18—.

Dear Sir:

Your proposal is quite unexpected to me, but it is made with such candor and frankness that I can take no offence. I cannot, in this note, give you a definite reply. Marriage is a very serious matter; and, while I regard you with the greatest favor, I desire to consult my near relatives, and consider the subject myself carefully for a few days, ere I give you a final answer. I think I can assure you, however, that you may *hope*.

Very Sincerely,

FANNIE KIMBALL.

Letter from a Young Man Who Proposes Marriage and Emigration.

482 —— St., April 16, 18—.

Dear Clara:

You have doubtless heard of my intention to go West in the coming month. Though surrounded here with my relatives and all the many friends of my boyhood, I have an intense desire to try my fortune amid new scenes, feeling that the fetters that now bind me and seem to hinder my upward progress will then be broken.

I shall sunder my ties with some regrets, but, to commence my business career as I am desirous of doing, I must make the sacrifice; in doing so, I do no more than thousands have done before me. In the great, broad fields of the growing West, a young man of resolution, ambition, honesty, temperance and perseverance cannot fail, I believe, to better his condition much more rapidly than he can here; you will, I think, coincide with me in this opinion.

Dear Clara, of all my farewells, none will be so sad to me as that I shall bid to you. Dear, dear Clara, you cannot be indifferent to the fact that I have long devotedly loved you; and, at the hour of parting, I feel that I cannot go without telling you my heart, and asking you if I may not have your love in return. And now, while I am asking, will you not take me and my heart, and in turn allow me to be your protector through life?

Dearest, I am going to press my suit still further. Will you not be mine before I go, and accompany me on my journey? I know this is asking a great deal of you. To accept of this proposition, is to take you from a home of affluence, where you are surrounded with every desired comfort. I have no right to ask the sacrifice; and yet I have resolved to make bold before I go, and tell you all. If you accept my offer, and will consent to cast your fortunes with me out in the great Sea of the Hereafter, I can assure you that no trouble or sorrow will come to you through me; and that, as you will be my dear, dear companion and sacred trust, so will I be to you all that a lover and husband can be.

Now, dearest, if you will accept my future as your own, and place yourself by my side, accepting the sorrow and partaking of the joy that is in store for me, you will make me the happiest of men. If you assent, God grant that you may never regret your faith. Do not decide the question hastily. The sacrifice is such, in leaving home and kindred, that you may not accept of my proposal even though you love. When you have fully determined, however, please send the answer, which I shall most anxiously await. Ever, Dear Clara,

Your Affectionate,

HENRY ADAMS.

Reply.

172 —— St., April 16, 18—.

Dear Henry:

I can make a reply to your candid question at once. I do not need to deliberate upon it long. I love you; I confide in you. I will trust you; I will go with you; I will accept the love and the future you offer. You may have many joys; you may experience some sorrows: I will share and bear them all with you, trusting that patient, earnest, willing effort may crown our labors with success. Believing that God will guide and prosper us, I can only add, hoping to see you soon, that I am, Ever yours,

CLARA DUNHAM.

A DICTIONARY OF THE LANGUAGE OF FLOWERS.

VERY charming and interesting method of communicating thought is by the aid of flowers, their language and sentiment being understood by the parties who present them. Although the following list is very complete, this vocabulary may be still enlarged by the addition of other definitions, the parties having an understanding as to what language the flower shall represent. Thus an extended and sometimes important correspondence may be carried on by the presentation of bouquets, single flowers and even leaves; the charm of this interchange of thought largely consisting in the romance attendant upon an expression of sentiment in a partially disguised and hidden language.

Of course much of the facility with which a conversation may be conducted, thus, will depend upon the intimate knowledge possessed of the language of flowers and the variety from which to select.

ILLUSTRATIONS.

A declaration of feeling between a lady and gentleman may be expressed by single flowers, as follows:

The gentleman presents a Red Rose—"I love you." The lady admits a partial reciprocation of the sentiment by returning a Purple Pansy—"You occupy my thoughts." The gentleman presses his suit still further by an Everlasting Pea—"Wilt thou go with me?" The lady replies by a Daisy, in which she says—"I will think of it." The gentleman, in his enthusiasm, plucks and presents a Shepherd's Purse—"I offer you my all." The lady, doubtingly, returns a sprig of Laurel—"Words, though sweet, may deceive." The gentleman still affirms his declaration by a sprig of Heliotrope—"I adore you." The lady admits a tenderness of sentiment by the Zinnia—"I mourn your absence."

LANGUAGE OF THE BOUQUET.

A collection of flowers in a bouquet may mean very much. Thus a Rose, Ivy and Myrtle will signify "Beauty, Friendship and Love." A Bachelor's Button "Hope," and a Red Rose "Love," will indicate that "I hope to obtain your love."

I DESIRE TO MARRY YOU.
Jonquil—Linden.

I HAVE SWEET MEMORIES IN MY SOLITUDE.
Periwinkle—Heath.

PRAY FOR ME IN MY ABSENCE.
White Verbena—Wormwood.

Thus longer and shorter sentences may be readily expressed by flower-language; and by agreement, if the variety of flowers is not sufficient, a change of definition may be given the more common blossoms and plants, whereby the language and correspondence may be conducted without inconvenience.

Flowers and their Sentiment.

Acacia, Rose ------------ Friendship.
Acanthus --------------- Art.
Adonis, Flos ----------- Painful recollections.
Agnus Castus ----------- Coldness; life without love.
Agrimony --------------- Gratitude.
Almonds ---------------- Giddiness; heedlessness.
Aloe ------------------- Bitterness.
Amaranth --------------- Immortality; Unfading.
Amaryllis -------------- Beautiful but timid.
Anemone, Garden -------- Forsaken; Withered hopes; Illness.
Amethyst --------------- Admiration.
Anemone, Windflower --- Desertion.
Angelica --------------- Inspiration.
Apple Blossom ---------- Preference.
Arbor Vitæ ------------- Unchanging Friendship.
Arbutus ---------------- Thee only do I love.
Ash -------------------- Grandeur.
Aspen ------------------ Sighing.
Asphodel --------------- Remembered beyond the tomb.
Aster, Double German -- Variety.
Aster, Large flowered -- Afterthought; Love of variety.
Bachelors' Button ------ Hope; Single Blessedness.
Balm, Mint ------------- Pleasantry.
Balm of Gilead --------- Healing; I am cured.
Balsamine -------------- Impatience.
Barberry --------------- Petulance; Ill temper.
Basil ------------------ Give me your good wishes.
Bay Leaf --------------- I change but in death.
Beech ------------------ Lovers' tryst; Prosperity.
Begonia ---------------- Deformed.
Bindweed --------------- Humility; Night.
Birch ------------------ Grace; Elegance.
Bittersweet Nightshade - Truth.
Blackthorn, or Sloe ---- Difficulties.
Bladder Tree ----------- Frivolous amusement

Blue Bell -------------- Constancy.
Blue Bottle ------------ Delicacy.
Borage ----------------- Abruptness.
Box -------------------- Stoicism.
Briers ----------------- Envy.
Broom ------------------ Neatness; Humility.
Bryony, Black ---------- Be my support.
Buckbean --------------- Calmness; Repose.
Bugloss ---------------- Falsehood.
Bulrush ---------------- Docility.
Burdock ---------------- Touch me not; Importunity.
Buttercup -------------- Riches; Memories of childhood.
Cabbage ---------------- Profit.
Calla ------------------ Delicacy; Modesty.
Camillia --------------- Gratitude; Perfect Loveliness.
Camomile --------------- Energy in Adversity.
Candytuft -------------- Indifference; Architecture.
Canterbury Bell -------- Constancy.
Cardinal Flower -------- Distinction; Preferment.
Carnation -------------- Pure and deep love.
China Aster ------------ Love of variety.
Cedar Leaf ------------- I live for thee.
Cherry ----------------- A good education.
Chestnut --------------- Do me justice.
Cereus, Night Blooming- Transient Beauty.
Chiccory --------------- Frugality; Economy.
Chrysanthemum ---------- A heart left to desolation.
Cinnamon Tree ---------- Forgiveness of injuries.
Cinquefoil ------------- A beloved daughter.
Cistus ----------------- Surety.
Clover, Red ------------ Industry.
Clematis --------------- Mental Beauty; Artifice.
Clover, White ---------- I promise.
Clover, Four Leaved ---- Be mine.
Cockle ----------------- Vain is beauty without merit.

Coltsfoot -------------- Justice shall be done you.
Columbine, Red -------- Anxious and trembling.
Coreopsis -------------- Always cheerful.
Coriander -------------- Hidden merit.
Corn ------------------- Riches; Abundance.
Cornelian, Cherry ------ Continuance; Duration.
Cowslip ---------------- Native grace; Pensiveness.
Coxcomb ---------------- Foppery.
Crocus ----------------- Cheerfulness.
Cresses ---------------- Stability.
Crowfoot --------------- Ingratitude.
Currant ---------------- Thy frown will kill me
Crown, Imperial -------- Power; Pride of birth
Cucumber --------------- Criticism.
Cypress ---------------- Despair; Mourning.
Dahlia ----------------- Dignity and elegance.
Daffodil --------------- Unrequited love.
Daisy, Garden ---------- I share your feelings.
Daisy, Single Field ---- I will think of it.
Dandelion -------------- Oracle; Coquetry.
Datura ----------------- Deceitful charms.
Dew Plant -------------- Serenade.
Dittany of Crete ------- Birth.
Dodder ----------------- Meanness; Baseness.
Ebony Tree ------------- Blackness.
Eglantine -------------- Poetry; I wound to heal.
Elder ------------------ Compassion.
Elecampane ------------- Tears.
Everlasting ------------ Always remembered.
Everlasting Pea -------- Wilt thou go with me?
Fennel ----------------- Force; Strength.
Fern ------------------- Sincerity.
Fir -------------------- Elevation.
Flax ------------------- I feel your benefits.
Flos, Adonis ----------- Painful recollections.
Forget-me-not ---------- Do not forget.
Foxglove --------------- Insincerity; Occupation.
Fraxinella ------------- Fire.
Fuchsia ---------------- Taste; Frugality.

A DICTIONARY OF THE LANGUAGE AND SENTIMENT OF FLOWERS.

Gentian............Intrinsic worth.
Geranium, Ivy..........I engage you for the next dance.
Geranium, Oak..........A melancholy mind.
Geranium, Rose..........I prefer you.
Geranium, Scarlet......Silliness.
Gillyflower, Common....Lasting Beauty.
Gillyflower, Stock.........Promptness.
Gladiolus..............Ready armed.
Goats' Rue.............Reason.
Gold Basket............Tranquility.
Gooseberry.............Anticipation.
Grape Vine.............Intemperance.
Grass..................Utility; Submission.
Greek Valerian.........Rupture.
Golden Rod.............Encouragement.
Gorse, or Turze........Anger.
Harebell...............Retirement; Grief.
Hawthorn...............Hope.
Hazel..................Reconciliation.
Heath..................Solitude.
Heliotrope.............I adore you; Devotion
Henbane................Blemish; Fault.
Hibiscus...............Delicate beauty.
Hoarhound..............Fire.
Holly..................Am I forgotten? Foresight.
Hollyhock..............Fecundity; Ambition.
Honey Flower...........Sweet and secret love.
Honeysuckle............Devoted love; Fidelity
Hop....................Injustice.
Hornbean...............Ornament.
Horse Chestnut.........Luxury.
Houstania..............Innocence; Content.
Houseleek..............Domestic economy.
Hyacinth...............Constancy; Benevolence.
Hydrangea..............Vain-glory; Heartlessness.
Ice Plant..............Your looks freeze me.
Indian Plum............Privation.
Iris, Common Garden....A message for thee.
Iris, German...........Flame.
Ivy....................Friendship; Marriage
Jasmine, White.........Amiability.
Jasmine, Yellow........Grace and elegance.
Jonquil................Desire; Affection returned.
Jumper.................Asylum; Aid; Protection.
Laburnum...............Pensive beauty.
Ladyslipper............Capricious beauty.
Larch..................Boldness; Audacity.
Larkspur, Pink.........Lightness; Fickleness
Laurel, American.......Words, though sweet, may deceive.
Lantana................Rigor.
Laurel, Mountain.......Glory; Victory; Ambition.
Laurestine.............I die if neglected.
Lavatera...............Sweet disposition.
Lavender...............Mistrust.
Lemon Blossom..........Prudence; Discretion.
Lettuce................Cold hearted; Coolness.
Lichen.................Dejection.
Lilac, Purple..........First emotions of love
Lilac, White...........Youth.
Lily, Water............Eloquence.
Lily, White............Majesty; Purity.
Lily of the Valley.....Return of happiness.
Linden, or Lime........Conjugal; Marriage.
Liverwort..............Confidence.
Locust Tree, Green.....Love beyond the grave
Lotus Leaf.............Recantation.
Lucern.................Life.
Lupine.................Dejection.
Madder.................Calumny.
Magnolia...............Love of Nature.
Maiden Hair............Discretion.
Marjoram...............Blushes.
Manchineel Tree........Falseness.
Mandrake...............Rarity.
Maple..................Reserve.
Marigold...............Sacred affection.
Marigold, Garden.......Grief; Chagrin.
Marigold, Rainy........A storm.
Marigold and Cypress...Despair.
Marshmallow............Beneficence.
Marvel of Peru.........Timidity.
Mayflower..............Welcome.

Meadow Saffron.........My best days are past
Mezercon...............Desire to please.
Mignonette.............Your qualities surpass your charms.
Milfoil................War.
Mint...................Virtue.
Milkweed...............Hope in misery.
Mistletoe..............I surmount everything
Mock Orange............Counterfeit; Uncertainty.
Monkshood..............Treachery; A foe is near.
Morning Glory..........Coquetry; Affection.
Mountain Ash...........I watch over you.
Moss...................Maternal love.
Mourning Bride.........I have lost all.
Mugwort................Good luck; Happiness
Mulberry, Black........I shall not survive you
Mulberry, White........Wisdom.
Mullen.................Good nature.
Mushroom...............Suspicion.
Musk Plant.............Weakness.
Myrtle.................Love in Absence.
Myrrh..................Gladness.
Narcissus..............Egotism; Self-Love.
Nasturtium.............Patriotism; Splendor
Nettle.................Cruelty.
Nightshade.............Dark thoughts; Sorcery.
Oak....................Hospitality; Bravery.
Oleander...............Beware.
Olive..................Peace.
Orange Flower..........Chastity.
Orchis, Bee............Error.
Orchis, Spider.........Skill.
Osier..................Frankness.
Osmunda................Reverie.
Oxalis.................Wood sorrel.
Pansy, Purple..........You occupy my thoughts.
Parsley................Festivity; Banquet.
Passion Flower.........Devotion; Religious fervor.
Peach Blossom..........I am your captive.
Peony..................Ostentation; Anger.
Persimmons.............Bury me amid Nature's beauties.
Peppermint.............Warmth of feeling.
Pennyroyal.............Flee away.
Periwinkle.............Sweet memories.
Phlox..................Our hearts are united.
Pimpernel..............Rendezvous; Change.
Pine...................Endurance; Daring.
Pine Apple.............You are perfect.
Pink, Red..............Pure love.
Plane, or Platane......Genius.
Plum Tree..............Keep your promises.
Plum, Wild.............Independence.
Polyanthus.............Heart's mystery
Pomegranate............Conceit.
Pompion, or Pumpkin....Grossness; Coarseness
Poplar, Black..........Courage.
Poplar, White..........Time.
Poppy, Corn............Consolation.
Poppy, White...........Sleep; Oblivion.
Potatoe................Benevolence.
Primrose...............Modest worth; Silent love.
Privit, or Prim........Prohibition.
Purple Scabious........Mourning.
Queen of the Meadow....Uselessness.
Quince.................Temptation.
Ranunculus, Garden.....You are radiant with charms.
Reeds..................Music.
Rest Harrow............Obstacle.
Rhododendron...........Agitation.
Rhubarb................Advice.
Rosebud................Confession of love.
Rosebud, White.........Too young to love.
Rose, Cinnamon.........Without pretension.
Rose, Hundred leaved...The graces.
Rose, Austrian.........Thou art all that is lovely.
Rose Leaf..............I never trouble.
Rose, Monthly..........Beauty ever new.
Rose, Moss.............Superior merit; Voluptuousness.
Rose, Musk.............Capricious beauty.
Rose, Red..............I love you.
Rose, White............Silence.

Rose, Wild, Single.....Simplicity.
Rose, Yellow...........Infidelity; Unfaithfulness.
Rosemary...............Remembrance; Your presence revives me
Rue....................Disdain.
Rush...................Docility.
Saffron, Meadow........My best days are past.
Saffron, Crocus........Do not abuse me.
Sage...................Domestic Virtue; Esteem.
St. John's Wort........Animosity.
Sardonia...............Irony.
Satin Flower...........Forgetfulness.
Scratch Weed...........Roughness.
Scotch Thistle.........Retaliation.
Sensitive Plant........Sensitiveness; Modesty.
Serpent Cactus.........Horror.
Service Tree, or Sorb..Prudence.
Shepherd's Purse.......I offer you my all.
Silver Weed............Naiveté.
Snapdragon.............Presumption.
Snowball...............Goodness; Thoughts of Heaven.
Snowdrop...............Consolation; A friend in adversity.
Sorrel.................Parental Affection.
Speedwell..............Fidelity.
Spindle Tree...........Your charms are graven on my heart.
Star of Bethlehem......Reconciliation; Purity.
Straw, Broken..........Quarrel.
Straw..................Agreement; United.
Strawberry.............Perfect excellence.
Sumach.................Splendid misery.
Sunflower, Tall........Lofty and wise thoughts.
Sunflower..............False riches.
Sunflower, Dwarf.......Adoration.
Sweet Flag.............Fitness.
Sweet Pea..............A meeting.
Sweet Sultan...........Happiness.
Sweet William..........Gallantry; Finesse; Dexterity.
Syringa................Memory; Fraternal love.
Sycamore...............Curiosity.
Tare...................Vice.
Teasel.................Misanthropy.
Thistle................Austerity.
Thorn Apple............Disguise.
Thrift.................Sympathy.
Thyme..................Activity.
Tremella...............Resistance.
Tube Rose..............Dangerous Pleasure; Voluptuousness; Sweet voice.
Tulip, Variegated......Beautiful eyes.
Tulip, Red.............Declaration of love.
Valerian, Common.......Accommodating disposition.
Valerian...............Facility.
Venus's Looking Glass..Flattery.
Verbena................Sensibility; Sensitiveness.
Verbena, Purple........I weep for you; Regret.
Verbena, White.........Pray for me.
Vervain................Enchantment.
Vernal Grass...........Poor, but happy.
Vetch..................I cling to thee.
Violet, Blue...........Faithfulness.
Violet, White..........Purity; Candor; Modesty.
Volkamenia.............May you be happy.
Wall Flower............Fidelity in misfortune.
Weeping Willow.........Melancholy.
Wheat..................Wealth.
Whortleberry...........Treachery.
Willow, Common.........Forsaken.
Willow Herb............Pretension.
Wood Sorrel............Joy.
Woodbine...............Fraternal love.
Wormwood...............Absence.
Yarrow.................Cure for the heartache.
Yew....................Sadness.
Zinnia.................I mourn your absence.

Speeches for Various Occasions.

FORMS OF ADDRESSES

SUITABLE FOR

Introductions, Inaugurations, Valedictories, Celebrations, Funerals, Reunions, Banquets, Anniversary Exercises, Fairs, Commencements, Improvement Meetings, Etc.

SUGGESTIONS FOR BEGINNERS.

The Fourth of July Oration.

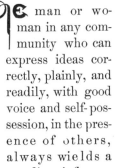

The man or woman in any community who can express ideas correctly, plainly, and readily, with good voice and self-possession, in the presence of others, always wields a commanding influence—provided this accomplishment is guided by good judgment, which teaches *when* to speak, *where* to speak, *what* to speak, and *how* to speak.

The art which enables an individual, when standing on the feet, to express a thought methodically and clearly to an intelligent and critical audience, in a manner such as will influence and instruct the auditors, is one very much to be desired. Can it be acquired by the average individual? The consideration of that question is the purpose of the following chapters.

MANY people who have an ambition for public speaking do not awake to the necessity and importance of this subject until the period of their school-days has long passed, when the conviction is likely to force itself upon their minds that they are too late to acquire the art. Such, however, should not be discouraged. To begin practice in extempore speaking, establish a debating club, which should include a membership of half a dozen or more persons, to meet regularly during the week, at stated times, for the discussion of current topics of the day, either at a private residence, some hall chosen for the purpose, or at a schoolroom; the exercises of the occasion being interspersed with essays by members of the club, the whole to be criticised by critics appointed. A few weeks thus spent will oftentimes develop in the club several fluent essayists and speakers.

If desirous of distinction, it is not enough that the speakers simply utter their own thoughts. There should be especial effort made to present the idea in an original, attractive and efficient form. To be effective, the speaker must exhibit variety in gesture, tone of voice, and method of illustration. Gestures and sentences should be gracefully rounded; the illustrations, in strong and telling words, should be so proportioned, and the arguments so arranged, as to grow stronger from the beginning to the end; while the thoughts should be so presented as to be appropriate, and in harmony with the occasion.

The speakers and essayists whom we know as wielding the greatest influence in the world's history, added to these graces of oratory depth of investigation, independence of thought, and freedom of expression. They scorned to traverse the beaten paths, simply because of custom and popularity. They chose to be independent. Rather than follow, they preferred to lead the opinion of others.

The following suggestions give an outline of what is necessary for the production of a ready, easy speaker.

The Cambridge Literary Club in Session.

THIS Society, organized for the purpose of Social, Literary and Oratorical Culture, meets weekly at the residence of its members.

ORDER OF EXERCISES:—Calling meeting to order by President; Roll Call and Reading Minutes of previous meeting by Secretary; Music; Recitation; Essay, by a member selected at previous meeting, which takes fifteen minutes to read. · Four critics, appointed by the President, make each a five minutes' talk upon the subject of the essay; Music. *Recess of Ten Minutes.*

Twenty minutes devoted to reading, by the editress, of the "Vanguard," the paper of the club, composed largely of contributions from different members of the society; Announcement, by the President, of subject for debate; Four debaters consume each five minutes in discussing the subject; Music; Announcement of time, place and Essayist for next meeting; adjournment.

The foregoing programme of exercises is subject to variation according to vote of a majority of the club, or as the President may think best.

First. The foundation of the discourse should be thoroughly fixed in the mind, and the order of succession in which the arguments are to follow.

Second. These should be so arranged that one thought should be the natural outgrowth of the other, and each idea should be so distinctly marked out as to be in readiness the moment it is wanted.

Third. The speaker should vividly feel all that he may design to speak, in order that clear ideas may be expressed. The mind should not, however, be so absorbed with the subject in hand as to prevent its acting readily in the development of the topic under consideration. It is possible for the feelings to become so vehement in their expression as to paralyze utterance from their very fullness.

Fourth. The feelings, in speaking, must be resolved into ideas, thought into images, to express which there must be suitable language. While the main idea should be firmly grasped, in its elucidation it should be separated into its principal members, and these again divided into subordinate parts, each under perfect command of the speaker, to be called upon and used at will, until the subject is exhausted.

Fifth. The full, complete and ready use of the imagination is of the greatest importance to the extemporaneous speaker, which power may be greatly cultivated by reading the works of Walter Scott, Dickens, and other standard writers who excel in imaginative description. To hold up before the audience a clear, distinct outline of the subject in hand, and paint the picture in fitting language so vividly that the auditors will delightedly follow its progress, step by step, is the distinguishing excellence of the off-hand speaker. With many persons of real talent, the powers of imagination work too slowly to hold the attention of the audience. This hindrance, however, can be largely overcome by practice.

Sixth. The difficulty of embarrassment, which afflicts some people upon public appearance, is overcome by practice, and by having a perfectly distinct understanding of what is to be said, which consciousness tends to give confidence and self-possession. To obtain the ability to present this clear conception of the subject, the speaker should study logic, geometry, and kindred subjects, that arrive at conclusions through a process of analytical reasoning. The speaker should be able to think methodically, being able to decompose his thoughts into parts, to analyze these into their elements, to recompose, regather, and concentrate these again in a manner such as will clearly illustrate the idea sought to be conveyed.

Fig. I—The Dandy
Who fails on the Platform because the diamond and fancy clothing detract attention of the hearers, and convey the impression that he gives more thought to dress than he does to ideas.

Fig. 2—Solid Man
Whose unostentatious yet substantial appearance is so much in his favor, when before an audience, as to make him a person of very considerable power, however little he may say.

Seventh. One of the most efficient aids to public speaking is the ability to write. The public speaker will do well to commence by writing in full what he is desirous of saying. He should, at the same time, make a study of the various masters of oratory. Writing gives great clearness to the expression of thought, and, having plenty of time in its composition, the mind is able to look at the subject in every phase. With the main idea clearly defined and kept constantly in view, let the speaker examine the subject in every light, the different faculties of the mind concentrating upon a single point. Thus, step by step, the subject is considered in all its bearings, the various details of the idea being completely studied, and the whole matter thoroughly developed, until the subject has reached its perfect form.

Eighth. The daily study of synonymous words and their meanings will give greater facility of expression. The mind should also be stored with a variety of information on subjects pertaining to the arts and sciences, from which one can constantly draw in cases of emergency. It is impossible for the speaker to extemporize what is not in the mind. And, further, all reading and study should be done with such care that every idea thus acquired will be so thoroughly impressed on the mind as to be available when we wish to communicate our ideas to others.

Ninth. In public speaking, one of the great secrets of success is a knowledge of human nature. To acquire this, the speaker should carefully study men—the passions and impulses that influence mankind—their phrenological characteristics, and know them as they are. To do this, he should freely mingle in society, interchanging ideas, and seeking every opportunity for the practice of extempore speaking.

Tenth. An important element necessary to success in the off-hand speaker is courage. While it is essential that he use choice and fitting language in the expression of ideas, let him not hesitate, when he has commenced a sentence, because he cannot readily call to mind the exact language necessary to beautifully clothe the thought. Push vigorously through to the end, even though at a sacrifice, for a time, of the most perfect forms of speech. This courage that dare stand up and speak a sentence ungrammatically, even, is necessary to make the good speaker of the future.

Finally, while all cannot become equally proficient in oratory, the industrious student of average talent, who earnestly resolves to win success as an extempore speaker, will find himself, in the majority of cases, in time, self-possessed in the presence of others. With ideas clear and distinct, vivified and quickened by imagination, clothed in fitting words and beautiful language, he will be enabled to instruct and entertain an audience in a manner vastly better than most people would suppose who may have listened to his maiden efforts in the commencement of his public speaking.

Instruction and Practice in Elocution.

Facts relative to Oratory, Eloquence, Expression, Gesture and Personal Appearance.

AS MEN began to multiply upon the earth, the uses of language increased and assumed new expressions in accordance with the desires and needs of individuals. Thus, affection required one tone of voice and one collection of words and phrases especially adapted to its communications. The voice of petition gave utterance to another class of tones and sentences expressive of its wishes. Anger, and fear, and hope, and every sentiment common to humanity, each found a rhetoric of its own, of such a distinctive character that it could not be easily mistaken for another. The cry of grief, the exultation of joy, differed then, as now, as widely as the East from the West, and the ear conveyed to the brain the peculiar sound of each. By-and-bye, when savage-life gave way to civilization, new sentiments were born, and nature and custom have given language to all.

In the calm home-life the voice is modulated

Fig. I.—Careless,
Ungainly and slovenly in appearance, consequently lacks the power to favorably impress his hearers as a public speaker, although he may possess real talent of a high order.

Fig. 2. —Orderly,
Self-poised, genteelly dressed, and has large influence with his auditors, because of fine personal presence, though he may lack the genius that makes the finished orator.

to sweetness and the earnestness of true confidence. In the school, in the various trades and occupations of men, in the halls of legislation, in the courts, on the platform, in the pulpit, and in the drama, nature and art have established utterances greatly diversified. Language has thus become a power in our human existence, and on the lips of the orator can sway the nations, as the winds awaken and arouse the sleeping ocean.

The human voice has been created an instrument in which are united the melody of the flute, the violin and the organ. The lungs supply the air, and the throat and nostrils serve as pipes for the construction of sweet sounds, producing tunes and all the changes of expression required by every consonant and vowel, and by every varying sentiment. So perfect is this arrangement for the formation of language, that rapid speakers are enabled to pronounce from 7,000 to 7,500 words an hour, or about two words in a second.

The art of correct and impressive speaking embraces elocution, oratory, eloquence, rhetoric, emotion, feeling, agitation, and logic, or the power of demonstration.

Elocution is the correct method of giving utterance to a connected discourse, either long or brief, before an audience, accompanied with appropriate gestures.

Oratory is the highest degree of elocution, and is the art of presenting a subject in its most effective and eloquent manner.

Eloquence is the expression of a great degree of emotion, whether pleasurable or sad, with such earnestness and skill as to excite a similar emotion in the breasts of the audience. With fervency and fluency it utters the most elevating thoughts in the choicest language, and with the most appropriate and graceful movements of the entire physical organization.

Rhetoric is the art of framing correct, forceful and elegant sentences, either in writing or speaking, and these may, on the lips of an acknowledged orator, supply the place of genuine emotion. Rhetoric may thus become an artificial eloquence, conveying powerful sentiments which the speaker may not feel in his heart. A true actor on the stage, or platform, may become so perfect in the rhetoric of his performance as to represent the

Disadvantages in Public Speaking.

THE above illustration shows the following unfavorable conditions for the speaker.

1. If in the day-time, the light in the hall, coming wholly from windows in the rear of the speaker, throws a shadow whereby his face cannot be seen.

2. If in the night, the unshaded lights, in the vicinity of the speaker, upon which the audience are compelled to look, will pain the eyes and divert attention of the hearers.

3. The disordered condition of maps, pictures, etc., upon the wall will annoy and hold the attention of some auditors who have large order and are keenly sensitive to disorder.

4. The holding of the manuscript by the speaker, in front of his face, will break the magnetic connection between himself and hearers, and then the audience will become listless and inattentive.

5. The balustrade and table in front of the speaker prevent the effect that may be exerted upon an audience by gesture and posture of the lower limbs.

6. The seating of a small audience in the rear of a hall gives an empty appearance to the room, alike depressing to speaker and hearers.

7. The scattering of an audience apart breaks magnetic conditions that are favorable to a speaker when the audience is seated closely together and near the platform.

8. Members of the audience communicating one with another, reading newspapers, moving about the room, or going out, make conditions unfavorable to the speaker and those who would listen to the discourse.

most varied and strongest emotions of human nature without experiencing them.

Emotion, Feeling, and **Agitation** are varying results of true oratory, and are produced by the eloquence of the speaker. Emotion is a mental excitement, inducing pity, grief, fear, joy, enthusiasm, or other natural passions. Feeling applies to a sympathetic condition of either mind or body, and is manifested with less excitement than emotion. Agitation is the violence of intense excitement, arising from physical or mental disorder.

Logic is the art of reasoning systematically upon any subject, and embraces its cause, progress and effect. "Pure logic" is the formal expression, governed by general rules, of any idea that may present itself. "Applied logic" is the application of this method and these rules to any specific topic on which an argument is proposed. Logic was first used as a form of reasoning by Aristotle, the great Greek philosopher, who, indeed, gave form and character to the principles and practice of public speaking.

Aristotle divided oratory into three classes, as follows:

The Demonstrative, which embraces praise in a high degree, as eulogies of great men; censure, reproach, or severe accusation against individuals, the acts of public bodies, or of governments; philosophic addresses, etc.

The Deliberative, which includes debates on subjects of national or district importance, in the halls of legislation or other public places, educational or moral lectures, etc.

The Judicial, which relates to the oratory of the courts of justice, where cases are pleaded or defended under the rules of current law practice.

All of these classes admit of the purest and most brilliant elocutionary efforts. Aristotle also classified rhetoric into three distinct parts—persuasion, expression, and arrangement. In *persuasion*, the orator presents himself, his motives, and the object of his discourse, in a persuasive attitude, with the design of obtaining the confidence of his hearers. In *expression* he treats of the arguments to be advanced in support of his object, and in this division he exemplifies the use of logic as a means of making his arguments clear and strengthening them. In *arrangement*, he teaches the proper method of presenting the argument, arranging propositions in the most effective manner, delivering them in appropriate language, and enforcing them with suitable and impressive gestures.

Conditions Favorable for the Public Speaker.

THE following arrangements in a hall favor the speaker, who would have the best conditions by which he may have influence with an audience.

1. The stand used for manuscript should occupy as little room upon the platform as possible.

2. All lights in the vicinity of the speaker, or upon the platform, should be so shaded that the audience cannot see them.

3. If convenient, the auditors upon the platform should be so seated that the speaker can occasionally turn and address them also.

4. The less the speaker is confined to manuscript, if thoroughly conversant with the subject, the better will be the effect of his speech with the audience.

5. The speaker should be carefully and well dressed, but not in the extreme of fashion. A Prince-Albert or dress-coat becomes the platform speaker who would appear to the best advantage before a fashionable audience.

6. The front part of the platform should have nothing upon it that can obstruct the view of the entire figure of the speaker. The position of the feet and lower part of the body frequently have much to do in enforcing an idea when accompanied by suitable words.

7. A large audience, a congregation well dressed, a handsomely furnished hall, an audience composed of the most respectable and influential in the community, and who give close attention—all these are favoring conditions, calculated to assist the public speaker in making a good impression.

In Oratory, the features and the hands perform an important part, introducing illustrations of the topic under discussion, emphasizing the language as it varies

"From grave to gay, from lively to severe,"

and vividly depicting each emotion or passion as it is indicated by the tongue.

True oratory springs from the impulses of the inner life as affected by outward circumstances, and the true orator is " a man terribly in earnest." Such a speaker needs no manuscript to aid him in his discourse. Observe the impassioned eloquence of Patrick Henry, on the eve of the American Revolutionary war:

"There is no retreat but in submission and slavery. Our chains are forged! Their clanking may be heard on the plains of Boston...The next gale that sweeps from the North will bring to our ears the clash of resounding arms! ...I know not what course others may take; but as for me,—give me liberty, or give me death!"

That was *natural oratory*, and no studied composition could carry with it the eloquence and power of these few simple sentences.

The man who is confined to his manuscript composition on the platform is not an orator—he is only a *reader*. In this respect he lacks freedom of gesture, and is unable to face his audience and allow them to see the varying emotions caused by his subject reflected in his features.

How differently does the true orator appear! Untrammeled on the platform by papers, he stands before his audience in the dignity of human nature, every feature enlivened by the thoughts that fill his brain, a clear, ringing voice to give them expression, and body and limbs all alive with harmonious and touching gestures. Such a man is a power in the land, for good or evil, swaying the masses, pleading the cause he advocates with earnestness, fidelity and eloquence, and leaving the impress of his intellect upon the minds and hearts of his hearers.

The distinguishing mechanical features of a finished address are distinct articulation, inflections, accent, emphasis, modulation and gesture.

Articulation is the art of using the vocal organs, including the teeth, with such ease and perfection that every portion of a word or sentence is distinctly uttered, every vowel and consonant fully pronounced, and no words or letters clipped off, as it were, or omitted from any sentence. Beginners, especially children, in their haste to get through a sentence, when "speaking a piece," often do this in a very ridiculous manner, but no finished orator is guilty of the practice. In the sentence, "He could pay nobody," the words, by careless speaking become, "He could pain nobody." This example will serve to show the necessity of a clear enunciation of every word and syllable, lest the entire passage be changed and its sense destroyed.

Inflection is a slide, or a change of the voice. The monotone is devoid of any rising or falling changes; hence the term "monotonous" is ap-

Fig. 1—Bashfulness. Fig. 2—Self-possession.

The above illustrations represent the effect of practice and culture. While speaker No. 1, by his unpolished manner and diffidence, is an object of pity or ridicule, as a public speaker, No. 2, representing a well-known orator, as he apostrophizes a glass of water, entrances his audience by his self-possession, his earnestness, and his naturalness.

plied to a continuous flow of words in a single tone of voice. Still, the monotone, as the expression of great sublimity of thought, is sometimes used by the best orators and readers. While it may serve to express earnestness, it does not convey the idea of deep emotion.

The rising inflection may start a sentence with a monotone, but becomes louder and more significant as it proceeds. It is strongly marked in the asking of a question, as: "Where were you yesterday?"—throwing the emphasis on "yesterday," with a gradual raising of the voice.

The falling inflection begins with a high tone of voice and ends the sentence in a moderate one; for example: "Yesterday I stayed at home," answering the question and emphasizing "yesterday," also, because that word covered the principal object in asking the question.

The circumflex tone begins with the falling inflection and ends with the rising one, as: "I went out *yesterday*, but I stay here *to-day*,"—"to-day" elevated.

The word *or* in the sentence: "Will you stay —or go?"—throws the rising inflection on "stay," and the falling on "go."

In the negative sentence: "Study not for recreation, but for instruction," the rising inflection is on the affirmative, "instruction," while "recreation" has the falling tone.

Affection or tender emotion requires the rising inflection, coupled with softness: "Then spake the father, Come hither, my child."

These inflections enter into all the expressions of the human voice, ever varying, according to the sentiment to be promulgated. Nature teaches them and frames their utterances, while art acquires and simulates them on the stage, on the platform, in the pulpit, in the halls of legislation, or in the legal tribunal.

Accent is a peculiar force of the voice displayed in the pronunciation of a particular syllable in a word, or a particular word in a sentence, to make it more effective. A variety of English words have two or more accentuations. Thus the word "ac-cent," in the sense here used, has the accent on the first syllable —"ac"; but if we say that such a word should be accented, the "cent" is most strongly pronounced.

Emphasis is a stronger expression given to the utterance of a word or sentence, for the purpose of impressing it upon the mind, than can be given by inflection or accent alone; requiring elevation of tone, indicating either earnestness or emotion, or calling attention to some peculiarity of thought or argument advanced by the speaker. In writing, the emphasized word is usually underscored; in type, it is put in *italic* letters.

Modulation is the natural or acquired melodious form of utterance to suit the sentiment with musical precision. Indeed, modulation is a feature of music as well as of elocution, giving sweetness of tone and variation to the voice. It combines articulation, inflection, accent and emphasis, and enriches the entire discourse with harmony of expression.

Gesture is any natural movement of the limbs or body that indicates the character of the prevailing feeling or emotion of the heart. It appeals at once to our sympathies with far greater eloquence than words, and when combined with oratory makes the latter more effective. Without proper gestures, an orator loses much of his power to control the thoughts and opinions of his auditors; they add to the earnestness of his expressions, increasing his eloquence, and carrying conviction with every proposition advanced. In real oratory the eye speaks as well as the lips; the motions of the arms, and hands, and head, and body, are all brought into subjection to the dominant argument, and the grace and dignity of the human form are exhibited in all their

brilliancy. "Hamlet's" advice to the players —"Suit the word to the action, and the action to the word," is worth heeding. A downward movement of the arm or hand at a rising inflection would be but a burlesque.

Volume is the character of the voice as determined by the utterance of various emotions, in which the throat expands or contracts, producing whispers, wailings, etc., and is expressive of the inward emotion, whatever it may be.

Time is a slight pause made by the speaker, with the design of giving an opportunity to consider the importance of the word or phrase to which he would call specific attention.

Pitch represents the proper elevation of the voice, and its use in elocution is to regulate the tone of the discourse to its character. If not regarded as it should be, the delivery becomes faulty and disagreeable.

Force applies to the energy which is given to certain words and phrases, as expressive of the earnestness with which they should be received. It is *mental emphasis*, laying stress, in degrees, upon whatever is uttered.

Avoid talking through the nose and getting into a sing-song strain of delivery. Do not take the other extreme and become too grand in language for the subject. Speak of common things naturally, distinctly and intelligently. Do not use great, swelling words, chosen from the dictionary, for the sake of "showing off." The Anglo-Saxon tongue is filled with short, expressive words—words of one or two syllables, that point a sentence with wit and eloquence better than a flow of dissyllables.

Pitch the tone of voice no higher than is necessary to reach the ears of the person farthest from you in the audience, but be sure that it reaches its limit without losing its distinctness. In this lay one of the strongest features of the eloquence of the lamented Wendell Phillips.

Oratory should express in the features, the position of the body, and the movements of the head and limbs, the emotions which govern the utterances of the speaker, as indicated in the figures, explanations and examples which follow:

FACIAL EXPRESSION AND GESTURE.

As Illustrated by Drawings Prepared Expressly for this Work.

FOR THE purpose of setting clearly before the student in elocution and oratory the gesture, posture, and expression of face appropriate to the delineation of an emotion or thought of the mind the accompanying illustrations are given.

They are prepared by us from attitudes representing Prof. Walter C. Lyman, a teacher of elocution and voice culture in Chicago, who has graduated from his classes many superior readers, several of whom have been successful in attracting to themselves upon the stage much attention, because of their faithful rendition of character.

Following these fourteen illustrations, representing the Professor in various attitudes, are twelve representations by Miss Mamie T. Short, of Chicago, a pupil of Professor Lyman's.

Much care has been taken in the production of these illustrations to truthfully represent natural posture, and a correct, clearly defined expression of the face, when actuated by passion, sentiment, or emotion. To the multitude of students in the field of elocutionary study, these examples from life will be invaluable as giving needed instruction in this important art.

An interesting study is found in the contrasts of the appearance of the individual when representing these various sentiments and emotions.

While Dignity expresses manhood in its self-possessed and energetic mood, Fear cringes and shrinks, and trembles, and the two serve to show the effect of inward emotions upon the outer man. Expectation displays eagerness, hope and forwardness of purpose, while Horror reverses the *pose* and the expression, with shrinking, repulsive movements.

Supplication exhibits desire and humility, while Despair indicates the absence of all emotions but one —the sense of loss in its most extreme form. Other contrasts are shown in the following:

Unexcited.

Weeping—Violent Grief.

ALL the muscles of the features, limbs and body are relaxed; the eyes assume a mild and quiet expression; the brow is expanded and unwrinkled; the arms and hands hang idly by the side; one foot is slightly advanced, but the body rests lightly upon both; the voice is natural and cheerful, as illustrated in the following example:

LADIES AND GENTLEMEN—In compliance with the request of the publishers of this work, I herewith submit to you the following illustrations as representations of the gesture, posture and facial expression, indicative of the emotion, thought, or sentiment, which may stir the heart under varying circumstances.

The highest degree of power by the orator is attained when burning words, born of the time and appropriate to the occasion, are accompanied by natural and graceful gesture.

THE head droops, inclining to one side; the eyes overflow with tears; the lips and countenance are drawn downward; the body inclines forward; the hands are wrung; the lower limbs are relaxed and retiring; the movements are slow, and the voice low, unless the grief is excessive, and the breath comes and goes with agitation, broken by moans and sobs.

EXAMPLE—"Oh, my sorrow is more than I can bear!

My wife, my child, all gone—wrecked—swallowed in the great deep, and that too, when I was so anxiously watching—waiting their coming; and they so near the land!

A few hours more I would have clasped them to my heart. Alas, that the storm should rise when they, in glad anticipation, were so near their haven, and so near the husband's and father's arms!"

IN this illustration, representing the emotion of **Love**, the whole being is subdued, the head and body inclining forward; the forehead is tranquil; the eyebrows droop; the eye sparkles with affection; the palm of the right hand is pressed over the heart, and the left hand, with open fingers, is folded over the right wrist; the lower limbs stand together in easy position, with the right foot in advance; the voice is low and musical, and often there is an air of melancholy thought.

Love.

EXAMPLE—"I love you, Margery dear, because you are young and fair,
For your eyes' bewild'ring blueness, and the gold of your curling hair.
No queen has hands that are whiter, no lark has a voice so sweet,
And your ripe young lips are redder than the clover at our feet.
My heart will break with its fullness, like a cloud o'ercharged with rain,
Oh!—tell me, Margery darling, how long must I love in vain?"

THE head is either erect or thrown slightly back, in **Laughter** and **Mirth**; the forehead is smooth; the eyes are partly closed and full of cheerful expression, sometimes filled with tears of joy; the mouth is open and extended; the shoulders are elevated; the elbows are spread, the hands resting on the sides of the body below the waist; and the voice is loud and joyous in tone. Should the mirth, however, be inward and silent, the form is convulsed with emotion, as in the expression of grief.

Laughter—Mirth.

EXAMPLE—"So he took me for a Priest, did he?
Ha! Ha!! Ha!!! Ha!!!!
Couldn't he tell the difference between a saint and a sinner?
Ha! Ha!! Ha!!! Ha!!!!
Why, that man don't know the difference between his heels and his head,
Ha! Ha!! Ha!!! Ha!!!!"

THE height of enthusiasm, the wildness of **Madness** or insanity, the struggle going on within, are manifested in this character. The head is dishevelled and uneasy; the arms and hands are moved about—now pressing the head, now thrown convulsively from it. Every movement of the body is irregular, rapid and reckless; the eyes, with fearful effect, turn uneasily from object to object, dwelling on none; the countenance is distorted, and the world is a blank.

Madness—Insanity.

EXAMPLE—"Mark how yon demon's eyeballs glare.
He sees me; now, with dreadful shriek,
He whirls a serpent high in air.
Horror! the reptile strikes its tooth
Deep in my heart, so crushed and sad.
Aye, laugh, ye fiends, I feel the truth,
Your work is done—I'm mad!—I'm mad!!"

FIRST, in **Horror**, the head is thrown forward, then upward, and then drawn back; the eyes, with fierce expression, stare wildly at the object; the countenance is distorted and affrighted; the form is contracted and half-turned away from the object; the lower limbs droop and are slightly thrown apart; the elbows are thrust out from the body; the hands are raised and open, with the palms outward, while the fingers seem contracted; and the voice is an excited half-whisper.

Horror.

EXAMPLE—"Which of you have done this?
Avaunt and quit my sight! Let the earth hide thee!
Thy bones are marrowless, thy blood is cold;
Thou hast no speculation in those eyes,
Which thou dost glare with.
Hence, horrible shadow!
Unreal mockery, hence!"

UNDER a feeling of **Disgust**, the head and body are turned away from the object; the lower limbs are parted, with the feet at right angles, the left being advanced; the forehead and the eyebrows are contracted; the mouth is slightly open; the eyes indicate the feeling within; the left hand is held partly in front of the face, with the fingers extended and the palm outward, as if pushing away the hated object, while the tongue utters a short and sharp guttural exclamation.

Disgust.

EXAMPLE—" She did not all too early die....
Unchecked the course of true love ran;
I married my Louisa Ann.
There the romance, however, ends;
Dear reader, you and I are friends!
You don't *like* my Louisa Ann—
No more do I—I never *can !*"

WHEN the individual is moved with **Anger**, the head is erect; the eye burns and flashes; the lips are compressed; the brows contracted, the nostrils are distended; the body is convulsed with passion, the fists are clinched; and the lower limbs are spread, with one foot strongly planted in advance of the other; the voice is either low or suppressed, or harsh, loud and quick; the whole appearance indicates agitation, fierceness and conflict, and every movement indicates energy.

Anger.

EXAMPLE—" Now imitate the action of the tiger,
Stiffen the sinews, summon up the blood;
Lend fierce and dreadful aspect to the eye,
Set the teeth close, and stretch the nostrils wide;
Hold hard the breath,
And bend up every spirit to its full height. "
" In the contempt and anger of his lip. "

IMBUED with **Earnestness**, the entire form stands erect; the brow is expanded; the eyes express sincerity and a desire to convince the hearers of the truth and importance of the subject under discussion; the chest is thrown well forward; the lower limbs are slightly parted, with the feet at right angles; the left arm is extended, with open hand; the right hand is closed, and the voice is full and distinct, and moderate or elevated, as the theme or the feelings may suggest.

Earnestness.

EXAMPLE—" Ye call me chief; and ye do well to call him chief, who for twelve long years has met upon the arena every shape of man or beast the broad empire of Rome could furnish, and who never yet lowered his arm. If there be one among you who can say that ever, in public fight or private brawl, my actions did belie my tongue, let him stand forth, and say it. If there be three in all your company dare face me on the bloody sands, let them come on. "

WITH the sense of **Dignity**, or self-valuation, the head is held erect, or thrown slightly back; the form is straightened and raised to its fullest height; the forehead is expanded; the eyebrows are raised; the eyes indicate a subdued fierceness; the lips are compressed, and the countenance firm; the arms are folded across the chest, or the left hand is thrust into the bosom; the lower limbs are straight and together, with the feet at right angles; the movements are slow and methodical.

Dignity.

EXAMPLE—" I am a Roman citizen....Here,in your capital,do I defy you. Have I not conquered your armies, fired your towns, and dragged your generals at my chariot wheels, since first my youthful arms could wield a spear? And do you think to see me crouch and cower before a tamed and shattered senate? The tearing of flesh and rending of sinews is but pastime compared with the mental agony that heaves my frame. "

EXCITED with joyous **Expectation,** the chin is thrown forward; the eyes open, and beaming with anticipation, are directed towards the desired object; the countenance and lips express earnestness; the body inclines towards the object; the hands are clasped; one foot is advanced; the movements are slow and graceful; the voice is cheerful and moderate; the forehead is unwrinkled, and the expression, not only of the countenance, but of the whole being, is pleasing.

Expectation.

EXAMPLE—"There has fallen a splendid tear
        From the passion-flower at the gate.
        She is coming, my dove, my dear:
        She is coming, my life, my fate;
        The red rose cries, 'She is near, she is near;'
        The larkspur listens, 'I hear, I hear,'
        And the lily whispers, 'I wait.'"

BORNE down with a feeling of **Despair,** the head is bowed, the chin resting upon the breast; the eyebrows are depressed; the eyes are rolled downward and express agony; the muscles of the face are convulsed and tremulous; the mouth is opened; the nostrils are expanded; the hands are tightly clasped, or wrung as if in pain; the teeth gnash; the body sways violently to and fro; the voice, if heard at all, is little better than a groan, and the breath is a succession of sighs.

Despair.

EXAMPLE—"O my offence is rank, it smells to heaven;
        It hath the primal eldest curse upon 't,
        A brother's murder!—Pray I cannot,
        Though inclination be as sharp as will;
        My stronger guilt defeats my strong intent;
        And, like a man to double business bound,
        I halt in pause where I shall first begin."

DISTRACTED by **Fear,** the head is thrown forward, especially the chin; the eyes stare wildly at the object; then turn away; the shoulders are elevated; the body shrinks and contracts; the lower limbs are relaxed and droop, with one foot thrown back; the hands are contracted, with the palms outward, in front of the breast; there is a convulsive motion of the chest, the breathing is explosive, and the voice is rapid, high and broken. Fear causes the form and limbs to contract.

Fear.

EXAMPLE—"In thoughts from the visions of the night, when deep sleep falleth on men, fear came upon me, and trembling, which made all my bones to shake. Then a spirit passed before my face; the hair of my flesh stood up; it stood still, but I could not discern the form thereof; an image was before my eyes; there was silence, and I heard a voice saying, Shall mortal man be more just than God?—shall a man be more pure than his Maker?"

IN the act of **Supplication,** the head is held back; the eyes, lips and countenance express earnestness; the body is bent forward; the hands are either spread heavenward, are clasped, or wrung, in intense emotion; one or both knees are bent to the ground; the movements are still or restless, according to the condition of the mind, and the voice is regulated by the same influence—sometimes slow, moderately fast, low and pleading, or high and exultant with praise and thanksgiving.

Supplication.

EXAMPLE—"'Gitchie Manito, the mighty,'
        Cried he, with his face uplifted,
        In that bitter hour of anguish; 'give your children food,
        O Father!—
        Give us food, or we must perish;
        Give me food for Minnehaha!
        For my dying Minnehaha!'"

RESULTS OF HIGHER CIVILIZATION.

THE civilization of the age is signalized by the advancement of woman to a higher plane of thought and action than she formerly occupied. Among the savage nations, woman's condition is that of the very lowest; in the semi-civilized countries she is largely regarded as fit only for menial labor, and even in civilized Europe, to-day, among the lower classes, the woman, harnessed with a dog, transports a large share of the produce to market, and in the same manner she serves as a creature of burden in scavenger and other work.

Only back to the first of this century, among the most intelligent of our best society in America and Europe, woman was thought unworthy and incompetent to perform work requiring any great degree of intellectuality. She was permitted to teach primary schools at a very low salary; beyond that, very few intellectual pursuits were open to her outside of literature.

Gradually, however, woman has beaten her way to the front, in spite of ridicule, jealousy and opposition. College trustees have resisted the opening of their doors to her; the managers of higher institutions of learning have opposed the idea of employing her as the superintendent of their schools. Physicians have fought against her invading their domain. Churchgoers have insisted that they would never listen to a woman-preacher. Lawyers have laughed at the suggestion that she might enter their profession, and judges in authority have refused her admission to practice in certain courts.

But the march of progress has been forward, and the intelligent sentiment of the age has demanded that woman be allowed to enter any pursuit, the work of which she could perform just as well as men. The result has been the filling of hundreds of clerkships in the Treasury Department at Washington with women, very satisfactorily to the government and all parties concerned. Large numbers have entered the postal service, holding various important positions. Thousands have gone into the educational field, and as teachers, managers, and heads of academies, seminaries, and advanced public schools, have demonstrated both business capacity and intellectual talent of a high order.

A large percentage of women are successfully engaged in mercantile pursuits. She is well represented in the medical profession, she is fast entering the pulpit, and the time is not far distant when on the platform, whether engaged in general lecture, moral teaching, political discussion, or legal argument, she will be found the exponent of truth and co-worker with man in reform. And while all this transpires she will be no less the kind mother, and the devoted, faithful wife.

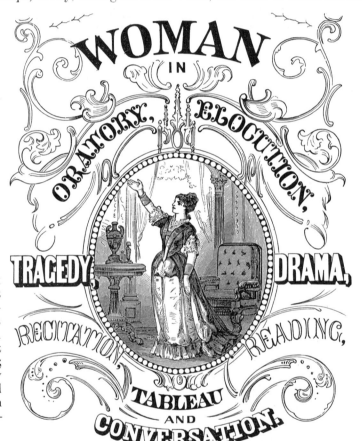

IN the illustration of **Dignified Repose**, the position is erect, quiet and graceful; the right foot is a little in advance of the left; the right arm and hand listlessly pend at the side, with the left forearm resting easily upon a book or table; all the muscles are relaxed; the eyes express tranquillity; the forehead is free from lines of care; the voice is subdued, but natural and cheerful, and the whole appearance of the individual evinces inward and outward contentment.

Dignified Repose.

EXAMPLE—"DEAR LADIES: With the multitude of ignorant people about us who need education, shall we not lend our assistance towards making the world wiser and better? To do this we should make the most of the privileges presented through the power of language; but to give words their greatest effect, these arts, including tone of voice, facial expression and gesture, must be studied and mastered, if we would use language to the best advantage."

BOTH feet, in **Anger**, are firmly planted apart upon the floor; the upper part of the form and head energetically incline forward; the forehead contracts; the eyebrows lift; the eyes fiercely flash; the arms rigidly stretch down the sides, with the hands clinched; the breath comes quick and heavily; the voice is shrill and harsh. The emotion of anger, under a sense of personal injury, may develop into resentment or revenge, and become furious or sullen, according to temperament.

Anger.

EXAMPLE—" Smile on, my lords!
I scorn to count what feelings, withered hopes,
Strong provocations, bitter, burning wrongs,
I have within my heart's hot cells shut up,
To leave you in your lazy dignities;
But here I stand and scoff you! here I fling
Hatred and full defiance in your face!"

EVERY indication of **Laughter** is represented here. The face, beaming with wreathed smiles, is slightly elevated; the form is sprightly and elastic, and convulsed with joyousness; the right arm and hand are extended, with the open palm turned towards the object of ridicule; the mouth opens widely to give vent to laughter, and the voice is loud and musical with gayety. Laughter is also a peculiar feature in representations of scorn. This is easily distinguished.

Laughter.

EXAMPLE—"What *I* in love! ha! ha!—the idea! and with *that* fellow! The thought is so supremely ridiculous! My name to be changed to Mrs. Philander Jacob Stubbs! And on the strength of the report—ha! ha!—Philander Jacob came around to see mother last night! I think I feel a pain in my heart already—ha! ha! Mrs. Philander Jacob Stubbs, indeed! Laughable, isn't it—ha! ha! ha! Mrs. Stubbs!—Mrs. *Stubbs!*—ha! ha! ha!"

ABSENCE of all hope creates **Despair**, and according to the sharpness of suffering the expression varies—sometimes indicating bewilderment and distraction; a look of wildness, and then a laxation of vitality bordering on insensibility; again, a terrific gloom of countenance; the eyes are fixed; the features shrunken and livid, and the muscles of the face are tremulous and convulsive; occasionally tears and laughter alternate, but frequently stupidity and sullenness appear.

Despair.

EXAMPLE—" Me miserable!—which way shall I fly
Infinite wrath and infinite despair?
Which way I fly is hell; myself am hell;
And in the lowest deep a lower deep,
Still threatening to devour me, opens wide,
To which the hell I suffer seems a heaven!
....Farewell, remorse! All good to me is lost!"

TO represent the expression of **Love** with fidelity to nature, the gaze should be intently fixed upon the object of affection, with mingled tenderness and admiration; the hands are clasped in the fervency of emotion; the head and body incline forward; the features indicate earnestness, the lips being slightly parted, the lower limbs are firmly balanced upon the feet, and the voice is mild and melodious, in harmony with the thoughts of the heart. Love is a beautifier.

Love.

EXAMPLE—" Come in the evening, come in the morning,
      Come when you're looked for, or come without warning;
      Kisses and welcome you'll find here before you,
      And the oftener you come the more I'll adore you!
      Light is my heart since the day we were plighted,
      Red is my cheek that they told me was blighted;
      How sweet is the thought, to be ever united!"

AGITATION and disorder mark the whole appearance in **Madness.** Every movement is sudden and irregular, quick and uncontrolled; the eyes, extended to their utmost limit, protrude wildly and turn rapidly from object to object; the hair is tossed loosely about the head and face; the open hands are thrown upward to the head, and press and clasp and tousle it as if to drive away the agony of the brain; the breath comes and goes excitely; the countenance is distorted.

Madness.

EXAMPLE—" Here have I watched, in this dungeon cell,
      Longer than memory's tongue can tell;
      Here have I shrieked in my wild despair,
      When the damned fiends from their prison came,
      Sported and gamboled, and mocked me here,
      With their eyes of fire, and their tongues of flame,
      Shouting forever and aye my name."

REPRESENTING **Dignity,** the step is firm; the body is stretched to its full height; the head is elevated and poised a little to one side; the eyes are wide-open, "with a downward tendency;" the brow is expanded; the right arm is thrown energetically across the chest, asserting the right to speak and the will to enforce that right; every muscle is firmly set, and the voice is slightly raised, with a tone of command that signifies possession of a perfect womanhood.

Dignity.

EXAMPLE—" I perjure myself,—I sink my soul in falsehood to gratify your greed for gold?—never! Out, wretch! leave my sight forever! Think you that I have no knowledge of the difference between right and wrong? Think you I would blast the happiness of another and carry in my heart forever the knowledge of a lie for a few paltry dollars? And you thought to tempt me to this by an offer of money. Base creature,–I despise you! Begone!–never let me see you more!"

IN **Earnestness,** the form assumes its full height; the head is erect, with the features slightly elevated; the breath has a firm, quickened movement; the eyes are clear and the brows knit; the voice is deep; the lips are slightly compressed; the countenance is fearless; the right arm is extended, with the open palm of the hand turned upward, and there is a dignified air.

Earnestness.

EXAMPLE—" You think I love it! If this nerveless hand
      Could gain immortal strength, this very hour,
      I'd sweep this hellish traffic from the land,
      And crush its blighting, maddening, nightmare power
      Yea, now, with all my latest dying breath,
      I'll curse the thing that drags me down to death!—
            Aye, curse it ever, ever!"

THE head and bust, in **Fear,** are first thrown forward and then recede: the chin is drawn toward the chest; the mouth opens; the eyes are expanded and gaze upon the fearful object; the face is distorted, and contracted; the lower limbs tremble; the hands, outspread, are held, with the palms outward, before the face and chest in great disorder; the voice is very high and abrupt, and the breathing convulsive. Fear, protracted, becomes dread, terror and fright.

Fear.

EXAMPLE—" Oh, take it away !—take it away—the evil thing! Ah, how its cruel eyes, and blasting breath, and flashing tongue, image of Eden's destroyer, blight my very soul! Take it away! Oh, how it chills my blood and clogs my breath! Away with it—away! Its ghostly hiss, its slimy folds, whisper of death! O! Save me from its fangs! Oh, this is terrible!—Help! help! help!—I faint!—Help! help! Oh, take it from me!"

AN exaggerated species of dignity, **Scorn,** is expressed in the straightened and rigid form; the elevated eyebrows; the scowl upon the forehead, as the lady turns slightly away from the object; the closed lips; the right hand thrown well forward, with the palm bent downward; and the voice, as manifested in bitter laughter, sarcasm, or disgust, varies in its tone and expression. The emotion of scorn frequently involves the display of either derision, mockery, contempt, or all combined.

Scorn.

EXAMPLE—" Is the obligation to our fathers discharged? Is the debt we owe posterity paid? Answer me, thou coward, who hidest thyself in the hour of trial! If there is no reward in this life, no prize of glory in the next, capable of animating thy dastardly soul? Think and tremble, thou miscreant! at the whips and stripes thy master shall lash thee with on earth,—and the flames and scorpions thy second master shall torment thee with hereafter!"

VIOLENT agitation pervades the form in the expression of **Horror ;** the chest and head are thrown backward and to one side; one hand flies to the head, while the other, with open palm and outspread fingers, appears to be warding off the terrible vision; the eyes stare wildly at the object, with elevated brows; the lips and other features have a contorted appearance, and there is an inward shrinking of the entire form, one foot being thrown far back.

Horror.

EXAMPLE—"Oh, Horror! horror!—The vessel is on fire! See the red flames bursting through the deck, twining and climbing up mast and rope! The sails are a sheet of flame, and higher, higher still, the fire ascends! See the poor men and women huddling at the stern as the fierce winds blow the vessel onward! Oh, who will save them now? Is there no hand to help—no power to quench the flame?— Oh, horror, horror, horror! They are lost!"

THE attitude and the expression of **Supplication** are represented as follows: Either one or both knees rest upon the ground; the features assume an earnest appearance; the hands are tightly clasped beneath the chin, and the emotions of the heart are reflected in the movements of the entire form. These and the voice are regulated by the fervency of the petitions offered, being sometimes very subdued in tone; at times rising to an ardent key, and tremulous with feeling.

Supplication.

EXAMPLE—" With flashing eye and burning brow,
The mother followed heedless how,
And kneeling in his presence now—
' O, spare my child, my joy, my pride!
O, give me back my child!' she cried:
' My child! my child!' with sobs and tears
She shrieked upon his callous ears."

PRESENTATION AND OTHER SPEECHES.

THE presentation speech should be short. It may allude to the work that the individual has accomplished, by which he or she is entitled to the gift. It may appropriately speak of the high regard in which the recipient is held by the donors of the gift, and it may bespeak a delightful, prosperous future for the person addressed, besides being brimful of good wishes; but the speech should come early to the point and close.

In the meantime it may be well for the managers of the affair to have some one besides the recipient of the gift appointed to make an appropriate response, unless he or she is thoroughly capable of making a suitable reply. In most cases it is a relief to the recipient to be informed of the intended presentation, as he or she, in that case, can make a response that will be more satisfactory than if taken by surprise and without time for preparation. As a rule, the article should be concealed from view until it is spoken of in the presentation, when it will create renewed interest.

Lady Presenting a Flag.

Presentation of a Flag by a Lady

To a volunteer company of the state militia, the flag being held by a gentleman while the lady makes the address.

CAPTAIN ARTHUR BENSON AND MEMBERS OF COMPANY H OF THE FIRST REGIMENT OF THE NEW YORK VOLUNTEER MILITIA—GENTLEMEN: In recognition of the public spirit, the patriotism and the bravery that move you to form an organization for the protection of your homes and your country, should you be called upon to fight in their defense, it becomes my duty, in behalf of the ladies of this town, to present you a silken flag.

This emblem of our nationality has been fashioned into these stars and stripes, has been trimmed and embellished as you see it here, by hands that will never tire of working for you. As you look upon its silken folds you may understand that it is the grand emblem of our country's greatness, and it is more. It is the bearer of the hope and love of the donors who present it—whose hearts will go with you to the end, should fate determine that it shall be carried into the battlefield.

Our hope is that it may never do other duty than rustle peacefully above your heads, a silent token of our respect and regard, but should necessity require, we are confident that in brave hands it will lead to success, and in the hours of trial will be wherever it shall wave the signal of victory. Into your hands we now place it. God grant that the need of trailing it in blood may never arise, but should duty or your country call, we know it will wave over the heads of brave men —we know you will do it honor.

Response of the Captain.

MISS CHANDLER: Responding, in behalf of my company, to the sentiments you express, I but speak the words which my comrades would utter, when I say that we deeply feel and most highly appreciate this appropriate and beautiful gift which we receive at your hands.

If it shall be our mission to unfurl it only when peace and harmony shall prevail, it will be well. Should it be our fate to go forth in defense of home and loved friends, we shall carry it as a token of the love, the respect and the solicitude we bear for those who remember us thus kindly.

The sight of this will ever nerve our men to greater bravery—it will be an inspiration. We thank you for this offering, and for the sentiment that comes with its presentation.

We shall carry it fearlessly in peace and in war; and throughout the length and breadth of this country we propose it shall wave over States ever loyal and true to the government—we resolve that it shall ever be the emblem of a nation that shall never be dismembered or disunited. Again tendering you our high regard for this testimonial, our color-bearer will now receive it, while the band will express our heartfelt appreciation of your gift as they render the "Star-Spangled Banner."

Presentation Speech at a Silver Wedding.

MR. AND MRS. ———: It becomes my pleasant duty, in behalf of your friends assembled here to-night, to remind you that we are not forgetful of the fact that you have turned a quarter of a century in wedded life. This of itself, in an age when marital separations are so common, is worthy of recognition; but it is not alone that fact that causes your friends to convene at this time.

For years it has been our privilege to know your household in genial friendship. In the varied walks of neighborly and social intercourse, you have contributed abundantly toward the making of life pleasant in the circle in which we have moved. We do not forget that when the laugh was merriest your happy presence added pleasure to the scene; and when sorrow visited our homes your words of consolation and sympathy made the sorrow lighter.

There comes a time, at various periods in life, when we can honor and reward those whom we esteem. Such is the present occasion.

Recollecting our many obligations for kindness you have rendered, and the pleasant years made agreeable through your acquaintance, your friends herewith present you this tea-service and desire your acceptance of the same.

The gift, while appropriate as a memorial of twenty-five years of wedlock, is presented as a token of the high favor in which you are held by your many friends.

May it adorn your table in the future, and may the refreshing beverage you shall sip from these silver goblets be such as will aid in prolonging your lives to that time when, at your golden wedding, we shall, by the sight of these present gifts, be reminded of the pleasant scene that took place twenty five years before—the delightful occasion which we celebrate to-night.

Reply to the Presentation Speech.

DEAR FRIENDS: It is at such a time as this that words fail to express the feelings of the heart. There comes occasionally a period in life when our unworthiness is made all the more manifest by the bestowal of kindness upon us. It is true that we have mingled in your society for years. But while, in our humble way, we may have contributed some pleasure to those about us, we have ever been the recipients of continued enjoyment at your hands; and it is *we* who are under obligation—not yourselves.

We accept these gifts to-night, dear friends, with a full appreciation of the kind motives which presented them, and not that we deserve them as free gifts at your hands.

There may be some things in our lives commendatory. We have journeyed together in married life for twenty-five years. Some shadows have crossed our path in that time, and many joys have illumined our way. Upon the whole, we have had more happiness than sorrow; more roses than thorns have strewn our pathway. Thus in this twenty-five years of consort together we have our recompense.

We have striven to do our duty as neighbors and friends, and for the little we have done we have, in all our intercourse with you, been repaid a thousand-fold.

We accept these gifts, therefore, with a sense of deep obligation to those kind friends by whom they are presented, and we shall use and cherish them, in all the years to come, with the earnest hope that, at like anniversary festal gatherings we may have frequent opportunity to repay the kindness which you have thus bestowed.

Speech, Presenting a Book,

By the pupil of a school to a teacher at the close of her last term.

MISS WILLIAMS: I am appointed by the pupils of this school to present you, in their name, this volume—a cyclopedia of poetry, containing the poetic gems of ancient and modern times.

In presenting this testimonial, I assure you in behalf of your pupils that, as a patient teacher, a wise counselor and a most excellent instructor, you will ever be remembered by the students of this school with feelings of the highest regard and esteem.

We look back over the period during which we have received instruction from you with sincere pleasure. We recollect your efforts in our behalf with grateful remembrance, and we learned of your intended resignation as a teacher, and the leaving of this school, with sincere regret.

In the turning of the pages of this volume you will, we hope, be reminded of those who presented it. In that remembrance of us please do not recollect the dullness we have often shown, and the disobedience, we fear, we have sometimes manifested. But please remember that we shall strive, in the hereafter, to profit by the instruction you have given, and when we are far separated from each other, it may please you to know that we consider that we are better and wiser from the instruction we have received from you.

Response of the Teacher.

MY DEAR PUPILS: I receive and accept of your elegant gift with much pleasure; first, because the volume, of itself, is one of rare value, which I shall highly prize, and, second, because it comes to me as a token of your appreciation of my efforts since I have had the pleasure of being with you.

I assure you I will turn its pages in happy recollection of the pleasant faces I have met in this room during my school duties. I will always remember your willing hearts, your kind intentions, your many evidences of love and regard for me, and your unceasing efforts to make my work as light and agreeable as possible.

I thank you for this beautiful testimonial, and also for the assurance you give me, that, as I read its pages, I may be reminded that the donors not only hold me in kindly remembrance, but they are resolved to profit by the teaching that has been given here.

My earnest hope is that your future life may realize all that your studious habits and school-days now seem to promise. Knowing you as I do, I expect you, in noble manhood and womanhood, to honor this school by your future lives of usefulness, prosperity and happiness.

Speech Upon being Nominated as a Candidate for Office.

MR. PRESIDENT AND FELLOW CITIZENS: My thanks are due for the compliment paid in selecting me to represent this district in the State senate. As I desire to go into the legislature unpledged and untrammeled, I shall make few promises as to what I shall do if elected.

It may not be amiss, however, to state that there is certain work which our representative, whoever he may be, should feel himself bound to perform, should he occupy a seat in the legislative councils. And of this may be mentioned the establishment of a reform school in this portion of the State in which can be received and trained a large number of boys who now bid fair to become ultimately permanent inmates of our prisons. The law should be stronger relating to the preservation of game. The rate of taxation on certain manufacturing industries should be lessened. The law relating to less hours for laboring men in the State service should be enforced, and much other needed legislation is evident.

So far as *I* am concerned, I can only say, if elected, I propose to do my duty as I understand it. That duty I conceive to be consists in working for the best interests of the constituency, and in serving the State and the entire people faithfully. Should it be my fate not to be chosen to fill the place for which you have placed me in nomination, the sun will probably rise and set as it has done heretofore, and I will console myself with the thought that there is a blessing in defeat. But should I be elected, I shall hope that my efforts may avail in accomplishing some work that will be beneficial to yourselves and the State.

Again thanking you, gentlemen, for your generous support, I can only hope that the expression you give here will be the voice of the people, and that our party in the coming election may carry the banner of victory.

Speech of Congressional Candidate from Hotel Balcony,

In reply to a serenade at the Clarendon House.

FELLOW CITIZENS: In response to your call for a talk from me, I beg to assure you that I appreciate the honor you do me in this gathering. But while I tender you my thanks for this ovation, I am not unmindful of the fact that the cause on this occasion is greater than any man. We are in the midst of an exciting political contest, in which principles are involved of the utmost importance, and

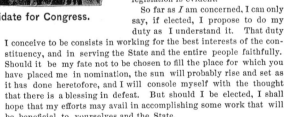

Speech of the Candidate for Congress.

whether those principles shall triumph or not, in the coming election, is the question of vital significance.

It must be clearly evident to the unprejudiced mind that the machinery of government is seriously destroyed, when so many of our people, in the midst of an abundance, should be compelled to beg for common necessaries of life. The fact is as plain as the unclouded noonday sun, that a government is wofully weak that will compel tens of thousands of strong, able-bodied men, anxious to work, to stand idle, while their families suffer for the means of maintaining existence. We are in the midst of plenty. The factories, shops and warehouses are full to repletion with goods that people require. The fields are teeming with grain, the banks are plethoric with money, and yet, in the midst of all this abundance, there is not wisdom enough in our national legislators to secure a proper division of this wealth among those who have produced it. But, fellow-citizens, I shall not now take your time in a discussion of the cause of hard times and the remedy.

I can only say that as your candidate for Congress, I deeply feel the need of prompt and efficient action by our general government; and if I am elected, I hope to faithfully perform my part in the work that so greatly needs to be done. I thank you, gentlemen, for this personal compliment to me, and with you I pray for the success of that cause which is righteous and just.

Speech when Presenting a Prize

To the successful competitors in a boat-race.

GENTLEMEN: Much discussion has been developed from time to time (in country school-houses and village debating clubs) as to the relative superiority of mind over muscle. Indeed, the question has been many times definitely settled (by these authorities), and yet it is ever bobbing up in actual life and begging for a final decision. Gentlemen, I am not here to solve the problem—I only rise to do honor to the union of mind and muscle that has brought victory to your banner and made you the proud recipients of this beautiful prize, the gift of fair hands, which you have so gallantly won.

I see in your frank and youthful features the glow of health and energy; I see in your bared arms the cord-like sinews that denote strength and endurance; and I see in the successful management of your boat the expression of an iron will to accomplish, whatever the opposition, and of a skill indicative of the intellect that controls your muscles and makes your manhood great.

Yours was not an easy triumph. Seven clubs competed with you for this rare and beautiful prize. I see in their crews, as they stand around you, skill and energy which you may be proud to have defeated. But in you they acknowledge the possession of superior skill, a superior force, and I doubt not that next to winning this prize for their respective clubs they rejoice most in your talents and success.

Gentlemen, you are young. Soon you will be entering for a greater race than this. The contest of life is before you. The prizes are honor, prosperity, wealth and influence. These are within your reach, for the same energy, the same skill, the same spirit of emulation, that you have manifested to-day, will be requisite if you desire to "go in and win" fame and fortune in the future.

There are lessons to be learned in this regatta from which you will be the gainers if you heed them. In the systematic training, the physical preparation for this contest, you have been taught the value of healthful diet and judicious exercise. To everything that tended to insure success you gave the closest attention. You avoided anything that was likely to weaken your bodily energies. You practiced temperance and sobriety. You gave up late hours and dissipation; you studied your own organization, and day by day you saw the benefit you received from systematic and self-denying regimen. All pointed to this crowning victory.

. So, in the mastery of life, in business vocations, in hours of recreation, the same careful watchfulness over yourself—the same sobriety and temperance, the same healthful treatment of your vital powers, will well repay you.

There is one thing, however, in this regatta that you will have to avoid in the race of life. As your oars harmoniously swept your boat along towards the home-stake, I noticed that you looked one way and sped another. In the life-contest you will do otherwise—or fail. You will be your own look-out, your own steersman, and you will need to keep a keen watch before you if you would win. To-day the course has been clear. In the course of life you will encounter snags and fogs, and other boats will cross your bows, and all your skill and energy will be required to keep your way clear, to avoid damaging collisions, and to hold your own.

But you tire of these allusions, and wonder where I will take you to in these airy flights. So I return to this present place and time.

Gentlemen, this richly ornamented silver vase that I hold before you is yours. You have worn it fairly, and these fair donors gladly give it to you. Altogether it is a fair operation. And as I hand it over to you, Mr. Captain, and retire to private life, I but echo the sentiment that so generally lights up every face about me when I say, "Long life and success to the Arrow Club."

Speech Accompanying Presentation of a Watch to a Clergyman.

REVEREND AND DEAR SIR: For more than twelve months past, we, as members of your church and congregation, have profited by your ministrations, and within that period you have greatly endeared yourself to us by your suavity, your amiable character, your earnest devotion to duty, and the hearty interest you have ever manifested in our welfare as a people.

In the sacred desk you have faithfully advocated your religion and ours, have wisely warned us against the evils that beset us in our everyday life, and have earnestly pleaded with us to seek our truest happiness in the paths of rectitude and sobriety.

In our homes you have been our sincere and sympathizing counselor and friend. In our hours of pain and sorrow you have spoken gentle and soothing words to our troubled hearts; our children have profited by your instruction; you have united our sons and daughters in holy wedlock; your benediction has rested upon us in our domestic and business affairs, and in all things you have proven yourself our competent and loving pastor.

With a deep sense of your many benefactions, those assembled here have requested me, in their name, to present to you this WATCH, as a token of our mutual and increasing admiration and esteem for yourself, and of our gratitude for your labors in our behalf. We ask you, dear sir, to accept it as freely as we offer it; for it is fitting that you who are daily and hourly preparing us for the joys of Eternity, should bear about you this monitor of passing Time, ever marking, as we sincerely hope, hours, days and many years of happiness for you and yours.

The Clergyman's Reply.

FRIENDS AND BRETHREN: Rapidly as time has passed with me since I first came among you, a perfect stranger, you have in one short year become very near and dear to me, and we are no more strangers. On the contrary, you have so freely bestowed upon me your confidence and generosity that it seems as if I had always known and loved you in the bonds of gospel truth. Busy as I have been in forwarding the interests of this church and society, I have received from you so many tokens of esteem and affection that my duties have been greatly lightened, and I have found time to institute new labors in your behalf. At all times your sympathy and encouragement has been freely given, and gratefully appreciated. As I receive this beautiful WATCH, which all must greatly admire, my heart warms with renewed joy in your service, for it assures me that your friendship is not for an hour, or a day, or a year, but for all time; and it shall be my heart's endeavor to merit in future, with renewed energy, the esteem which you have thus so bountifully expressed. I pray you to accept my thanks for your beautiful gift and the kind words accompanying it. As pastor and people, may our ties unite us closer and closer in the bonds of Christian love throughout time and eternity.

Speech at Old Settlers' Reunion.

FELLOW CITIZENS—OLD NEIGHBORS AND PIONEERS IN HALLOCK COUNTY: Forty years ago, in company with Old Benjamin Crawford, who died last year, I hunted for ducks on this very block of ground, worth to-day a large fortune of itself. At that time there were only seventeen white persons in the town, three or four blacks, and a tribe of Winnebago Indians, encamped, at that time, about three miles west of our village.

There were two frame-houses in the place. The rest were made of logs, containing usually about three rooms, with sometimes a chamber. In a careful review of my own life and recollection of those who were here in those early days, I doubt if there has ever been a period in all our experience when we had a greater amount of happiness than fell to our lot in those pioneer days.

Everybody had work—plenty of it. Nobody feared being discharged on Saturday night because of over production. Good health generally prevailed, the result of exercise, fresh air, hard work and sound sleep. There were no cliques in society, no aristocracy, no snobbery, no bankruptcies, no envy, and no distress because certain men were getting very rich while others were very poor.

There were no heart-burnings because one neighbor had a better furnished house than the others, and the women—they were women in those days—had no worry because they had nothing to wear.

Old Deacon Towne told me, on one occasion, when we were talking of the old times, that himself and family came from a handsomely furnished house in Troy, New York, to his log cabin, up near the big woods, and in all his experience he never saw such genuine hospitality, nor such a genial and happy time as his neighbors all had on their plain fare and the few opportunities around them. Yes, we lived right down to the barest necessaries in those days, and in doing that we learned that our real wants, in order to make us happy, are very few.

Forty winters, since some of us came here, have spread their white covering, and as many beautiful springs have brought the birds and flowers to us, returning every season to a vastly larger population than we had the year before. But I cannot tell you how, step by step, we have grown. I will leave that for others, who will give you the history of these forty years more in detail. Suffice it to say, the early settlers in this locality have been most fortunate in the peace and happiness which surrounded them in their pioneer days, in the wealth which has been showered upon them, and in the privileges which they enjoy to-day.

Speech at an Improvement Meeting.

MR. PRESIDENT: While it is unquestionably true that the manufacturing of articles that may be sold abroad is a most prolific source of revenue and ultimate wealth to a town, it is equally important that a healthy atmosphere be about us, and that our homes, by their charming surroundings, be such as will cultivate those graces of nature which enable a people to make the right use of wealth when it is acquired. I have therefore this to suggest as a means of beautifying this city: That the inhabitants upon any street, for the space of one block, form an improvement society for that block, to do the following:

First—To take away all front fences from before dwellings.

Second—To set elms by the roadside and a sufficiency of ornamental trees to suitably shade the streets.

Third—To secure a smooth stone sidewalk, at least eight feet in width.

Fourth—To grade the front lot from the house to the roadway, and cover the same with sod.

Fifth—To have the street swept as often as may be necessary to keep it clean, and the lawns all mown and kept in excellent order.

Sixth—To have all alleys and foul places carefully cleaned, and put into a condition such as will make the atmosphere in the immediate vicinity perfectly healthy.

The taking down of fences, setting trees, and putting grounds in order, will not be very expensive in the first place, and the keeping of them in fine condition afterwards can be done with comparatively small expense, the labor being performed by men who need this employment.

When these improvements which I have indicated are carried into effect generally, throughout the town, ours will be one of the healthiest and one of the most beautiful cities in the world.

Selling Goods at Auction.

The business of disposing of goods at auction is one of large magnitude. Frequently, when all other means prove futile in getting rid of property, the auctioneer's persuasive language, added to the inherent impression that auction prices are invariably *low*, entails spirited competition, and thus the figures realized often exceed the most sanguine expectations. As in other classes of trade, there are men engaged in this pursuit who are utterly unprincipled, and who are very properly dubbed "Peter Funks;" while on the other hand individuals, whose character and honor are as high as the highest and as good as the best, also discourse on the auction-block. In Trinity building, the great real-estate mart of New York city, millions of dollars of property change ownership " under the hammer" each year—and in all the leading cities of the Union vast quantities of dry-goods, boots and shoes, and staple articles, reach the jobber through the same channel.

At the beginning of an auction, the terms of sale are stated. If it be a vendue of merchandise, the crier or auctioneer commences about as follows:

The Words of the Auctioneer.

LADIES AND GENTLEMEN: These goods are to be sold to the highest bidder, without reserve. If I accept the first bid and get the second, then the article must be sold. Strangers will be required, in every case, to pay a deposit. Bid promptly, and I will dispose of the goods quickly. I begin the sale by offering this splendid photograph album, known as the Superdonbonsical brand; it is manufactured in the city of Berlin by Henri Von Hytenschnitzenheimer and cost twelve dollars, besides import-duties. How much am I bid to start it? Start it along, —it is for sale at your own price; how much do I hear for it? One dollar! One dollar is no money for it,—but no matter—I'm bid a dollar for it—One dollar. One dollar—one dollar—one dollar—one dollar—one dollar; at one dollar—one dollar—and a quarter I *have*—one dollar and a quarter—and a quarter—and a quarter—will you go the half?—*half*, I'm bid; one dollar and fifty, one dollar and fifty—will you give the seventy-five? Why what are you people thinking about?—one dollar and fifty cents would not pay the import-duties on this magnificent, hand-made, morocco-bound album, with separation pages, a hinge to every leaf and a patent back and spring clasp—seventy-five—one dollar and seventy-five I am bid—and now will you make it two dollars? *at* one dollar and seventy-five—two dollars will you make it? Will you *go* the two—do I *hear* the two—shall I have the *two?* One dollar and seventy-five—going at one dollar and seventy-five—going going at the low price of one dollar and three-quarters—once! twice! one dollar and seventy-five,—fair warning and a fair sale—going, going, going, gone! Next lot.

Fourth of July Oration.

FELLOW CITIZENS: The Declaration of American Independence, adopted by the Continental Congress at the State House, Philadelphia, July 4, 1776, to the reading of which we have just been listening, stands to day the charter of our national liberty. It was the first grand step of American freedom and progress in their march across this continent, whose influence now binds together a nation extending from Lake Itasca, on the north, to Mexico, on the South, and bounded respectively, on the east and on the west, by the Atlantic and Pacific oceans. It was the death-knell of England's power over her American colonies, and severed the ties that bound them to contribute to her support without a voice in their own government.

At this distance from the occurrences of that day, when the enthusiastic and just indignation that prompted this immortal State paper has passed away, the allegations against King George and his ministers have, to a certain degree, lost much of their interest; and yet those wrongs still stand, and will continue to stand while the world lasts, a momentous page in our national history. At this period, when all nations have learned to respect us, and we count England among our best friends and commercial allies, the bitterness of these charges against her has, in *our* minds, faded away. In the bosoms of the Revolutionary fathers, however, they created a fervor of patriotism stronger than the love of life and property, and in defense of their principles these men took up arms, defied tyranny, fought, bled and died. With them, as the great orator, Patrick Henry, defined it, the issue was simply "liberty, or death!" To gain the one, they braved the other, regarding their sufferings as a sacrifice to secure the prosperity and political freedom of their posterity. Nowhere is this sentiment more forcefully, more brilliantly expressed than in the closing sentences of the Declaration itself: "With a firm reliance on the protection of Divine Providence, we mutually pledge to each other our lives, our fortunes, and our sacred honor."

It was no empty boast. Living or dying, whatever might be the result, they went forth to battle for their rights with such earnestness, such fidelity to each other and their country, that they won the prize for which they fought, and the American Republic, born of patriotism and of strife, won victory and peace for succeeding generations. Such a spectacle entranced the nations, and the colonies did then, in deed and in truth, "assume among the powers of the earth the separate and equal station to which the laws of nature and of nature's God entitled them."

The one great principle established by the triumph of the American colonies was this: The equality of all men under the law, possessing the inalienable rights of life, liberty, and the pursuit of happiness, as one common heritage.

That principle prevailed, with one exception, through all the vicissitudes of the young republic, fortified by the wisdom of a Washington, a Jefferson, an Adams, and a Hamilton, and the result of their deliberations was that grand guarantee of our liberties, the Constitution of 1788–'79. At that time negro slavery was viewed with different eyes from those that witnessed its horror in after-years, and its enormity was not appreciated by the founders of the government; a fact that has led to many sneers, that while the continental patriots fought for their own liberty, they forged the chains of their slaves, and thus cast discredit upon their motives for freedom. This criticism, though severe, had a particle of reason in it; but in that day, and among that people, slavery was considered no offense against Divine or human law.

The benefits secured to every individual (excepting slaves) were representation in the national councils, the right of equal suffrage, trial by jury, freedom from unjust and onerous taxation, protection to life, and peaceful possession of individual property. And these rights and privileges are our heritage to-day.

It is in honor of these rights and privileges under the Constitution, secured to us by the valor of our forefathers, that we celebrate this day. In the long strides of the civilization of the nineteenth century, our nation has kept step with the progress of the world, and, under our Constitution and beneficent laws, every encouragement has been afforded us for the development of the arts and sciences; labor has been appreciated as a source of wealth and improvement, and has attained to a high position in the work of perfecting the great enterprises of the age; inventors and inventions have been encouraged and patronized; literature has achieved honor by its freshness and brilliancy, and everything that comfort or luxury could suggest has been multifariously furnished at prices within the reach of moderate incomes. To enumerate the blessings we have in this way enjoyed under the provisions of our national charter would be a herculean labor; and in any other country such progress as we have made in one hundred years would have required two or three centuries.

Above me wave the stars and stripes of our country among the peaceful branches of the grove, and the shadows of the flag we love and venerate as the ensign of our liberties flit over the happy faces of our sturdy yeomanry and their comely wives and daughters. The birds are singing in our leafy bowers; flowers and fruits, and waving fields of grain, enrich our soil; peaceful homes dot the landscape all around us, and the voices of merry children fall sweetly upon our ears. These are the blessings of peace wrought out for us by the hardy Continentals and their brave and wise leaders of the American Revolution. To-day we venerate their memory; and if from their spirit-homes they are permitted to witness our happiness and the blessings they purchased for us in those rugged times and dark days, I am sure they must rejoice with us in the triumph of the principles they established, and in behalf of which they laid down their lives by the wayside and on the battlefield. Let us never forget these men, nor those noble mothers, wives and daughters of the Revolution, whose patriotism was no less sincere and enthusiastic than that of the men they encouraged to take up arms against tyranny, and was only less demonstrative because of the gentleness of their sex.

The lessons which the lives and deaths of these brave and noble men and women bequeathed to us are worthy of our consideration, and I would dwell upon some of the peculiarities which made them great and sustained them in the hour of trial and danger. I have already referred to the deep, inborn patriotism which the rule of oppression to which they were subjected so thoroughly developed. It was a sentiment born of the period and the circumstances of their existence—a sentiment that subdued all selfish propensities and found expression in actions of just defiance and heroism.

They were men of simple habits, living lives of industry in their several vocations, and overcoming difficulties by their energy and perseverance.

They were men of integrity and honor, knowing and doing their duty as citizens in all the relations of life.

They possessed no false ambition to become rich by speculation and fraud, nor to aspire to stations of honor and profit for selfish purposes; nor did they encourage hurtful extravagance.

They respected the laws of the government under which they lived, until those laws became unjustly oppressive and destructive to the best interests of the entire colonies.

They encouraged morality and truth in their dealings with each other and also toward strangers with whom they came in contact, and were severe in punishing infractions of law and evil practices.

Such were the men and women in "the times that tried their souls," and such were the examples which they left for us to follow.

Young ladies and gentlemen, whose beaming eyes gaze into mine as I look around over this assemblage, in your blooming manhood and womanhood remember these dead heroes and their families, their sufferings and their endurance, their unselfish patriotism, and, above all, the examples of their private virtues. The world needs such men and women as they were every day, and it is in your power to emulate them in all that reflects honor upon their memories. There are battles to be fought against wrong and oppression in numerous forms, social obstacles to overcome, love of country to cherish and maintain, truth and honor to be upheld, and it will soon devolve upon you to govern this broad nation, with all its interests confided to your care. In the near future this responsibility will fall like a mantle upon your shoulders, and it will behoove you to see that the trust is not misplaced. To-day there is not one of the old Revolutionary patriots alive. They did their work, and did it well, and then passed on. Other generations came upon the stage of action, but through all the years that intervened between then and now, their staunch principles and sturdy teachings were owned and heeded. Will you own and heed them also? If you will, I may safely prophesy from this stand that the glory of the Union will not depart from it in your day and generation, and I foresee, in that case, greater wonders awaiting our second centennial birthday than we in the last century have witnessed. Revere the stars and stripes forever. They are the symbols of our prosperity as well as our integrity—the mementoes of a past age—the hope of our country's future.

CELEBRATING THE FOURTH OF JULY.

History of the Day and Forms for its Observance.

FROM 1761 to 1773 the thirteen American colonies owned and controlled by Great Britain were in a continuous state of excitement caused by the excessive taxation imposed upon them, the arbitrary rule of the home government in their affairs, and their insufficient representation in the national councils of legislation. The colonists felt justly aggrieved, and the spirit of revolution was strongly manifested on several occasions; so much so that in one or two instances their public demonstrations of indignation resulted in the repeal of certain obnoxious measures.

After several serious collisions between the colonists and the national authorities, owing to the increased taxation and oppression of the government, this spirit of rebellion culminated, in 1773, in the destruction of three cargoes of tea sent to Boston, on which the colonists were required to pay an onerous tax. This bold act brought a new crisis into colonial affairs. The colonists were in open rebellion, and the military forces of the government were increased, with new powers, to subjugate the rebels. In the contest which ensued the colonists were frequently victorious, and their enthusiasm in the work of freeing themselves from the dominion of Great Britain was unbounded.

for an early separation of the colonies from the home government.

June 7, 1776, Richard Henry Lee introduced in Congress his famous resolution, "That these united colonies are, and of right ought to be, free and independent states; that they are absolved from all allegiance to the British crown, and that all political connection between them and the state of Great Britain is, and ought to be, totally dissolved." This resolution was adopted by twelve of the colonies, July 2, 1776. On the fourth, the Declaration of Independence, prepared by Thomas Jefferson, was adopted amid great rejoicings and the wildest enthusiasm. Wherever the news spread, it was greeted with shouts, bonfires, processions, and other unusual demonstrations of delight.

This is "the day we celebrate," and the reason why its joyful observance is so general throughout the land and in other countries wherever Americans can assemble in its honor. That it should be so widely recognized and celebrated is only a just tribute to the patriots who secured to us the liberties we enjoy.

Years ago John Adams said: "It will be celebrated by succeeding generations as the great anniversary festival. It ought to be commemorated as the day of deliverance

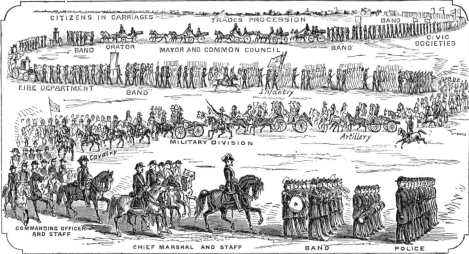

How to Organize a Fourth of July Procession.

THIS illustration represents a lengthy procession, composed of many distinct parts, among them the various trades organized to celebrate the Fourth of July. In this the orator of the day occupies a central position. Before his carriage come the fire companies, the military display, chief marshal and the police, who may be detailed for the day; next behind is the orator's carriage, with the distinguished guests and others to appear on the platform; next follow the mayor and aldermen, in carriages, succeeded by the civic societies; next come the different trades-wagons, the rear being made up of citizens in carriages; several bands scattered throughout the procession, each placed at the head of a distinct division, add much to the attractiveness of the occasion. The interest is increased when the cavalcade exhibits a large amount of variety.

The legislative body which they formed, known as the Continental Congress, was organized and composed of the most brilliant intellects and patriotic spirits in the country. It began its first session at Carpenter's Hall, Philadelphia (afterward known as Independence Hall), September 5, 1774, continuing until near the end of October. Little was accomplished at this session, beyond giving earnest expression to their determination to secure civil and political liberty.

The year 1775 was marked by the battles of Lexington and Concord, the capture of Fort Ticonderoga, the battle of Bunker Hill, the evacuation of Boston by the British, and other stirring events. The second session of the Continental Congress began at the Pennsylvania State House, May 10, and continued throughout the year, encouraging the efforts of the patriots in the field, and stimulating the project

by solemn acts of devotion to Almighty God. It ought to be solemnized with pomp and parade, with shows, games, sports, guns, bells, bonfires, and illuminations, from one end of the continent to the other, from this time forth, forevermore."

In the celebration of the day the managers should seek to present a large and varied programme, both in the procession and upon the speaker's stand. No exercise should be unduly long. The procession, formed at ten o'clock, and commencing to move at eleven, should exhibit a variety of that which will instruct and amuse; bands of music being judiciously distributed through the same so that the music of one will not interfere with the other. On the platform, there should be prayer, singing by glee-club, poem, reading Declaration of Independence, music by the band, oration, singing by quartette, announcement of afternoon exercises, music, and benediction.

Pen and Pencil Flourishing.

PRIZE

WHEREAS

THE·PUBLISHERS·OF·THE

Fireman's Herald,

OF
New York City,

UPON THE 19TH DAY OF   JANUARY, 1882,

OFFERED

a prize of an engrossed pen and ink premium for the best set of

COMPANY BY LAWS, BLANKS AND ROLL.

THIS IS TO CERTIFY THAT

THE Passaic Steam Fire Engine Co No 1

OF
PATERSON, N.J.

HAS BEEN AWARDED THE

SAID PRIZE.

In Testimony Whereof we the undersigned Judges have hereunto affixed our signatures on this the twelfth day of October A.D. 1882.

(The signatures of the committee of award are here omitted for want of room.)

INSCRIPTIONS
FOR
ENGRAVERS
ON
METAL.

Engravers' Inscriptions.

Wording and Punctuation of Inscriptions for Engraving.

Forms of Wording, appropriate in marking Rings, Spoons, Pins, Coffin-Plates, Cane-Heads, Watches, Silverware, etc., for use in Presentation on the occasion of Weddings, Marriage Anniversaries, Birthdays, etc., etc.

STYLES OF LETTERING.

NSCRIPTIONS to be engraved on metal, should be in as few words as possible. It is important always that the person furnishing the copy to the engraver should write the words to be engraved in the plainest manner, not even omitting the punctuation. Care should be taken to plainly distinguish the I from the J, and other letters, that in script are likely to be taken for others. Special care should also be observed in spelling.

The following forms of wording, styles of lettering, punctuation, and arrangement of sentences will be found serviceable, both for the engraver and those persons who wish to have engraving executed.

Carrie Jane.	I. O. O. F.	Charles Horton.
MINE EVER.	To My Husband.	REMEMBER.
Mrs. D. Williams.	To My Sister.	FORGET ME NOT.

From a Friend.

Mary.

Christmas, 1870.

Chas. O. Wilson;

From a Friend.

XMAS.   1872.

C. D. Briggs & Minnie Buck.

July 7, 1871.

Martin Wells to May King,

December 26, 1869.

William H. Brown.

JANUARY 1, 1869.

Jas. H. Kendall.

Aged 25 y'rs, 3 m's.

OUR

Little Willie,

George K. Hoyt.

Born, May 12, 1835.

PRESENTED
—TO—
Hoyt L. Wilson;
BY
EMPLOYEES, CAR DEP'T,
N. W. R. R.
April 4th, 1873.
Chicago, Ill.

TESTIMONIAL
—TO—
Perry Knight;
FROM
HIS FRIENDS,
L. Jackson, W. W. Coy & H. Munson.
Buffalo, N. Y.,
November 1, 1868.

TO
Capt. A. Benson;
FROM
His Comrades of Co. E,
44th Regt., Ill. Vol's.
CHICAGO, ILL.
Jan. 1, 1863.

Mother;

From MARY.

CHRISTMAS, 1873.

Kittie;

FROM HER FATHER.

Lizzie D. Smith;

From Her Father.   May 12, 1873.

Fannie W. Brown;

From Her Mother.

18th Birthday,   June 10th, 1873.

Harvey D. Kent;
FROM
Father and Mother.
21st Birthday.

Mother;

From HER CHILDREN.

Christmas, 1872.

Mr. & Mrs. Jas. C. Black.

25th Anniversary Wedding;

August 17th, 1873:

FROM

THEIR MANY FRIENDS.

PRESENTED TO
Mr. & Mrs. R. Coy;
BY
Mr. & Mrs. Browning.
Apr. 1, 1868.

Mr. & Mrs. King;

FROM

Their Many Friends,

AS A TOKEN OF

Esteem and Respect.

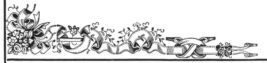

Tomb-Stone Inscriptions.

Wording and Punctuation.

USUAL recent wording of Tomb-Stone Inscriptions is shown in the following. In comparison, it will be seen that the modern inscription is generally much more brief than that of the olden time. Formerly it was customary to chisel in rude letters epitomized biographical histories of the deceased on the tomb-stones that marked their last resting place. Among such are many quaint, curious and foolish inscriptions that, so far as perpetuating the memories of the deceased was concerned, had better never have been engraved on the headstones.

The lesson taught in these examples is, that the more concise the inscription, the more favorably coming generations will judge of the handful of dust that lies beneath the leaning tombstone. The most approved modern forms, accompanied by epitaphs, are shown herewith, together with the correct grammatical wording and punctuation of the same. The following appropriately accompany the inscription.

Brief Epitaphs.

Father.	Our Mother.	Charlie.
All is Well.	Gone Home.	Christ is my Hope.
Darling Sister.	Gone, but not Forgotten.	The Morning Cometh.
We will Meet again.	Rest, Darling Sister, Rest.	Dying is but Going Home.
Over in the Summer Land.	In after Time we'll meet Her.	There shall be no Night there.
Absent, not Dead.	Gentle, Sweet little Freddie.	They are not Dead.

Lillie.

She faltered by the wayside, and the Angels took her home.

MINNIE,

INFANT DAUGHTER OF

E. & M. Binninger,

—❖❖DIED❖❖—

Sept. 15th, 1873. AGED 1 Mo. & 15 D's.

Beneath this stone, in soft repose,
Is laid a mother's dearest pride;
A flower that scarce had waked to life
And light and beauty, ere it died.

TRUMAN MARTIN,

Aged 60 Years. August 2, 1870.

Harriet Theresa,

WIFE OF

F. D. Stevenson,

AGED 41 Years.   Oct. 4, 1872.

"I Fear not Death."

Little Johnny,

—❖❖DIED❖❖—

November 1st, 1871. AGED 5 Y's & 8 M's.

"'Tis a little grave, but O, have care,
For world-wide hopes are buried there;
How much of light, how much of joy,
Is buried with a darling boy."

Harvey J. Belden,

CAPT. OF

51st Regiment, Illinois Vols.,

Killed at the Battle of Perryville,

October 8th, 1863.

Aged 51 Y's, 6 M's, 10 D's.

Darling Freddie.

The Angels called Him.

MARY ELLEN,

WIFE OF

Chas. Williamson,

Born at Keene, N. H., Jan. 8, 1805.

Born into Spirit Life Sept. 6th, 1865.

NOT DEAD, BUT GONE BEFORE.

H. W. Billings.

December 1, 1872. Aged 36 Years.

CHARLES H.,

SON OF

Thos. & A. Smith,

—❖❖DIED❖❖—

December 25th, 1870. AGED 4 Y'S, 3 M'S & 4 D'S.

SACRED

to the Memory of

S. K. Mannering,

WHO DEPARTED THIS LIFE

August 10, 1871.   Aged 50 Years.

"I go to prepare a place for thee."

Rev. G. Wells,

BORN, —❖❖❖❖— DIED,

Sept. 21st, 1841.   Nov. 21st, 1872.

He Died as He Lived—a Christian.

Hon. M. Randall,

—❖❖DIED❖❖—

August 15, 1869. AGED 61 Years.

A Member of the U.S. Congress for 20 Years, he
died as he lived, a pure and upright man.

Wm. D. Hubbard,

Dec. 28th, 1873. Aged 92 Y's, 8 M's.

"Farewell to thee, my house of clay!
   Long have we two been bound together,
But I forsake thy porch to-day,
   And yield thee up to wind and weather.
Sleep, sleep at last! thy sleep shall be
My rest, my strength, my victory!"

Our Mother,

Died October 5, 1869. AGED 61 Years.

MINNIE B. PHELPS,

BORN INTO SUMMER LAND

Sept. 1st, 1872. Aged 19 Y's, 3 M's.

DARLING SISTER;

" Yet, though thou wear'st the glory of the sky,
  We know thou'lt keep the same beloved name;
The same fair, thoughtful brow and gentle eye,
  Lovelier in heaven a sweet climate, yet the same."

Mary L. Palmer,

ENTERED SPIRIT LIFE

September 9, 1872. Aged 38 Y's, 6 M's.

"O land beyond the setting sun!
   O realm more fair than poet's dream!
How clear thy silvery streamlets run,
   How bright thy golden glories gleam!
For well we know that fair and bright,
   Far beyond human ken or dream,
Too glorious for our feeble sight,
   Thy skies of cloudless azure beam."

Herbie:

**The angels called him on a sunny day,
August 15th, 1872.**

AGED 5 Y'S, 6 M'S, 4 D'S.

" We shall all go home to our Father's house,
   To our Father's house in the skies,
Where the hope of our souls shall have no blight,
   And our love no broken ties :
We shall roam on the banks of the River of Peace,
   And bathe in its blissful tide ;
And one of the joys of our heaven shall be,
   The little boy that died."

Importance of Early Moral Instruction.

To what may Failure in Life be Attributed.

IN CHILDHOOD and in youth the seeds are sown that determine the extent of the success we shall have, and the happiness we shall enjoy in later years.

Like the tender twig that bends with the slightest breeze, the child's mind is, in a very high degree, susceptible to the influence of good and evil. If favoring winds, a genial sun, copious rains and bounteous soil nurture the young plant, the tree in its maturity will be a noble specimen of its kind. So character in youth, impressed by every passing event, becomes evenly and harmoniously balanced in proportion to the fortunate circumstance of good birth, kind training in childhood, and wise government when the young are coming forward upon the threshold of active life.

President Garfield used to say that he never looked into the face of a boy, without a feeling of reverence at the thought of what the little fellow might achieve in future years. As we behold a group of children, of however humble and lowly condition, and contemplate the work that some of them may perform in life, we can well understand the sentiment that moved the martyred President, as he studied the face of a boy and thought of his future possibilities.

It is painful to contemplate how many bright, beautiful children come into this world of sunshine, to early sink into habits that will shadow their after-years.

In all the great cities, there are large numbers of women who have been unfortunate and have left all hope behind. There were periods in their childhood when, in their girlish dreams, the world seemed all beautiful and bright to them. Alas that they could not have been wise enough to have gathered a fair measure of the happiness that should be the right of woman.

In the haunts of vice and in the prisons there are tens of thousands of men to-day that stood, at one time in their childhood, where the road divides ; one path leading to indolence, intemperance and crime, the other to industry, morality, prosperity and happiness.

At the diverging point, a kind, judicious and wise teacher might have directed them into the better way, and thus they would have realized that fullness of success in life which is the natural ambition of man.

For that joyous, bright-eyed girl, for that laughing, happy boy, for the youth of the land everywhere, for all those who may be without the needed advice in the hour of trial, this chapter in the Album is prepared.

The hope is that those who read it will be so instructed by its perusal, that they will ever be thankful that they found and followed the lessons taught by these illustrations.

Right and Wrong Contrasted. Self-Willed and Obstinate. Kind and Obedient.

Willful and Disobedient.

A Kind and Obedient Child.

A COMMON character is here represented— the result of an evil and untrained nature, fostered by over-indulgence at home, and manifesting a sullen, disobedient disposition, which, unchecked, ripens into dangerous manhood and ends in disgrace and misery.

HOW pleasant is the contrast in this picture. Here is a gentle child, loving and obedient, confiding in his mother, and delighting in her instructions. As he advances he is likely to be a studious scholar, a faithful employe, and a kind employer.

The Trouble that Follows Falsehood. The Reward of Truth.

Telling a Falsehood.

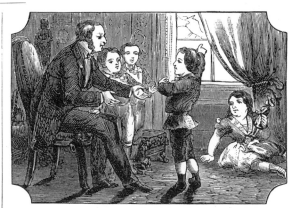

Explaining How it Happened.

WHO broke the window? The boy denies it to his father, and escapes punishment for the time. But, unless restrained by future discipline, he will grow up a deceitful youth, a dishonest man, trusted by none, and despised by all.

WE SEE this manly little fellow who has broken a window telling the story of his carelessness truthfully, his fine features glowing with the candor of his soul. In youth and manhood his unswerving love of truth will win confidence and success.

Quarrelsome Children in Contrast with Those of Sweet Disposition.

Engaged in a Disgraceful Fight.

Children that Know How to be Happy.

FEW scenes are more painful than a street fight between lads of tender years, who, unrestrained by proper training, give vent to their passions. In after-years the quarrelsome boy is likely to become a harsh and cruel man, unfitted for good society or companionship.

QUIET groves, green grass and summer air, where happy little children sport innocently amid the beauties of nature, speaking kind words and engaging harmoniously in their plays, shadow forth the peaceful dispositions and pursuits of their future lives.

The Effects of Good and Bad Company Illustrated.

Getting into Bad Company.

Good Society Brings Prosperity.

NO matter how good a boy is, if he falls into the society of vicious lads, and suffers himself to listen to their vile language and wicked schemes, he soon loses his innocence, gradually sinks into immoral habits, and becomes a *criminal*.

BY associating only with the pure and good, an innocent boy will save himself from falling into many hurtful snares, and in such society he will find healthful restraint and great encouragement, which will better prepare him for a prosperous manhood.

Evil Effects of Pernicious Literature upon Boys and Girls.

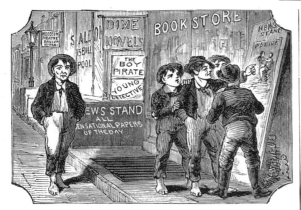

Looking Upon Obscene Pictures.

What Shall Our Young People Read?

THE disgraceful pictures at the news-stands corrupt the morals of boys and girls by presenting to their imaginations the vilest passions, leading to vice, destroying the innocence of youth, and reaping crime and degradation in their later lives.

A GOOD book or paper for a child is like a companion, and its influence is very similar. The child who reads nothing but romances and sensational literature weakens its intellect, depraves its morals, and is unfitted for the duties of a useful life.

The Advantage of the Sunday-School as a Means of Moral Instruction.

Sunday Work and Amusement.

Benefits of the Church and Sunday-School.

THE opportunities for needed moral improvement are to be had in nearly every locality, and yet, as shown in the above illustration, many in the desire for sensual enjoyment neglect to acquire that moral training which is essential to permanent success.

MANY an aged man and woman look back with peaceful remembrance to the hours of youth which they passed amid scenes like this, learning valuable lessons of natural and spiritual truth never to be forgotten, and never to be regretted.

Boys that are Honest Become Prosperous Men.

Thieves Engaged in Stealing.

Returning Lost Property to the Owner.

FROM petty thieving to robbery the road is short. The boy who allows himself to take what is not his own, be the article ever so small, is on the road to prison. Beware of the first wrong-doing. The coveting of the property of others often leads to crime.

BOYS should remember that property found and not restored to its owners, if possible, is *stolen*. It is something gained, but it does not belong to the finder, and gains made dishonestly are losses in the end. Always endeavor to give to all their due.

Youth who Respect the Aged and Profit by their Advice.

Lack of Respect for the Aged.

Kind Care and Regard for Old People.

MAKING sport of old people and cripples is inhuman. Yet how few young boys and girls remember to honor the aged, to assist them in their labors, and to cheer and comfort them in their troubles. Only the unkind and wicked ill-treat the old.

VERY few traits in youth are lovelier than this here indicated. Around the venerable, white-haired man stand youths, with heads uncovered, and listening to his counsel with the closest attention. With such respect should old age ever be treated.

The Difference in Conduct of Young Men Toward Ladies.

Corner Loungers Commenting on Passers-By.

Genial, Pleasant and Gentlemanly.

THE corner-idler, chewing tobacco, or smoking, lounging on boxes or against posts, talking foolishly and profanely, and leering at ladies as they pass, is an object of scorn and hatred, foreshadowing the depraved and dissolute man he will become.

IN HIS intercourse with women, the young man who has a proper estimation of himself will always be polite, friendly and agreeable to the young ladies, manifesting respect and gentleness toward those who are older. Early politeness paves the way to successful manhood.

The Refining Influence of Home Illustrated.

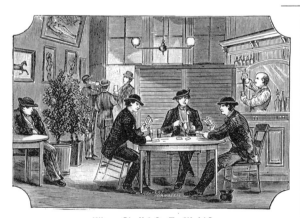

Where Shall I Go To-Night?

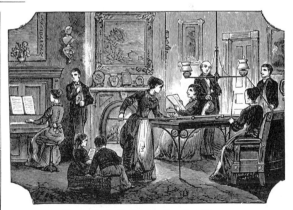

Home Made the Most attractive Place..

MANY are the resorts open to youth who seek amusement outside the family circle. Brilliant lights, music, exhibitions, games of chance and skill, and delightful beverages are fascinations hard to be resisted. But danger lurks beneath these attractions.

LET none forget that the young must be amused. Time properly allotted to each will afford ample opportunity for work, for study, for play and for rest. Home, by all the attractions with which love surrounds it, may be made the dearest spot on earth.

To What the First Step in Crime Ultimately Leads.

First Theft and Robbery—Then Murder.

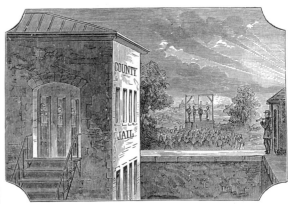

From Jail to Execution.

THE steps from house-breaking to murder are but few. Too often, from the effects of evil associations in childhood, our worst thieves and burglars are young men in their teens, and almost as frequently we find them taking life in order to gain money.

PROPERTY and life must be protected against dangerous criminals. When it is discovered that a boy or man is disposed to take for his own the property or life of another, the time has arrived when it becomes necessary to visit upon him the severest penalties.

Appropriating the Money of the Bank and the Final Consequences.

The Dishonest Confidential Clerk.

Sentenced to Imprisonment for Ten Years.

A YOUNG man, lacking moral principle and possessing ambitious desires, is entrusted by his employer to handle large sums of money. He sees his opportunity to speculate and make money, and cannot resist the temptation to steal. Too late he finds that he is ensnared.

ONLY a little time has elapsed since he stole his employer's money, yet he has been detected, tried, convicted and sentenced to imprisonment at hard labor. Reputation gone —prospects blasted—degraded to hardship and prison fare for ten long years—How sad the story !

Extremes of Pleasure To-Day. Sickness To-Morrow.

Excesses of Various Kinds.

Excesses Yesterday. Sickness and Sorrow To-Day.

SOCIAL pleasures, carried to excess, expose young men and women to danger of moral corruption and physical disorders. The feast, the dance, the social glass, immoderately indulged in, with late hours and evil associates, have often wrought ruin to the pure and good.

NATURE will rebel when the physical system is subjected to unwholesome excesses. As the people in this scene sowed, so have they reaped. Dissipation sapped the vigor of their constitutions, and debility, sickness and death have followed.

Sin Hides Behind Bolted Doors. Righteousness Does not Fear the Light.

The Guilty Flee when None Pursue.

Happiness at the Fireside.

BOYS who began their careers of wickedness in infancy have grown to manhood, laden with crime, outlaws of society, fearful of arrest at every turn, enjoying no peace even in their barred and bolted homes, where every noise startles them lest it be an officer of the law.

CONTRASTED with the opposite scene, behold a charming home, where father, mother, sons and daughters gather about the evening lamp and enjoy the life that honest competence, unselfish affection, intelligent and cheerful conversation brings.

As we Sow, we Shall Reap.

Poverty, Squalor, Intemperance and Crime.

Pleasant, Beautiful, Happy Homes.

THE neighborhood here shown is a representation and true type of hundreds of localities which exist all over the face of this fair land. The scene tells its own story—a tale of brutal passion, poverty, base desires, wretchedness and crime.

HOW great the difference! Intelligence, refined taste and prosperity are indicated in these beautiful dwellings. There may be error committed even here, but whatever morality, good sense and culture can do to make people better and happier is to be sought in such homes.

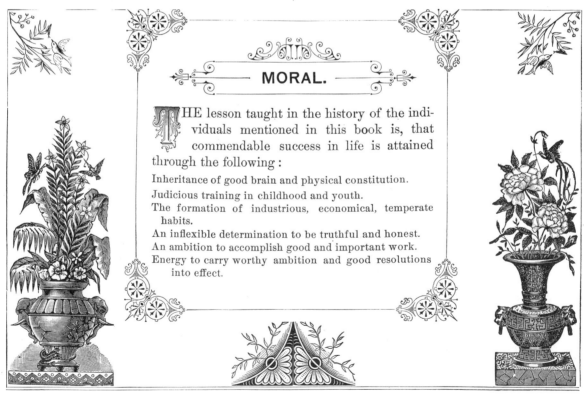

MORAL.

THE lesson taught in the history of the individuals mentioned in this book is, that commendable success in life is attained through the following:

Inheritance of good brain and physical constitution.

Judicious training in childhood and youth.

The formation of industrious, economical, temperate habits.

An inflexible determination to be truthful and honest.

An ambition to accomplish good and important work.

Energy to carry worthy ambition and good resolutions into effect.

How Training and Circumstances May Change the Mind.

What the Boy May Become.

IN THE success and failures of life much allowance must be made for training and circumstances. The inheritance at birth of a favorable temperament, physical constitution, and mental organization, is, in the beginning, a most important factor toward the accomplishment of grand purposes in life. To be born of evil parentage, to inherit weaknesses and gross appetites, to have bad training in infancy—these are circumstances that will very probably strongly tend to consign the individual to the lower walks of life. And yet, notwithstanding bad parental influence and inferior mental endowment, the course of life can be so regulated through education as to enable the person to become a respected and honored citizen. On the contrary the individual, though the possessor of naturally superior qualities of mind, may pursue a course which will bring sorrow and unhappiness through life.

The illustrations upon this page show the "**Two Roads**," which the boy, as he journeys toward manhood, may travel, the result of surrounding circumstances favorable or otherwise. Temptation crosses the pathway in youth. Possibly wise counsel comes at an opportune time, and the lad is thus enabled to resist the evil. No guiding hand, however, coming to the rescue, and adverse influences being at work undoing good admonitions, he falls into evil ways and wrecks the happiness and usefulness of his after-life. The following pictures tell the fact more forcibly than pen can portray.

The Downward Path.

—No. 1.—

THAT the debased man may have been a guileless youth, in the beginning, we show here the innocent face of the lad as presented in **No. 1**.

—No. 2.—

AGAIN we see him in **No. 2**, when the effect of evil company, late hours, profanity, neglect of personal appearance, and irregular life, begin to make themselves manifest.

—No. 3.—

YEARS go by, and at **No. 3** we see our boy, fair-faced in the beginning, now a listless lounger, with little ambition above tobacco, liquor, and the gratification of his low appetites.

—No. 4.—

BROKEN down and worn-out much before his time, we see him lastly at **No. 4**. The face tells its own story of dissipation, crime, degradation, and final misery.

Happy, Prosperous Life.

—No. 5.—

AGAIN we see, at **No. 5**, the guileless face of the boy, before whom the world stretches so far and wide with its opportunities and its temptations.

—No. 6.—

A FEW years and our boy is a smooth-browed, clear-eyed youth, whom we see at **No. 6**. He is living correctly, and he is doing rightly. This is shown in every lineament of his face.

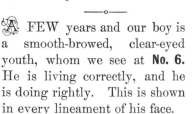

—No. 7.—

OUR boy has matured into manhood, at **No. 7**, with an evenly balanced mind, and aspirations all in the right direction; consequently success and prosperity greet him at every turn in his career.

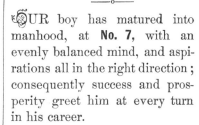

—No. 8.—

LIFE has been well-lived, and his last years find him, as seen at **No. 8**, in the midst of plenty, honored and beloved, resting serenely at the close, ready to live and ready to die.

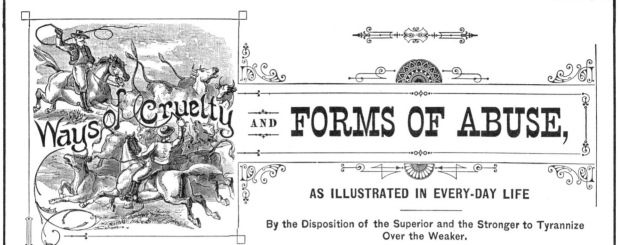

Ways of Cruelty AND FORMS OF ABUSE,

AS ILLUSTRATED IN EVERY-DAY LIFE

By the Disposition of the Superior and the Stronger to Tyrannize Over the Weaker.

ONE OF THE first instincts of nature among all mankind is to ornament. The savage will ignore all comfort—will sleep on the cold, wet earth—will endure the pangs of hunger—will undergo every privation, but in the midst of it all he will indulge himself in paints, beads, feathers and various modes of ornamentation.

Years pass and opportunities come for more real comfort to be attained, but the untutored man will be very slow to avail himself of the means which bring physical enjoyment. He will yet neglect to cook his food, he will be unsheltered and un-clad, but through it all the disposition to ornament remains strong and conspicuous.

This love of display runs through all grades of mind and all phases of civilization, to the exclusion of comfort. In fact, it is show first and comfort last. The belle will compress her waist until ruin of health and death result, for the sake of winning admiration. She will endure untold torture from tight shoes and uncomfortable dress for the love of display, and seek ease only at the end.

In all ages the fondness for show and neglect of comfort has been a characteristic of the human mind. The ancients were noted for their works of art, their superior frescoes, their grand architecture, but they had few conveniences. Little attention was given to wholesome cookery, little to ventilation, little to comfortable dress—all was for appearance.

Comfort is a modern institution. It has come with a later civilization. All the multiplied inventions of travel, correspondence, and methods of saving labor, are the result of a later intellectual development which has discovered that life is made happier by increase of comfort.

Man's Willing Servant.

WE SEE in this illustration a fair representation of one of the various breeds of horses now in use by civilized man. This picture is from real life, being a truthful portraiture of an intelligent horse—a beautiful dapple—as he stands ready to do his master's bidding.

It seems hardly possible that man should be so ignorant as to attempt to improve this animal's appearance by docking his tail, shearing away his hair, shutting out his sight by a blinder, and taking the arch out of his neck by a check-rein; but the folly of men is such as to cause them, because of fashion, to do all this.

To the disfiguring of the horse is added also a willingness to over-drive, under-feed, whip, over-load and otherwise ill-treat the animal according as impulse or passion may dictate, partly the result, often, of maliciousness on the part of the owner, and largely owing to man's carelessness and ignorance.

As with man himself in the past, so has it been with him in the treatment of the animals in his charge. His dog, if of a certain breed, must have his tail cut off and his ears clipped for style. And his horse, formerly dressed in elaborate trappings, with its tail cut short and turned upward, must yet have its hair clipped and its head held in a certain position, and all for show. Whether this affords the horse comfort or produces torture is a matter of no consequence to the owner.

A few humanitarians throughout the world have been thinking upon the subject, and have arrived at the conclusion that animals have some rights which should be regarded by their superiors. That among these is the right to all the enjoyment which may reasonably be had. That needless torture is a wrong which reacts upon the person who inflicts it. That all animals have their use in the economy of nature. That many of them have much more intelligence than they have been given credit for, and that all the domestic animals are entitled to kind treatment.

Gradually this sentiment has been spreading, until to-day, throughout the world, there are hundreds of humane societies whose expressed purpose is to suppress the cruelty which heretofore has been, and at present is, inflicted upon the helpless. As an aid in the furthering of that work the following original illustrations have been prepared, with the view of presenting the common cruelties practiced upon various animals, particularly the horse, one of the most intelligent, beautiful, serviceable and greatly abused of all.

The chapter closes with directions for the humane and efficient treatment of domestic animals.

HOW THE UNWISE USE OF THE CHECK-REIN DESTROYS THE BEAUTY OF THE HORSE.

Illustrations Showing that Holding the Horse's Head in Position by the Over-Check Does Not Improve His Appearance; on the Contrary it Very Seriously Mars its Beauty Besides Inflicting Torture.

AS WILL be seen below, the horse, which is one of the most beautiful animals in existence, is largely so because of his fine proportions and gracefully curving outline.

In all her objects of beauty nature furnishes the curve. She never allows a straight line. We see this in the outer form of the bird, leaf, blossom, tree, forest, mountain and planet. This is strikingly shown in the human countenance, which when wasted by disease loses its beauty through becoming thin, angular and full of straight lines. With returning health the face

The Horse in Natural Beauty,

becomes more full, more curve and color come into its lines, and beauty is restored.

Horsemen, in the dressing of the horse, should understand this law. As a well-cared-for, well-groomed horse cannot be improved in appearance by harness, there should be just as little of it used as possible, and every strap should be made as small as safety will allow. In short, the harness should be such as will allow the perfect outline of the animal, in all its parts, to stand freely forth.

IN THIS illustration we see the law of curved line violated. Not only is the strap running over the head made unduly conspicuous, but a straight line running thus over an arching neck is as much out of place as a straight pole would be by the side of a bed of roses. Again, this straight strap is not only a disfigurement

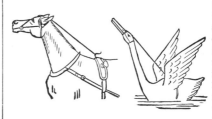
The Horse with Over-check.

of itself, but it is still further injurious to fine appearance in consequence of taking the curve from the horse's neck and converting it into a straight line, besides deranging, tangling, wearing off and breaking to pieces the mane, which in many horses is a leading and prominent feature of beauty.

It will also be seen that the grandeur of the animal's bearing and noble poise of head are all destroyed by this peculiar method of checking, which turns the eyes upward, the nose outward, and makes the neck appear considerably smaller than it really is.

It is impossible to resort to a device that will more effectually destroy the handsome appearance of fine horses than does this foolish appliance for raising the horse's head by means of the over-check.

The Folly of the Over-Check as Shown on Man and Horse.

THE over-check ruins the horse's appearance, and it does more: it inflicts a most cruel torture, which drivers can best appreciate when fastened in this position themselves. Suppose we fasten their heads back and give them a trial.

The first ten minutes these men will probably endure this constraint without much complaint; but as hours go by and pain in the neck becomes excruciating, and the mouth bloody from efforts to get the head down, they will understand and appreciate what causes the continual restless tossing of the head which a horse exhibits when he is thus tortured

Let the Drivers Try it Themselves.

by the over-check. To add to the pain arising from this terrible, unnatural position, let these men, while the sun is blinding their eyes, with their burdens to draw or carry, unable to see where they are to step, be whipped into a run over the rough roads of the town, and we have the brutality of the exhibition complete.

WE SEE here the contrast between the horse that is allowed to hold its head in natural position and that disfigured and tortured by a strap extending over the head.

This over-check contrivance was originated a few years ago by a noted horse-jockey, whose horse, when rapidly driven,

The Two Methods of Checking.

with the driver pulling upon the rein, made a whistling noise. To obviate this annoyance, he devised an iron martingale which held the nose upward. To avoid being laughed at while his horse wore this ridiculous arrangement, he advocated the idea that a rapidly driven horse could breathe more freely with its head held up. He made a good many horsemen believe this nonsense, and actually created a demand for something that would fasten the head into this unnatural position. The demand thus made was finally supplied by one Kimball Jackson, who introduced the silly contrivance known as the over-check.

Illustration of Check-Rein Cruelty.

TO FULLY realize the barbarities practiced upon some of our best horses, watch that beautiful team which stands at the church door, or in front of some store while the occupants of the carriage are engaged elsewhere.

Possibly the heads of the horses are held in torturing position by the side-check, which oftentimes holds the head painfully high, but quite likely it is the over-check. See the vigorous pawing of the earth, the champing of the bit, the throwing of the head, and restless turning of the neck from side to side in their endeavor to loosen the check, and get relief.

See the ignor-ant driver perched on the

Cruelly Tortured by High-Checking.

seat, all oblivious to the restlessness and frantic efforts of his horses to free themselves from their terrible pain. He supposes spectators will think that all their uneasiness and foaming at the mouth is an indication that they have high mettle.

THE team shown below represents the nervous, restless horses seen in the opposite picture. Before, they were unable to keep themselves quiet from the torture they were under-going. At the present, their checks are so easy as to give them no discomfort, and they restfully stand with arching neck, in their proud beauty, real objects of worthy admiration.

In Easy, Graceful Position.

Reader, we ask you to be a commit-tee of one to inter-est everybody you meet in the subject of loosening the check-rein. Par-ticularly do we ask you to kindly whis-per in the ear of the fair occupant of the carriage who rides behind these horses, that it be-comes her, while she enjoys the shopping, or en-gages in her devotions at church, to know that the animals which are patiently waiting her coming are not being tortured while in her service. Surely the natural sympathy of women would rectify these abuses if their attention could be drawn to the subject.

Sight Obscured by the Blinder and Strength Destroyed by the Check-Rein.

IT IS NOT alone the fine horse that has to suffer from the high check-rein. Too frequently the work-horse is compelled to draw the heavy load up the hill and out from the excavation with head fastened in such position as to make the effort to draw doubly laborious. This illustration represents the struggle of the team to pull the over-loaded wagon up the hill, their heads fastened by the check-rein. In the frantic en-deavor to accom-plish this work, one of the horses has broken its check and brought its head into natural posi-tion for draw-ing, while the other suffers both from the driver's lash and the in-ability to draw.

The kind mas-

The Check-Rein on Work-Horses.

ter will always loosen the check when his horse has a long hill to climb or heavy load to draw, and sensible horsemen dispense alto-gether with blinders and check-reins on their work-horses. It is beginning to be understood that all horses do better when blinders are not used.

BELOW is represented a common scene in front of the village groggery or the country store. The countryman came with his horse to town in the early morning, and has found refuge, drink and amusement in the saloon. The horse, fastened by the roadside, has stood through pelting storms of sleet and rain and snow, quite likely, from morning till night; and possibly, while its owner has been sleeping off a drunken de-bauch, has re-mained there all night and into the next day, and per-haps longer. The course for the humanely dis-posed to pursue with the horse found thus left by its master, ex-posed to inclement weather, is to make complaint to

All Day Suffering in the Storm.

the first police officer found, or to some one in authority, who should place the animal in a near, warm stable, to be cared for until the owner calls for his animal and pays for its keeping. If the authorities decline to act, the humanitarian should take the respon-sibility himself.

Though Ill-Treated all its Life, Struggling Faithfully to the Last.

AS IT IS always unfortunate for the helpless to be at the mercy of the cruel, so it is a sad misfortune to the horse to fall into the hands of an ill-tempered master.

The animal can never tell us what sufferings it endures from poundings in the stable, from the lash as it is being driven, and from beatings it is liable to receive upon any occasion. The picture here shown is a common one. The horse has in some manner given offense, and with a piece of board the master is pounding it over the head. Of course this brute in human form should have immediate arrest, as should any man who allows himself to inflict torture upon his

Beaten by a Cruel Master.

horses, or give vent to his passions by whipping the dumb and helpless animals in his charge when he is himself under the influence of anger.

It is unnecessary to add that however kind the disposition of this horse may have been in the beginning, it is soon spoiled by this cruel treatment.

POSSIBLY the horse that so faithfully serves the family for long years, as his vigor and sprightliness depart, is sold to a teamster, who often compels it to draw such heavy loads as to cause lameness and general worthlessness. Having become feeble with age and hard labor, the horse, by a kindly disposed master, should then be shot and its trials ended. But this is not

The Last Days of the Old Family Horse.

usually done. Instead, the animal is again sold to the junk or fruit peddler, who, in many of the cities throughout the country, may be seen with his blind, old horse in such lame and decrepit condition as to be barely able, under the influence of vigorous whipping, to draw its load about the town. In many cases the old horse owes its extreme feebleness to lack of necessary food as well as general abuse. If, upon complaint, the owner refuses to take the creature from service, the officers of the law should immediately terminate the life of the animal, and arrest its owner for compelling it thus to continue such a miserable existence.

The Willing Horse Driven to Its Ruin by the Reckless Driver.

WE HAVE here a scene by far too common. It tells its own story. The liveryman has horses to let. Two roughs appear at the stable, apply for a horse, and get it. The owner should have known from their appearance that they would ruin his horse, if allowed to drive it; but his desire for money causes him to yield the animal into their hands.

We see the bright, high-lifed animal as it starts from the barn, from the very first cruelly overchecked by its ignorant owner. This fine horse, with no loosening of the check, is driven up the hill and down the hill; is over-heated, has no water to drink, or too much, as the case may be; is

In the Hands of Fast Young Men.

compelled to stand, with foaming perspiration, in the wind, while the drivers carouse in some drinking place, and thus with the general ill treatment it has to endure throughout the day, the animal more intelligent in many respects than those who abuse it, has its strength and health forever destroyed.

NO ONE will require to have this picture described. The drunken men who have driven this faithful beast so nearly to death that it can scarcely stand, deserve severe punishment; and as the owner in his anger shakes his fist at the rowdies when giving his horse the first comfort of the day, as he lets its head down, we are inclined to think, by his high checking and

Ruined by Fast Driving.

hiring out the horse to these irresponsible fellows, that he has much blame to bear as well as the drivers who have ruined his horse. In either case, the livery-horse, through the mistakes of its owner and the ill-usage of all kinds of drivers, is liable to be very greatly abused.

Many people think, when a horse is being over-driven by strangers, that it is alone the business of the owner to care for his property; but public good requires that any one seeing a horse ill-treated should admonish the driver, and if he persists in this misconduct he should be turned over to the officers of the law.

Cruelties Inflicted While Conveying Calves and Cattle to Market.

NEXT to horses and older cattle, calves are subjected to the greatest amount of abuse at the hands of cruel men, the trials of these creatures often beginning when they are but a few weeks old, as shown in this illustration representing the butcher, who has been a dozen miles into the country to find his load of these young animals with which to supply veal for his market.

The scene in this picture is a true one. With feet closely tied, the poor beasts are packed promiscuously together, their heads dangling over the sides of the wagon, often torn and bloody by the wheels wearing into their flesh, and with eyes looking

Tortured While Being Transported.

pleadingly upon the passer-by, they are carried to the slaughter. Like all brutal customs, the sight of this begets a hardened feeling upon the mind of the spectator. Humanity, as well as regard for health, requires that all animals designed for food be kept in comfortable condition while being taken to market.

IF THE horned animal is allowed to grow to maturity, its sufferings will very likely commence when transported to market. The following is a common sight. Too many cattle are placed in the car. The weaker, when conveyed long distances, fall, and are trampled by the stronger. To avoid this the drivers, armed with sharp iron-spikes, prod the animal when likely to fall, until oftentimes the blood flows in streams. Cattle frequently arrive at their journey's end terribly mutilated from this horrible cruelty.

Another barbarity practiced is that of salting the animals before the journey is commenced, and giving them little to eat and no water,

Prodding Cattle with Sharp Irons.

though they may be insane from thirst, until arrived at the market, possibly two or three days after starting. The journey completed, the animals are allowed to gorge themselves with food and quench their thirst; their weight is greatly increased, and the driver realizes large profit on the sale of the hay and the water they contain.

Scenes that are Common in the Village and the Great City.

IT HAS fallen to the lot of this cow to be in the hands of an economical owner, who determines that she shall obtain her food in the streets. The cow that is consigned to the street has a terrible ordeal to pass. There will come the hot, dry, dusty days, when vegetation will cease to grow, and, enfeebled by hunger, she must starve or save herself by breaking into the yards where she sees green grass growing. Then come the hoots and yells of men and boys with stones and clubs, accompanied by the biting and tearing of her flesh by dogs.

The accompanying illustration, which is absolutely true to life, is the well-known village cow, with tail bitten off, and horn

Stoned by Boys and Bitten by Dogs.

torn away through the cruelties she has had to undergo. This animal, emaciated by starvation, that quenches her thirst at the putrid mud-puddle—that is chased, stoned and clubbed a dozen times a day, furnishes the milk that is expected to nourish, at the close of the day, a family of little children.

CHILDHOOD has an unwritten history of suffering that will never be told. We see faint glimpses of some of these in this picture.

There is the little waif in charge of the organ-grinder, who must tramp her dreary way, early and late, with her master and his monkey, the joy of sunny childhood unknown to her. There is the little bent form of a girl compelled to grow under loads of wood, which she constantly gathers for the family use; and there is also the frail beggar-girl, in her rags, trained by her master to assume a look of distress, who will know very little of happy girlhood.

Even the chil-

Methods of Cruelty to Children.

dren of the rich, through ignorance of parents, must often endure their trials, as shown in the warmly wrapped and hooded girl in the foreground, whose lower limbs are constantly allowed to be so exposed to even the most freezing weather as to subject her to sickness, suffering and an early death.

Trials Endured at the Hands of the Hard Master and the Brutal Husband.

WHILE depravity of the human mind is shown in the wanton cruelty which men will often needlessly inflict upon inferior animals, so the lower nature of human beings reveals itself in the disposition of the stronger man to gratify passion by bullying, browbeating and inflicting pain upon the weaker. As we look through the window on the picture we see this demon-

Under Control of a Hard Master.

strated in the larger boy, who is a rowdy and a rough. And in the foreground we have it very clearly shown in the beating which the master inflicts upon the boy in his charge, evidently in anger, and possibly for some trifling offense.

In a majority of cases, pain inflicted thus in anger debases the master and brutalizes the nature of the child. The boy who is much whipped and ill-treated is liable to lose self-respect, and to become coarse, vindictive, ill-tempered and cruel.

Our prisons contain many criminals who entered upon careers of vice because of the brutalities they had to endure in childhood

PROBABLY no greater misfortune ever happens to woman than that which comes from linking her destiny with a husband who turns out to be a drunkard with a vicious temper. To continually tremble lest the husband shall return in maudlin condition to embarrass the family, is suffering enough; but to wait and listen into the late hours of the night, dreading, fearing the

The Sufferings of Mother and Child.

uncertain approaching steps of that creature who asserts the right to enter, but who may be so crazed with drink as to take the life of all his family before the morning, is agony before which all other sorrows are but trifles in comparison.

Reader, we can present you a picture no more horrible than this. What a world of suffering, of heartache, of deprivation and cruelty it reveals, and that, too, while it is absolutely true. That poorly furnished room, the frightened, hungry, trembling little girl, the anxious, suffering mother—all tell their tales of sorrow.

Needless Torture of Birds, by Men and Boys, for Pleasure.

MAN IS said to be superior to the lower animals because of moral nature. This claim of human superiority, however, is denied by those who have given the subject thought, the argument being that while the lower animal will take life for food it is never known to wantonly torture for pleasure or to take the life of other animals as an amusement.

The innate enjoyment which men experience in witnessing the throes of death is strikingly shown in those countries where tribe wars with tribe—where the criminal is devoured by the wild beast, and where encouragement is given to bull-fighting and the contest between wild animals. This in-born cruelty in the

Killing Birds for Amusement.

human soul is still further shown in men, laying claim to superior intellectual capacity, moral endowment and a Christian education, who will assemble at stated times and places, and there waste time and money in the singular enjoyment and curious pleasure of shooting pigeons.

HUNTING for inoffensive and innocent animals for the purpose of taking their lives, as a sport, is a pastime in which many people delight to engage. Why men enjoy this taking of life as a pleasure, and without necessity, can only be accounted for on the ground that the barbarous in their nature still lingers as a relic of a past age, in which constant hunting

Cruel Acts by Man and Boys.

and killing was necessary in order to sustain life.

While the man, as shown in this illustration, is free to shoot the bird, it is very reasonable to suppose that boys, who imitate the example of their elders, will feel themselves free to indulge the cruelty of destroying birds' nests and of killing any of the little songsters that may be found or that come in their way.

This wholesale slaughter of birds is sometimes fraught with serious results, as was shown a few years since, when the grasshopper devastated the land in consequence of the general killing, by hunters, of the prairie-chicken.

The Savage Instincts of Men and Boys Illustrated.

IN CERTAIN parts of Europe there are men who support large numbers of servants, horses and dogs for the simple purpose of getting pleasure from chasing rabbits. The picture here shown is a common one in England and Ireland.

The grandee is out in full force—men, horses and dogs. The little animal fleeing for its life, and entirely innocent of doing the least wrong, will be captured ere long and torn by the dogs limb from limb. This will be occasion for great congratulation by the lords of the chase, and will end in a banquet and champagne supper. In the meantime the poor peasants, whose crops are destroyed by this troop of hunters across their little

Hunted and Mutilated for Sport.

fields, bemoan their fate; but they have no redress.

It is an honor to England that she was the first to inaugurate humane societies, whereby ultimately, the cruelties of the chase will be all banished from her soil.

CRUELTY and tendency to destroy are common with boys of a certain class; a fact to be deplored, as the youth who will deliberately pick a fly to pieces, step on a worm, or torture any helpless animal, will very likely develop into the selfish, base-hearted, cruel man.

The boys here shown are types of the rougher element in society,

Gratification of Savage Instinct.

who delight in tyrannizing over and frightening the weaker; their chief pleasure is in hurling some missile at the unoffending dog, the stray cat, or any animal that crosses their pathway. From this class come the dissolute, the reckless, the depraved and the criminal classes.

Even among the professedly refined people the spirit of mischief among boys, if not checked by wholesome instruction, is liable to develop into rudeness and cruelty. With some boys the simple fact that any small animal is unprotected is a signal for abuse.

The Street Fountain an Ever-Living, Public Blessing.

NO DETAILED description is necessary for this illustration. It speaks for itself. The boy has fallen from the pier, and the faithful, sagacious dog has rushed to the rescue. Well may we understand how the anxious parents grasp their drowning child when he comes within their reach, while they bestow every kindness thenceforth upon the faithful animal that saved him.

This is but one of thousands of instances of a similar kind. The calendar is full of accounts of great service rendered through the sagacity of the horse, and of property saved and human lives rescued through the affection and intelligence of dogs. Even down in the lower

The Fidelity of the Dog.

grades of animals the affection and fidelity they cherish for those who care for them make a strong claim upon our kindness and sympathy, and should impress the law of kindness so emphatically on our natures as to make it impossible to torture or to cruelly treat them.

WHAT a grand benevolence is steadily pouring forth in this public fountain! How the tired, hot, thirsty animal, that cannot tell us of its trials, drinks of the water and turns its face towards us in thankfulness! Here the dog is saved from madness, the bird dresses its plumage and the horse is strengthened for its labor. Even the wayfaring man, who

A Great and Constant Blessing.

otherwise might have sought drink in the saloon just across the way, slakes his thirst, is refreshed, and has saved his money and his mind.

For a people in any community, what a grand boon is conferred by the presentation of such a fountain! How much real comfort it affords! What an ever-flowing blessing to the thirsty wayfarers in the dusty city, whose privileges are few at best.

Like the donor of this fountain, who took delight in doing kindness, may it ever be our pleasure to make the pathway of the unfortunate easier, to alleviate suffering, and to "speak for those who cannot speak for themselves."

BAD HABITS OF HORSES.

Horse Made Cross by Teasing.

Their Cause, and How to Overcome Them Through Humane Treatment.

THE BAD habits of horses, as of men, are traceable either to inheritance from vicious parentage or the carelessness of their trainers. A horse's natural temper, like a man's, may display itself in its infancy, and be eradicated by humane and proper training; but if neglected, or perpetuated as something amusing, the mature animal will retain it to a vicious degree through life.

Among the most common of these evil habits are balking, kicking, crib-biting, running away, rearing, shying, pawing, and dislike to being mounted, and these, and the remedies to be applied for their correction, are here described, several of the suggestions being those effectually practiced by Mr. Pratt the noted horse-trainer.

To Prevent Pawing.

Attach a rope from the fore-feet to a ring in a surcingle, and thence to a crupper under the tail. Have this sufficiently tight to make a sharp pull on the crupper whenever the horse indulges in pawing, and the pain inflicted will cause the horse ultimately to cease the habit.

Rearing.

This habit is broken up by the use of a strong martingale. If a horse rears in a carriage, attach a cord tightly around the thickest part of the body, tied with a loop-knot, and have the other end in the carriage. Unable to expand its body on account of the rope around it, it is impossible for the animal to rear. This plan never fails.

To Make a Horse Get Up That Refuses to Rise.

A sulky horse, in the habit of lying down and expressing unwillingness to get up when told to do so, may be cured by lifting up the head and pouring a pint of cold water into the nostrils from a cup. The water stops the breath, as if in the act of drowning, and the horse becomes frightened and springs to its feet. The remedy is simple, but is said to be effectual.

To Prevent Crib-Biting.

Horses accustomed to crib-biting should have their mangers built on the floor. The attempt to gnaw it requires the animal to get his mouth below his chest, which prevents indulgence in the habit.

A remedy that will effectually break up the vice, is to cover the edges of the manger and hayrack, etc., with sheep-skins, having the wool outside, and the wool well sprinkled with cayenne-pepper.

To Prevent Running Away.

Horses will sometimes acquire this habit, possibly by fright at first, and afterward indulge in it viciously. A strong, cool-headed driver, a curb-strap and sharp bit is the best treatment known.

When the opportunity offers and the horse is resolved to run, a most excellent method of preventing the desire is to give the horse a full opportunity to run, and that, too, right under the whip, until the animal is badly exhausted. A few vigorous runs of this kind will remind the horse that running is not an agreeable exercise.

To Prevent a Horse Kicking at Persons Who Enter its Stall.

Put the Bonaparte bridle, elsewhere described, on the horse. Drive a staple at the side of the stall, near the manger, three or four feet from the floor, and fasten another staple at the entrance of the stall, the same distance above the floor. Pass the halter-cord through both staples and tie it at the outer one. When entering the stall, pull sharply on the rope, saying "go over." The head of the horse will be drawn towards the person and its heels to the opposite side. All danger is thus averted, and the horse soon learns to abandon its bad habit.

To Prevent Shying.

This fault is usually the result of early fright. To overcome the habit, lead the horse up to anything of which it is afraid, let it smell of the object and see that no harm comes from it. A plan pursued by some horse-trainers is to throw the animal, and when in this position rub the nose with a buffalo-skin, throw the skin upon its head, open and shut an umbrella over it, and thus familiarize the creature with the presence of those things at which it shies until it understands that these can do it no injury. The horse that shies in the blinder will frequently be found much more brave when the blinder is removed and the horse is fully able to see all the objects about him. Patience and gentleness must be exercised with the timid horse. Harshness and whipping only aggravate the difficulty.

To Prevent Pulling on the Halter.

Put a common halter on the horse from which the hitching-strap has been removed. Then double a small cord, about eighteen feet long, in the center, place the loop under the tail and cross the cords on the back; bring the ends of the cord each side of the neck and place them through the strap of the halter under the mouth and tie to a tree or post. Tie a strap from the mouth to a post or tree so that it will be one foot shorter than the rope after tightening it at the tail; then cut the strap half off, and afterward frighten the horse by rolling a barrel in front of it. This will cause it to dodge backward, breaking the strap, when it will be caught under the tail by the rope and be severely punished. After this process has been repeated two or three times the horse will learn not to pull on the halter again.

To Prevent a Horse Getting Cast in the Stall.

In the ceiling over the manger, at the side of the stall, drive a staple, and another in the center of the ceiling, over the horse's head. Pass a small cord through the staple at the side of the stall, and to the end of it attach a horse-shoe or piece of iron of about the same weight, so that the cord will not draw out of the staple. Then pass the other end of the cord through the staple in the center of the stall, bring it down within two and a half feet of the floor, cut it off and attach a common harness snap to it. Fasten a ring in the strap of the halter at the top of the horse's head and into this hook the snap. When the horse raises up its head the weight goes down, and when its mouth is on the floor it can lie down to rest, but it cannot get the top of its head down to the floor, and unless it can do this it cannot roll, and if it cannot roll it cannot get cast.

To Keep the Tongue in the Mouth.

The habit of allowing the tongue to dangle from the mouth may be prevented by a circular piece of leather on each side of the bit that extends down to the tongue when it is out. Attached to this leather should be sharp points, the pricking of which will cause the animal to withdraw its tongue. These pins thus worn for awhile, and the tongue severely pricked every time it is hung out, on one side or the other of the mouth, the horse will soon learn to keep its tongue where it belongs.

Another plan suggested is to take an ordinary straight-bit, five-eighths of an inch in diameter, and drill two holes, each one three-fourths of an inch from the center; then procure a piece of very small chain, attach to it iron bullets about the size of a musket-ball, and let them hang in the mouth about one and a half inches, by the chain, from the bit. Use this instrument and bit for a week or more.

To Prevent Uneasiness While Being Mounted.

Two causes make horses unsteady or uneasy while being mounted. Either it arises from eagerness to start, or unwillingness to be ridden, and in both cases it involves the rider in danger. Severity beyond firmness does no good, but is rather an injury. A strong, agile, energetic man is necessary to break the habit where eagerness to start causes it. The rider should be free from fear, carelessly and confidently approach the horse, gather the reins in his left hand and help himself quickly into the saddle with the other. Once there his energies must be exerted to control the motion of the horse, patting it and not permitting it to go forward until under perfect submission. If the uneasiness of the horse is due to unwillingness to be mounted or driven, to conquer it will require frequent contests of strength and waste of time, for the horse cannot be depended upon with any certainty after all attempts to subdue the habit.

To Cure the Habit of Kicking.

Raise one fore-foot of the animal and fasten it there. Then attach a strap to the hind foot and from thence to a rope around the neck of the animal. Release the fore-foot and let the horse kick. As every strike results in punishment to the horse itself, it will soon desist from further kicking. Another plan is to place a thorn-bush behind the animal and let it kick until it ceases from the pain inflicted upon itself.

Pratt's method was to throw the horse, as described elsewhere, while held with a strong and hard bridle in the mouth. While down, with a board he then irritated the legs, and every time the horse kicked he jerked upon the bridle and said "whoa." The horse was given to understand in this treatment that kicking meant punishment, and finally when it ceased and submitted to the rubbing of the board, he caressed the animal. Afterward the horse was allowed to rise and its power to resist the habit was then tried. If the animal kicked, a severe pull on the bridle and the word "whoa" was again a reminder that punishment followed kicking. Finally the horse was placed in a cart and every inducement given it to kick. If the horse yielded to the habit, vigorous jerking and the word "whoa" made the practice so very uncomfortable for the animal as to effectually overcome the habit.

To Overcome Unwillingness to be Caught.

Horses that are turned into pasture with a whoop and a blow as they jump over the bottom rail of the fence or gate-bar, are usually the ones which get into a habit of not liking to be caught again, through fear. To break up this habit its cause should be stopped, and the Bonaparte bridle should be used. Put the bridle on the horse and tie a knot at the mouth to prevent its slipping down to the teeth, lest it be bitten in two. Carry the cord up to the mane over the shoulder. Tie part of the mane together with a string. Pass the cord through the loop thus made in the mane, and bring it through a loop made in the same way in the tail, leaving the cord from ten to fifty feet long, dragging on the ground. To train the horse, carefully approach it from behind, grasp the cord firmly and say "come here!" at the same time pulling strongly on the cord. After three or four lessons the cord may be removed, but the horse will then have learned to obey the command—the effect of the punishment received from the cord at its mouth.

Another method of producing willingness to be caught when in the pasture, is that of frequently visiting the horses when in the field, calling them and feeding a small amount of grain, as a reward for their coming, at the same time caressing them. The confidence of almost any domestic animal can, by kindness, be secured in a manner such as to make it willing to serve us.

To Prevent Balking.

Time and much patience are necessary to remedy this fault, and various are the devices used to overcome the habit. One course to pursue, when a horse balks in a public place, is to speak gently to the animal, and while standing beside it, by little raps on the fetlocks, with the foot, cause it to set its fore-feet further and further forward until, gradually, it will move ahead.

Sometimes a pebble in the ear, dirt in the mouth, a nail under the harness or any contrivance that will divert the mind of the horse from its intention to stop, may effect good results. All or any of these serve the purpose better than harsh treatment.

Another method is to hitch the horse to a light load in an unfrequented street or road, and drive it moderately until it balks. Then tie the reins to the wagon, dismount and wait until the animal is ready to go on again, without remonstrance or other treatment of any kind. Hours may elapse before it will feel inclined to go forward, but its obstinacy will at last subside; especially if hunger prompts it to move homeward. Take it all as a matter of course, and after a few experiences of this kind, the horse will understand that nothing is gained by balking and give up the habit.

If the balk can be traced to too heavy a load for the horse to draw, it should be lightened before proceeding to other measures. To stamp, yell and flourish the whip, like one insane, can have no good effect on the horse, for such actions only serve to confuse its senses. If the collar galls its neck or chest, the pain may cause the balk; the remedy, then, is to apply proper padding to the chafed places, and gently encourage the animal to be led far enough to convince it that the soreness has been relieved.

TRICKS AND PERFORMANCES OF HORSES.

HOW HORSES MAY BE TAUGHT TO PERFORM.

The Means by Which Trick-Horses are Trained.

ANY CURIOUS performances of trick-horses at the circus and agricultural fairs attract the attention and excite the admiration of spectators. Among these are the following: To walk up and down stairs; to "laugh"; to push a vehicle; to sit down; to say "No"; to walk on its knees; to mount a box; to waltz; to walk on its hind-feet; to go lame; to drive a boy off a box; to bow, and to shake hands.

The first requisite in this sort of training is

A Bonaparte Bridle,

which is thus made and applied: Take a piece of clothes-line, or a cord a little larger, ten feet long; tie a loop at one end just large enough to loosely encircle the lower jaw of the horse when placed in its mouth; then pass the rest of the cord over the horse's head on the off-side, just behind its ears, bring it down to and pass it through the loop on the other side, pulling it firmly. The loop in the mouth forms the bit, the cord passed over the head makes the bridle, and the remainder of the cord is an effectual halter in the hands of the trainer. This bridle is recommended by Professor O. S. Pratt, the horse-trainer, author of a most excellent work entitled "The Horse's Friend," as a perfect restraint upon the movements of the horse while teaching him to drive, carry burdens, or amuse the spectators. To make this bridle doubly effective, after adjusting it as above described, pass the loose cord through the right hand; then with the left hand take the cord, place it over the top of the horse's head, bringing the cord down with the left hand under the upper lip, resting against the upper teeth, forming another loop.

Mr. Pratt instructed a horse to

Walk Up and Down Stairs

by putting a rope around the neck, bringing it down through the mouth and back through the loop on the neck; then he jerked the rope until the fore-feet were ever so slightly raised, and then stopped operations to caress and sooth the horse; then he checked the horse's head up to a surcingle—from the bit to the side-ring; then the cord was jerked again, saying, "get up, sir!" and causing the horse to rise on his hind-feet alone. By repeating these operations carefully, and caressing the horse each time that it does well, it may soon be made to perform the trick of going up and down steps by the motion of a whip alone.

Teaching the Trick-Horse.

To "Laugh."

The horse's lip is to be pricked with a common pin till it lifts its upper lip; then caress and pet it, and ere long, when pointed at, and hearing the word "laugh," it will know that its lip must be turned up or pricked.

To Sit Down.

This requires a tractable horse to begin with. Having put on the Bonaparte bridle, to control its movements, put a harness collar on the neck. Buckle a pole-strap around each hind leg, below the fetlock-joint, and to the other end of each strap fasten a cord ten or twelve feet long; then pass each cord through the collar towards the head, on each side of the horse; then bring the ends back behind the animal, at the same time holding the end of the Bonaparte bridle. Pulling strongly on both cords, repeating the words "sit down," the horse will be drawn backward until he sits down. This position should not last more than a few seconds at first. The operation having been repeated three times a day for about a week, the trainer indicating by a whip what is expected, and uttering the command, the horse will sit down when told to do so.

To Mount a Box and Push a Vehicle.

With the Bonaparte bridle lead the horse to the box—one eighteen inches high—and tell it to "mount it." Not understanding the order, it will not do it until it learns what is required. The trainer holding the horse by the bridle, the assistant gently lifts its fore-foot, places it upon the box, and leaves it there. Caress the horse while it holds its foot on the box, and give the command to "get down," backing it by a slight strain on the bridle. When the foot is taken down caress the horse again. Repeat the operation until the animal obeys both orders promptly, and then train it in the same manner to put the other foot upon the box and take it down. Then repeat again, placing both feet upon the box at once, and teach as in the first two instances. A little practice, with caresses to sooth the horse's nerves, will soon result in obedience without the use of the bridle.

MODERN FASHIONABLE CARRIAGES AND VEHICLES IN GENERAL USE.

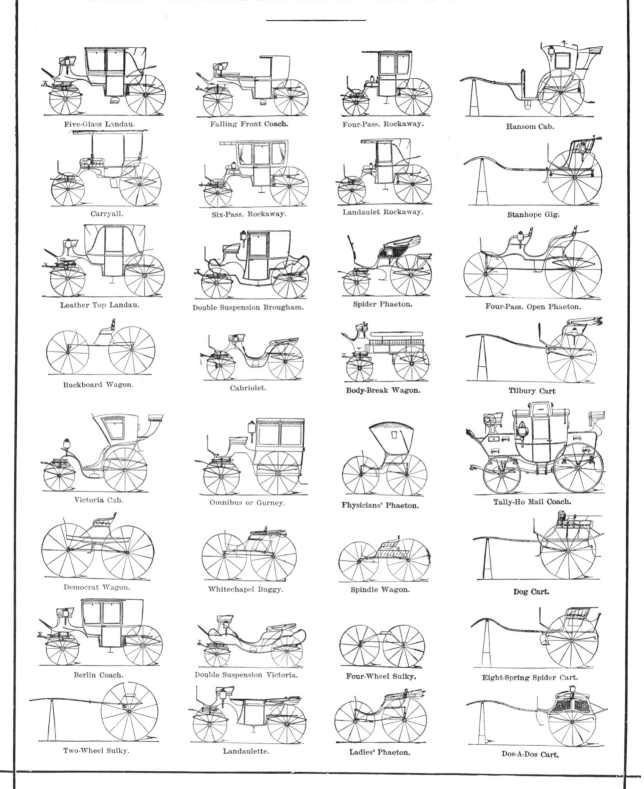

Five-Glass Landau.

Falling Front Coach.

Four-Pass. Rockaway.

Hansom Cab.

Carryall.

Six-Pass. Rockaway.

Landaulet Rockaway.

Stanhope Gig.

Leather Top Landau.

Double Suspension Brougham.

Spider Phaeton.

Four-Pass. Open Phaeton.

Buckboard Wagon.

Cabriolet.

Body-Break Wagon.

Tilbury Cart

Victoria Cab.

Omnibus or Gurney.

Physicians' Phaeton.

Tally-Ho Mail Coach.

Democrat Wagon.

Whitechapel Buggy.

Spindle Wagon.

Dog Cart.

Berlin Coach.

Double Suspension Victoria.

Four-Wheel Sulky.

Eight-Spring Spider Cart.

Two-Wheel Sulky.

Landaulette.

Ladies' Phaeton.

Dos-A-Dos Cart.

LATE STYLES OF FASHIONABLE CARRIAGES AND SLEIGHS.

Jump Seat Phaeton.   Tandem Dog-Cart.   Goddard Buggy.   Physicians' Rockaway.

Brougham.   Dos-a-dos Wagon.   Village Cart.   Vis-a-vis Phaeton.

Canopy Top Phaeton.   Victoria.   Surrey Wagon.   Four Passenger Wagon.   T-Cart.

Top Surrey.   Side-Bar Buggy.   Corning Buggy.   Concord Spring Buggy.   Depot Wagon,

Square Body Sleigh.   Shell Body Cutter.   Pony Sleigh with Rumble.   Victoria Shell Body Sleigh.   Six-Passenger Shell Body Sleigh.

Russian Cabriolet Sleigh.   Cabriolet Sleigh.   Russian Vis-a-vis Sleigh.   Victoria Sleigh.   Leather Top Landau Sleigh.

Copenhagen Sleigh.   Portland Cutter.   Jump Seat Sleigh.   Curricle Sleigh.   Russian Sleigh.   Albany Swell Cutter.

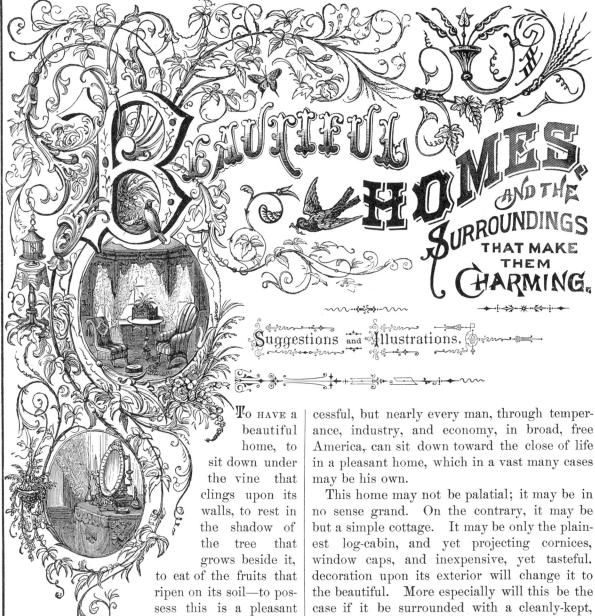

Beautiful Homes, and the Surroundings that make them Charming.

Suggestions and Illustrations.

To have a beautiful home, to sit down under the vine that clings upon its walls, to rest in the shadow of the tree that grows beside it, to eat of the fruits that ripen on its soil—to possess this is a pleasant dream and a worthy ambition. To fail of this is to largely miss life's purpose.

The pages of this book contain the record of many lives, all of whom have attained eminence in certain directions. They are presented as examples of the power to achieve. It is true that all cannot be equally great nor equally suc- cessful, but nearly every man, through temper- ance, industry, and economy, in broad, free America, can sit down toward the close of life in a pleasant home, which in a vast many cases may be his own.

This home may not be palatial; it may be in no sense grand. On the contrary, it may be but a simple cottage. It may be only the plain- est log-cabin, and yet projecting cornices, window caps, and inexpensive, yet tasteful, decoration upon its exterior will change it to the beautiful. More especially will this be the case if it be surrounded with a cleanly-kept, closely-shaven lawn, interspersed with winding pathways, trees, shrubs, flower-beds and arbors, arranged and constructed with artistic taste.

This closing chapter is, therefore, devoted to an exposition of that which offers to all a field in which to excel—a good and noble purpose— that of making for themselves or others BEAU- TIFUL HOMES.

Residence Architecture
—as—
A Fine Art.

Costly Residences
—and—
Elegant Grounds.

Fig. 34--View of Residence.

Results of Wealth.

FIG. 34 shows another beautiful American home, with Mansard-roof and tower, taken by permission of Messrs. Bicknell & Comstock, publishers, New York, from Croft's " Progressive American Architecture. " A low fence, which is little more than a coping, determines the outer edge of the lot. The curving walks, arching windows, and graceful fountain satisfy the desire for curves. The principles of contrast and proportion are here also finely shown.

As the best appropriately comes at the close of the feast or the entertainment, so the elaborate home shown in **Fig. 35,** comes at the close of this chapter. This represents the residence of Mr. J. C. Flood, the San Francisco millionaire, which is eligibly situated at Menlo-Park, California, a beautiful suburb twenty miles from San Francisco. The work upon this edifice occupied several years, and the cost of the residence, complete, was not far from $1,000,000. It is undoubtedly one of the very finest dwellings ever designed and erected in America. In it are combined all the

Architectural Achievement.

elements that make the beautiful in architecture and landscape gardening, as shown in its curves, its harmonious proportions, its bold reliefs, and its greatness and grandeur, which make the sublime.

While in this chapter have been shown mostly expensive dwellings, as illustrative of those which constitute the charming, the aim has been to show principles in such a manner as will teach the poorest to surround themselves with adornment that will make their homes, however humble, the abodes of beauty. Amid such surroundings may the children of coming generations be born.

The study of architecture, and of the embellishment of public and private buildings, is one of the most interesting that can occupy the lover of the beautiful in art and nature. In it are developed the richest gifts of genius, delighting the senses and filling the mind with the sublimest thoughts, and affording a wide scope for the imagination in the creation of the noblest forms, the ornamentation of waste places, and the decoration of the humblest abode.

Fig. 35--Residence of Mr. James C. Flood,
At Menlo Park, California. Augustus Lever, Architect, San Francisco.

COMMENDATIONS

FROM

DISTINGUISHED EDUCATORS AND EMINENT MEN.

NO work of an educational character, of late years, has met with such universal approval from teachers and learned men as this. While the book is most warmly welcomed by the illiterate, it is equally sought for by the educated. Hundreds of testimonials from distinguished individuals might be given similar to the following:

From Samuel Fallows, ex-State Supt. Pub. Schools, Wisconsin.

"I am highly delighted with the plan and execution of Hill's Manual."

From Prof. J. G. Cross, Principal of the Northwestern Business College, Naperville, Ill.

"It is a most valuable book, which ought to be multiplied as many times as there are families in the United States. I have adopted it as a book of daily reference for our business students."

From Theodore B. Boyd, Principal of the Louisville Commercial College.

"I have examined 'Hill's Manual of Social and Business Forms,' and am surprised at the amount of useful information contained in one volume. Prof. Hill seems to have studied the wants of every one. It is one of the most useful books that was ever laid upon the counting-room desk or the drawing-room table."

From D. S. Burns, Supt. Pub. Schools, Harrisburg, Pa.

"I know of no work that contains so great a variety of valuable information on social and business topics as 'Hill's Manual of Social and Business Forms.' I think it a work of special value to those who have not had opportunities of an extended school course, or becoming familiar by contact with the conventionalities of society."

From Wm. Cornell, Supt. Pub. Schools in Fall River, Mass.

"I most cheerfully recommend "Hill's Manual of Social and Business Forms' as a very full work on the various 'Forms' which every person is likely to have occasion to use in his relations with persons in society. A thorough study of the 'book' by our young men and women would repay them by their acquiring a large fund of very valuable and practical knowledge from its pages. It should meet with a large circulation."

From M. M. Ballou, Distinguished Author, formerly Publisher of "Boston Globe," "Ballou's Monthly," etc.

"'Hill's Manual' is one of those indispensable books of reference which both business men and families should always have at hand. It is such a natural outgrowth of the spirit of the age to condense and put in available form important information upon every subject, that, while we are much gratified to possess this volume, we are also surprised that such a book has not before been produced. It is exactly what its title indicates, a book of 'Social and Business Forms'; but it would require too much space to give even a synopsis of this valuable compendium of instruction and important knowledge."

From D. P. Lindsley, Author of Lindsley's System of Tachygraphy, Andover, Mass.

"'Hill's Manual' is really the most comprehensive, thorough and elegant volume, treating on 'Social and Business Forms,' that has ever been issued in this country."

From Gov. Gaston, of Massachusetts.

"'Hill's Manual of Social and Business Forms' *contains much valuable and useful information.* I think *it well meets a public want,* and can therefore be safely and properly commended to public favor."

From President McCollister, of Buchtel College, Akron, Ohio.

"'HILL'S MANUAL' is a timely book, meeting a public want which has not been filled before. Every family should own this book. It contains information important and useful to all classes. I feel all who examine it will want it."

From Wm. M. Cubery, of Cubery & Co., Publishers of the "Pacific Churchman," San Francisco, Cal.

"'Hill's Manual of Social and Business Forms' is not only a luxury, but a necessity — eminently serviceable in the social circle, and indispensable to the man of business who would save time and money. I keep a copy in my counting-room for ready reference."

From Stephen Walkley, Treasurer of the Peck, Stow & Wilcox Co., Southington, Conn.

"Hill's Manual is remarkable as containing a great variety of forms for numberless little things which all people have to do at sometime in their lives, but which most people do so seldom that they entirely forget the methods in ordinary use, and do them awkwardly or not at all. I have known even well-educated persons travel one or two miles to have a subscription paper drawn, just for the lack of such a book as this. I am surprised at the great scope of the work, and have yet to discover any social or business form needed by people in the ordinary walks of life which is not there given."

From Newton Bateman, ex-State Supt. of Public Schools, Illinois.

"KNOX COLLEGE, GALESBURG, ILL.
"'Hill's Manual of Social and Business Forms' is the best and most complete work of the kind that has yet fallen under my notice. Indeed I do not see how it could well be more comprehensive and exhaustive in respect to the matters of which it treats. It contains, in comparatively small compass, an immense amount of useful information upon a great variety of practical matters, general and special, with which every person in every community ought to be acquainted."

From Geo. Soule, President of Soule's Commercial and Literary Institute, New Orleans.

"I am pleased to say that I regard 'Hill's Manual' as one of the most valuable works for all classes of society which the nineteenth century has produced."

From Prof. Worthy Putnam, Author of Putnam's Elocution and Oratory, Berrien Springs, Mich.

". have bought Hill's Manual — I like it — I admire it; and so says my household. It is a little encyclopædia of use, ornament, and knowledge for both men and women. It is a gem of authorship, artistic execution and usefulness."

From the venerable Jared P. Kirtland, M. D., LL.D.

"After a THOROUGH AND CRITICAL EXAMINATION of 'Hill's Manual,' I have subscribed for three copies: one to accompany Webster's Unabridged Dictionary on my writing desk for my own use, the others for my two eldest great-grandsons. * * * It should be in the possession of every class of persons, from the young student to the most active business man or woman."   JARED P. KIRTLAND.

President Grant Subscribes.

The agent of Hill's Manual at Long Branch writes: "By ten A. M. I was at the president's cottage, tipped and doffed my hat, announced my business, when the president promptly said he did not want to subscribe. I obtained permission to show it to him, and did so very hurriedly. At the conclusion, he took my specimen copy, paid me the cash, and added his name to my autograph book."

From Major Merwin, Editor "American Journal of Education," St. Louis.

"After having given 'Hill's Manual' a very careful and thorough examination, I do not hesitate to say that it will be found one of the most *useful* and *practical* works to put into the schools of the country that has ever been published. IT IS A FIT AND ALMOST INDISPENSABLE COMPANION TO WEBSTER'S UNABRIDGED DICTIONARY; containing in a compact form just those things every person who transacts *any* business needs to know. There is scarcely a subject which comes within the purview of any individual, either in public or private life, but what is explained in this elegant volume. If it could be consulted in the drawing up of contracts, nearly all the mistakes which occur might be avoided, and the ill feeling and litigation growing out of misunderstandings would be a thing of the past. I wish every person in the State could be supplied with a copy."